W9-BSX-598

Mrs. Janet Owen
215 Tanglewood Dr.
Alexandria, LA 71303

WEEP
FOR THE
LIVING

BUTL

WEEP
FOR THE
LIVING

Anne Butler

BUTL

Copyright © 1998, 2000 by Anne Butler.

Library of Congress Number:		00-192331
ISBN #:	Hardcover	0-7388-4076-9
	Softcover	0-7388-4077-7

All rights reserved. No part of this book may be reproduced or transmitted in any form or by any means, electronic or mechanical, including photocopying, recording, or by any information storage and retrieval system, without permission in writing from the copyright owner.

This book was printed in the United States of America.

To order additional copies of this book, contact:
Xlibris Corporation
1-888-7-XLIBRIS
www.Xlibris.com
Orders@Xlibris.com

CONTENTS

OTHER VOICES, OTHER VIEWS

Cover photograph: Jacques Royal
Author photograph: Lily Metz

BUTL

"Stranger, if e'er these lines be read,
Weep for the living, not the dead."

Tombstone inscription from Locust Grove Cemetery in West Feliciana Parish near the author's home. It marks the grave of little Aurelia Ripley, who died in 1834, age one year. Her father, General Eleazor W. Ripley, was a hero of the War of 1812. The cemetery is on the site of Locust Grove Plantation, home of the sister of Jefferson Davis, president of the Confederacy. It is the final resting place of Sarah Knox Taylor Davis, his first wife and daughter of President Zachary Taylor; she died a young bride in 1835 at the age of 21.

FOREWORD

To an outsider, to one neither born nor accustomed by long acquaintance to its nuances, the deep south is a little strange. Spooky. Downright mysterious. Even in broad daylight there's a sense of things just out of view, hidden behind a courteous smile or a lichen-draped stone staircase that, everyone brightly explains, goes nowhere. (Although everyone knows it goes to the old cemetery where . . . well, never mind.) Anne Butler would label such observations as romantic nonsense. But, you see, that assertion is part of the mystery. And so is Anne Butler.

Not that I really know Anne Butler or the man who wished to murder her. Not that I, a mystery writer from California, may pretend any real understanding of Louisiana, West Feliciana Parish or the social undercurrents of an old Mississippi River settlement called St. Francisville. But I have been there several times. I have been a frequent personal guest of the principal actors in this drama. And this is what I do know. I know a mystery when I see one.

The origins of this mystery may spring from deep in the rich plantation soil from which generations of Anne's family wrested their livelihood. There are plantation homes all over the St. Francisville area, many now operated as tourist attractions, B&B's and restaurants. One of these is Butler Greenwood, Anne's "Tara" and her greatest love. Another, grimmer plantation lies just twenty-five miles away, and also figures in the bloody story of Anne Butler and Murray Henderson. Its name is Angola and it's now a maximum-security prison where thousands of men still slave in cotton fields under the blazing Louisiana sun. In West Feliciana parish, as Anne Butler will tell you, change is slow. Slow for prisoners. Slow for African-Americans. Slow for women. It's good-old-boy country. Best to remember that and not step out of line.

Except Anne Butler never stepped IN line. Not since she drew breath. Never. No one could own Anne Butler. And maybe that's why a former prison warden in an elegant shirt holding a black .38 eighteen inches from her abdomen shot her. Maybe that's why he then paced near her seemingly lifeless body for over an hour waiting for her to bleed out and die. Almost certainly, that's why she DIDN'T die. Anne Butler would live under no one's thumb, would not be owned and would damn well not be killed! A steel magnolia of the New South facing the bitter rage of a dying world in which white men once owned everything, including women. Perhaps especially women. Maybe. But such literary answers are the stuff of fiction. And this is real life.

I came to St. Francisville to work on a writing project with Douglas Dennis, a convict serving a life sentence at Angola. His life sentence was for murder. Over the years he and I discussed murder frequently. As a mystery writer, I write about murder. I wanted to know the answer to one question—"Why? Why commit murder?"

"Because at the time you think there is no other option," he said, over and over. "Because at the time there appears to be nothing else to do."

Murray Henderson and Anne Butler knew and were friends with Douglas Dennis and Wilbert Rideau of the award-winning prison magazine, THE ANGOLITE, and so as a professional writer I was invited to be a guest at Butler Greenwood whenever I was able to make the long trip to this isolated region. After grueling hours at the prison, I was grateful for the plantation's atmosphere. The oak-lined drive, the lawns and duck pond with its own floating duck house, the blessed swimming pool! Anne and Murray invariably treated me to gourmet dinners at the St. Francisville Inn, where Anne and I would engage in writerly chat while Murray sat ramrod straight in an impeccable three-piece suit, only occasionally joining the conversation when it swung to Angola and his role there.

Later, after the August phone call from a friend in Baton Rouge who said, "Murray Henderson has shot Anne and she's not expected to live," I thought of Murray at those formal dinners. My thoughts were chilling. Had his disinterested gaze at Anne as she talked animatedly of her books and her love of the area been TOO cool? Had he been angry at not being the center of these conversations? He was elegant. He was distant. I wrote fiction about precisely this sort of situation every day of my life. What had I MISSED? Why had Murray Henderson come to a point where there appeared to be "nothing else to do" but to kill Anne Butler, his wife? And to kill her, not cleanly with a bullet through the brain, but with an intent toward the slow, deliberate inflicting of pain?

Yes, perhaps he'd made a mistake in leaving his wife of many years to marry Anne. We all make such mistakes, but we don't torture and kill the lovers who fail our dreams. At seventy he had wanted the lively 46-year-old Anne, courted her, won her. "A less-formal arrangement, a simple affair, would have made much more sense," say we who live in other places. But we don't live in St. Francisville, Louisiana, and we aren't these two people. We don't know what forces drove them into the traditional cage that would later run with blood.

And the cage was in a lovely setting, although it was Anne's setting. She owned it then and owns it now. It's still there, the glassed-in back porch off the main house where they'd sit in the evening. Wicker furniture, books, coffee cups. Condensed humidity steaming the cooled glass, running in rivulets down the exterior side. Armadillos shuffling about in the St. Augustine grass between the kitchen cottage where I stood on the steps smoking and thinking about mystery novels, about murder, and that glassed-in porch. I did not include

BUTL

the gracious couple who were my hosts in these thoughts, although I did include the elegant, white-haired Murray as an INNOCENT character in a mystery short-story I fictionally based at Butler Greenwood. He was so Southern, I thought. Such a gentlemanly archetype. Vests and stickpins and starched shirts with French cuffs in 110-degree heat and drenching humidity. And so distant, so aloof.

Blonde and outgoing, Anne was not so distant. I erroneously never thought of her as "Southern," but rather as someone I might have known at my Midwestern college. Both writers, we had a shared universe of discourse and were immediately at ease with each other. I adored her books on regional folklore, especially a cookbook with such authentic and hysterically funny regional anecdotes that I bought a slew of them for Christmas gifts. We enjoyed morning coffee, talking of the latest news from Angola. At night I sometimes joined Anne in the poolside clubhouse, working out to Richard Simmons as we hoisted 28-ounce cans of red beans in lieu of weights, giggling.

On one of my visits all the cottages were booked and I stayed upstairs in the main house, where the early architecture of the region had precluded interior walls which would blunt air circulation. It was all one big room with expansive leaded glass windows dead-center in the front wall, affording a magnificent view of the lawn and oak-lined earthen drive. The airy absence of rooms and the regal view were "different" in a way I found hard to define. "What would it be like to grow up in such a place?" I wondered. "What would it be like to know such a place was YOURS?"

Virginia Woolf, I remembered, had said that each woman must have a "room of one's own." Anne Butler had a whole plantation. And like the rest of us who fiercely guard whatever little niche we manage to create for ourselves, Anne knew her survival depended on the maintenance of that place. Her place. Comparisons to Scarlet O'Hara are inevitable, but valid. Perhaps there's something Southern women know that the rest of us have forgotten. And perhaps that's part of the mystery. Anne's blood soaked into the ground of Butler Greenwood that hot August afternoon, but the ground gave something back. Anne Butler survived.

Anne survived and wrote a book about her experience, as any writer would. Anne's book, this book, isn't fiction. It isn't a mystery. Or is it?

I write mysteries. I should know. But I don't.

A crime was committed, a murder was attempted, a victim bled and fell. Before these events there was a love affair, two divorces, a marriage, then the slow accumulation of plot and characterization which would lead to the crime, the attempted murder, the fallen and bleeding body. After these events there was an investigation. There was crime-scene tape. There was whispering and rumor. Ultimately there was a trial, testimony, a judge and a verdict. Now the bloodied body has risen to write of its wounds and their healing, and the man who fired the gun so many times that hot afternoon, a former prison warden, is in prison. This sounds like a traditional mystery to me, except for one thing. There are still secrets.

In a fictional mystery the reader must be privy to every nuance, every motivation. The reason, rational or irrational, for the crime must be explained. The reader must understand why the crime took place, why the body bled and fell. There can be no sense of things just out of view, things hidden by design or by accident. There can be no secrets.

And yet the reason Murray Henderson shot Anne Butler, then roamed beside her still body for so long is still a secret. Many lives were dramatically altered by events on that hot August afternoon. One life was nearly lost. But why? Anne Butler here relates, with characteristic humor and inspiring forgiveness, her experience. She also does a credible and surprisingly unbiased job of accounting for her attempted murderer's personal history and character. And yet, and yet . . . this is not fiction.

It is only between the lines that the secret is revealed, if at all. For even the principal actors in this drama, so cloaked in the intriguing atmosphere of an elegant, isolated culture and its horrific prison,

BUTL

may not know the secret. It may, rather, lie deep inside each one of us. So read carefully, for what you are reading is a truth from which the secret may . . . or may not . . . be distilled.

Abigail Padgett

neighbors, upon whom our ancestors looked with great disdain. The early settlers here, by contrast, were nearly all patrician English or Irish or Scottish, coming down from the East Coast in large family groups around the time of the Revolutionary War, during which some were Tories, sympathetic to England but a great many fought on the American side. Regardless of wartime leanings, they all brought with them time-honored English culture and traditions still observed today.

There has almost always been a Butler or Flower or Mathews on the vestry since the church was begun in 1827, and there is usually still one today; in fact, the very first vestry had two Flowers (my grandmother's family) and one Butler as senior warden (my grandfather's family). Grace in the past was the church of choice for anybody who was anybody. It's not exactly that way today—but somebody forget to tell that to a lot of the congregation.

#

During the late lamented War Between The States, what was important in this area was control of the traffic along the Mississippi River, and there were federal gunboats on the river at St. Francisville during the bloody siege of Port Hudson, the last Confederate stronghold on the river. St. Francisville sits atop a heavily wooded bluff high above the riverbanks, and what was visible to the gunboats above the tree-line was the bell tower of Grace Church, upon which they set their sights and commenced shelling, causing considerable damage. The commander of the *USS Albatross* died during this minor engagement. He was not actually *killed*. Naval records indicate he took his own life during a fit of delirium, probably brought on by yellow fever.

A Mason, Lt. Commander John E. Hart had requested Masonic burial. St. Francisville just happened to have one of the oldest Masonic Lodges in the state, Feliciana Lodge No. 31 F and AM and, while its grand master was away serving in the Confederacy, its senior warden just happened to be in the vicinity, his "headquarters being in the saddle." And so as the surgeon and several other officers of the *Alba-*

19

tross, all members of the craft, struggled up the hill from the river with the coffin of Commander Hart, they were met by several local Masons.

Together they proceeded to Grace Church, where the Reverend Dr. Lewis, rector, read the solemn words of the burial rite and with full Episcopal and Masonic services, in one of those peculiar little interludes of civility in the midst of a terribly brutal war, this young Yankee naval officer who had died so far from his home in Schenectady, New York, was buried in Grace Church cemetery. (That some of the parishioners of the church he had been shelling considered it divine retribution is certainly understandable.) Then they all started shooting at each other again.

Now we re-create the burial of Commander Hart every year. The first year we did it on the Fourth of July, which turned out to be a bad idea because all the Civil War re-enactment troops were otherwise occupied and so all we had were some overweight Masons, with ill-fitting rented Confederate and Union uniform jackets uneasy with their polyester slacks, hauling a very heavy coffin up from the river in a wagon which, although appropriately mule drawn, had rubber tires. But it proved very popular with tourists and locals alike, and we'll continue to refine the performance, hold it on the proper date, and erase a few more of the modern intrusions.

#

During the struggling Civil War and Reconstruction periods, there were times when Grace Church's only contributor of record for the entire year was Harriett Flower Mathews, second generation in my house, willful woman who ran four plantations and had all her slaves baptized at Grace. Later one of the nearby plantations, Afton Villa, would donate land for a black church and the slave congregations would stop meeting in secret in the wooded hollows for services of their own.

In the midst of the Civil War, when New Orleans was an occupied city, Harriett Mathews, a stout elderly widow who by then had survived not only her husband but also both of her children as well and even a grandchild or two, insisted upon making the strenuous trip to the city by steamboat to check with her cotton factor and try to salvage something of her crop.

She also formalized the parlor at Greenwood, ordering a 12-piece set of rosewood rococo-revival style furniture upholstered in scarlet damask with matching damask lambrequins at the floor-to-ceiling windows and graceful porcelain and bronze calla-lily tiebacks to hold back the under-lying lace curtains, 10-foot-tall gilded French pier mirrors, Brussels floral carpet—all right as the Civil War began, not exactly an auspicious time to augment extensive interior redecorating projects, but no self-respect-ing Flower or Mathews or Butler would ever let a little inconvenience like a bloody war interfere with plans. Ensuing generations have taken such good care of the parlor set that each and every piece still sits exactly where it did in the 1860's, still in the original upholstery.

"The parlor at Butler Greenwood Plantation is one of the
finest examples of a formal Victorian parlor left in the
South, its scarlet tasseled lambrequins framing windows
draped with lace held back by rare porcelain calla-lily
tiebacks, separated by gilded French pier mirrors."

BUTL

The women of the family, like Harriett, always seemed to outlive the men by many years, maybe because of their well-deserved reputation for determination (some called it stubbornness back then, I suppose, and I know some who still do). Even as recently as the generation before my own, my mother began her reign at age five by clambering atop a very high outdoor barrel cistern for catching rainwater, from which dangerous perch she pompously fired the long-suffering lifelong family retainer, black Bertha, who was trying to coax her down. If this makes her sound like a snooty spoiled little brat, she *was* one, and she remained one until the day she died.

At LSU she learned how to fly—at five feet two inches, squeezing past the height requirements for the pilot program by stuffing cotton wads into her forties' hairstyle—and only the arrival of her first child, me, deterred her from ferrying planes overseas when World War II began (that may be why she resented me her whole life through). When she finally succumbed to cancer at age 60 she could still and often did turn cartwheels, usually in high heels and hiked-up straight skirts.

Of the current generation, me and my sister and our first cousins on this "Greenwood house side" of the family, we have among us eleven daughters and only two sons, and even in their tender years the daughters show signs of becoming typically strong rebellious women—not a docile one in the bunch.

Harriett Flower Mathews ran four plantations, surviving even the difficult years surrounding the Civil War. I've had my hands full trying to keep just one operating. But I've had four *husbands*; Burnett insists upon referring to them as my ex, my ex-ex, my ex-ex-ex, and the last one, Murray Henderson, I'm still married to as I begin to write this—but not for long. It took my own civil war to alter the dynamics of *that* one.

#

If you think the women of the family sound bad, the men were historically just as stubborn so I must get a double dose, from both

22

sides. The second generation removed from Ireland included five Butler brothers who served on George Washington's staff during the Revolutionary War and were known as Honor's Band for their fearlessness and integrity, several beginning the fight as mere teenagers and all ending up colonels or generals.

The next generation served with equal valor on Andrew Jackson's staff at the Battle of New Orleans, and Jackson himself visited in the family home here on his way back up the Natchez Trace. Several of the nieces and nephews of Jackson on his wife Rachel's side married Butlers, and their offspring ended up being raised by the Jacksons in The Hermitage due to untimely deaths.

But when General James Wilkinson—aspiring to egalitarianism in the new army—ordered all patriot officers to cut off their queues (those little pigtails favored by English gentry), one Butler brother, Colonel Thomas Butler who was my father's grandfather's grandfather, refused, doing so vigorously enough to be called up for court martial for insubordination. Before his appeal was heard by the Secretary of War, he died in 1805 of yellow fever in New Orleans and was buried in a coffin with a hole cut in the bottom so his queue could hang through.

#

There must be something in the water here which encourages rebellion, given the history since the first formal settlement centering around a small fort, Ste. Reyne aux Tonicas, was established by the French around 1729 and soon abandoned. When France lost the rest of Louisiana to Spain, her vast territory east of the Mississippi, including this parish, West Feliciana, went to England in 1763 and became known as West Florida; settlement there began in earnest in the late 1700's encouraged by large grants of land from England and later Spain.

In 1779 the governor of Spanish Louisiana, Bernardo de Galvez, ousted the British from the Felicianas. The Spanish themselves would

23

soon be ejected by the sturdy planters who settled here and carved the great plantations from the virgin woodlands, tilling the rich river bottomlands to subsidize lifestyles noted for fine architecture, refined culture, great educational achievement and a gracious standard of honorable and mannerly living.

After the Louisiana Purchase in 1803 left Feliciana still part of Spanish West Florida, there were two revolutions, the first, the Kemper Brothers' Rebellion of 1804, being more colorful than successful. When one brother was disciplined by Spanish militia, he and two siblings captured the local *alcalde*, declared their independence from the Spanish Crown and flung themselves—greatly outnumbered and poorly armed—against the fort at Baton Rouge. Captured by planters and turned over to Spanish authorities, they were daringly rescued and subsequently repaid one erstwhile captor by cutting off his ears, pickling them in wine and exhibiting them in the family tavern. Another captor was sent to an early grave when he was forced to spend damp sleepless nights in an open boat on the river to elude the brothers' revenge.

The Republic of West Florida, on the other hand, stemmed from the second and rather more respectable rebellion, which pulled off a successful coup in 1810, establishing for 74 days an independent republic with its capital in St. Francisville. This led to the desired annexation of the Felicianas into the United States by President Madison. Becoming part of the state of Louisiana in 1812, West Feliciana would fly its own independent banner only once more—upon secession from the Union at the outset of the Civil War.

One of the ten books I had written was the tourist guide to West Feliciana Parish, and my considerable research into the history of the area gave me a good bit of background knowledge about these earlier revolutions to illuminate the continuing rebellions swirling about me in my own lifetime.

CHAPTER 2

I always attended early services at Grace—not quite so fancy or formal as the later worship service—so I was home by 8:30 and then conducted a little tour for a group of visiting travel agents interested in my antebellum home and B&B, Butler Greenwood Plantation.

Using two historic structure—the original outside kitchen built in 1796, and the little 19th-century cottage where the plantation cook had lived just to the rear of the kitchen—and four newer ones I designed and my longtime master carpenter/associate and friend Burnett Carraway built, I provide overnight accommodations for international tourists, traveling businessmen and assorted state urbanites yearning for the peace and quiet of a country weekend.

"Pleasant cottages surrounding the duck pond at Butler Greenwood Plantation provide private overnight accommodations for B&B guests, while the smaller replica in the middle of the pond is safe nesting space for resident ducks and a fishing perch for visiting blue herons"

BUTL

And this *is* usually a place of peace and harmony, inspiring guests to write in our journals with surprising eloquence about the great sense of calm that washes over them as they enter our oak-lined drive and the deep appreciation for God's blessings and the beauties of nature that they experience here.

But an old home like this one, surrounded by antebellum gardens, is absolutely a bottomless pit, always requiring an endless round of repairs and continual expensive maintenance. For the first twenty years after I returned here from working in Washington, D.C., and California I had said "Never, Never, *Never*" about opening to the public, but eventually it becomes necessary to let an old place like this one help support itself, and I had devised a method of doing that while retaining some semblance of privacy and sanity for those of us living in the main house.

From 9 to 5, I conduct tours through the historic structure, but at 5 p.m. we turn off the lights and hide behind the sofa, providing overnight accommodation for guests only in the individual cottages scattered around the peaceful plantation grounds, not in the main house itself.

In a small rural area like this, you more or less have to make your own employment, resources being so limited, and if I do say so myself I had done a rather commendable job of turning a financial drain into a viable asset which would eventually support itself and my family as well, I hoped. Most especially, I hoped it would support the old house which I love so much.

Unfortunately, in my most recent marriage, I think the house served to accentuate our differences, old Louisiana family connections especially. It reminded me of the scene in John Berendt's *Midnight In The Garden Of Good And Evil*, where one character looks at some tattered needlepoint seatcovers and whispers knowingly, "*Old* money," the implication being that new money would immediately rush them off to be refinished, recovered, re-upholstered, all the better to impress impressionable visitors. Me, I clung to plenty of tattered and worn relics; to me, they represented character and history, they represented a long life well lived. It drove Murray crazy that I wouldn't re-do them. But I never had given much of a damn about impressing anybody else.

The first time we entertained together, Murray plopped his six-foot-plus frame down rather forcefully into an early 1800 Seigneuret armchair and broke it all to pieces, foretaste of the way he never would quite *fit* here in this house which was mine and never would ever become *ours*. He couldn't fit into my solid mahogany Victorian half-tester double bed, so we had to purchase a new kingsized one; his extensive wardrobe wouldn't fit into the antique Empire armoires that the rest of us used for our clothes and so we had to add on a whole new room as his closet. His *face* wouldn't even fit into the little wood-framed mirror with old crackled glass I had hanging over the bathroom sink, and so we had to install a giant new mirror covering the entire wall for him to be able to admire himself (to be perfectly honest, I must admit that since my old mirror was only about 9x11 inches, if it was hanging low enough for me to see into it, Murray really was too tall to use it). He *hated* living here.

He was the worst, but it was rather unfortunate but true that each of my four husbands had at some point during our marriage faced the fact that, like Scarlett O'Hara, I really loved my house and land more than I did any of them. And it usually turned out that this place was much more something I could count on than any of them ever were.

You could almost say I had made marriages just for the house, its demands sometimes taking precedence over my own, so that possession of a tractor, for example, or handyman skills might become all-important assets in a suitor. Each marriage, I'm sure, spoke to a specific need in my own life at the time as well, but needs change as time passes; it was not that my husbands changed or became less, but rather that I changed and needed more than they could give. Anyway, these relationships were hardly good bases for matrimonial contracts and never quite the help for the house I had hoped for, either.

#

Begun in the late 1700's when the family emigrated from Pennsylvania overland by wagon train, Butler Greenwood is a typical raised English-style cottage, as were all the early plantation houses in this particular part of Louisiana. It was really built for the climate more than anything else: simple floor plan without hallways so that every room opens directly to the outside for good cross ventilation, broad galleries surrounding the house, and hundreds of spreading live oak trees providing plenty of shade.

"Spanish moss hanging from hundreds of centuries-old live
oak trees softens the view and adds romance to the front
lawn at Butler Greenwood Plantation"

These were well-educated, cultured, well-traveled people, and the house they built was designed to support such a lifestyle. The library was filled with leather-bound first-editions of the world's literary greats; the music room boasted a golden harp and an 1855 French *Pleyel* concert grand piano of rosewood inlaid with brass; the walls were hung with fine oil portraits of all the early generations of the family—doctors, judges, lawyers, planters, congressmen and state Supreme Court jurists.

"The portrait of Harriett Flower Mathews, daughter of
Butler Greenwood's builder and mistress of the plantation
for nearly the entire 19th century, dominates the dining
room to this day."

Formal gardens with Victorian summer houses and boxwood *parterres* surrounded the home, filled with century-old camellias and azaleas, sweet olives and *magnolia fuscata*, thoughtfully planned like all the early gardens so that there was always something blooming, always a pleasing fragrance in the air.

29

Anne Butler

"A charming 19th-century Victorian summer house graces
the formal gardens bordering the plantation house at
Butler Greenwood, providing respite from the heat"

#

I have always loved this place. My grandmother and her elderly
maiden sister lived here when I was small, and I spent a lot of time
with them, summers and most weekends, even though my mother
and father actually lived in Baton Rouge, 25 miles south. During
World War II, my father was in the Corps of Engineers, building air-
ports and bridges on far-flung Pacific islands, so after I was born in
1944 my mother and I even lived at Greenwood during his absence.

Weep For The Living

As children the whole gang of cousins congregated at Greenwood, waded in the warm waters of Bayou Sara, hiked along its sandy banks finding Indian arrowheads and fossils, played with the resident population of hunting hounds and barn cats. We rode horses until we were bowlegged (I used to nap lying across the broad back of my favorite mare Nelly as she grazed in the backyard and stayed on her all day long, going nowhere) but only the older cousins got to go for exciting and dangerous moonlit rides. Hot summer days we fished for bream and catfish in the duck pond, and at night we savagely brandished tennis or badminton rackets against the ever-present population of bats in the upstairs hallway.

"Cousins Anne and Pat Butler on the lower step and
Virginia Bruns Marshall (with pigtails) and Eleanor Eustis
Young sit behind the Cook's Cottage after a summer day of
play at Butler Greenwood"

In the evening cool we joined the older folks lining the front gallery in the wicker-bottomed rockers, feet propped on the rail as conversation quieted and the cicada sounds rose in waves and a gentle sense of contentment settled over all, watching the dusk gather and the lightning bugs flicker through the oak grove. We learned our family history here, listening to the stories of ancestors and far-flung cousins: the Butler who went off to attend his class reunion at Princeton and didn't come home until three years later, much to his wife's chagrin; the Lawrason-McCutcheon widow whose dead body was washed out of her grave by Mississippi River floodwaters down near Ormond Plantation; the aunt whose Colonial Dames research led her to Wild Bill Hickok on one side of the family so that she decided to trace her lineage along the *other*, slightly more reputable side; my grandmother's father who as a boy was taken to Barcelona during the Civil War after his father, director of the Confederate port in New Orleans, had been locked up in a Yankee prison camp and who would grow up to serve in the honor guard in Robert E. Lee's funeral in 1870, carrying the ceremonial sword which now hangs in my music room—endless tales, endlessly fascinating.

We also ate plenty of good home-cooking straight off Celie's wood-stove in the old outside kitchen: okra gumbo, cornbread sticks, jam cake, biscuits with lots of dewberry jelly, fried chicken (watching the gruesome process of beheading dinner in the extensive poultry yard was always an eagerly awaited entertainment).

Despite the largesse of the kitchen at Greenwood, it couldn't hold a candle to the hospitality recalled by my grandfather's maiden sister, Miss Louise Butler of The Cottage Plantation, turn-of-the-century author and historian whose writings describing her beloved parish were published in historical quarterlies in the early 1900s. She writes vividly of a day's visit by neighboring plantation aristocracy, closing her reminiscences by citing at least one of the reasons for the passing of this lavish earlier way of life. Arriving with a touch of *mal de mer* from a rough coach ride, the visitors were fortified in proper

sequence with cordials, juleps, claret, sherry, champagne and spir-
ited coffee, so that they departed, "the gentlemen, especially, with
eyes considerably brighter than when they arrived. Dear, generous,
lavish, warm-heartedly hospitable old givers of pleasure! Many a one
of you literally entertained himself out of his home and into the
poorhouse!"

My grandmother who lived at Greenwood, a stout dignified elderly widow, was so tolerant she would let me, as a small child, braid
wildflowers into her long gray hair and to please me would wear these
colorful decorations all day long, much to the wonderment of visitors.
It took something extraordinary to get much of a rise out of her: bats
flying down the attic stairs and into the soup tureen during formal
Sunday dinners, or unruly uncles accidentally shooting holes in the
ceiling while cleaning their hunting rifles, or maybe the hard-drinking elderly bachelor cousin whose ancient car careened off the driveway and down the steep slopes of the sunken garden while arriving to
visit one day. When inmates escaped from the nearby state penitentiary at Angola, this same cousin would rush over on unsteady legs "to
protect the ladies," brandishing loaded firearms and fortified with
plenty of liquid courage.

#

I loved the place and everybody in it. It would always be the only
physical place to which I would give my heart, and I would be drawn
back to it again and again until, after working on both coasts and
traveling extensively in my 1960s footloose days, I would return to it
in 1970 and never leave again, at least not permanently. Even during
the period when "material possessions" were anathema to the counter-
culture and I was a long-haired liberal pseudo-hippie, I would sell all
my silver and crystal wedding presents at a California garage sale for
pennies but could never quite bring myself to part with anything old
which had come from Greenwood.

3UTL

Anne Butler

"Author Anne Butler has made her home at Butler
Greenwood Plantation for more than three decades now"

Weep For The Living

I had initially resisted what I considered the inexcusable laziness of standing on an ancestor's feet (and feats) instead of one's own. I would make my own way, be my own person, and I came into this little community as the resident radical liberal, straight from the wilds of crazy California. I was probably the only white person in the parish who voted for George McGovern for president; if there was another, it would have been Murray.

Coming from the impersonality of California, where no one asks or knows anyone else's business, I took immediate offense at the southern small-town inquisitiveness taken for granted by everyone else. Stopping by the one local drugstore to purchase some item soon after moving here, I was asked by the clerk if I lived around here. When I replied that I did, she responded, "Well, *I've* never seen you before." To which I coldly replied, "*So?*" and walked out the door. I certainly wasn't going to let them all stick their noses into *my* business.

Given time, though, I would come to appreciate the concern of small-town residents for their neighbors and the warmth with which they accepted returning offspring, however many generations removed from the original families. The small-town atmosphere so stifling to other transplants didn't bother me, as I've never much cared what my community approval rating might be. Besides, St. Francisville, for all the limitations of small-town life, has always been more open-minded and forward-thinking than its even smaller neighbor Woodville, where the daily sport is running down everybody else in town and the only moral imperative is keeping up with the Joneses.

When my daughter Chase graduated from the local high school as the outstanding student for the whole parish, her stirring address to the gathering focused on the message I had always tried to instill in her: being her own self, setting her own goals, daring to be different, taking that chance. Both of my children would grow up with extended families which included practically the entire community, answering needs and filling gaps in ways no longer possible in cold, impersonal big cities.

Anne Butler

"Chase and Stewart, children of Anne Butler, with the furry
family dog and a cement cherub"

And I too would feel, in my house, the enveloping love of eight generations of family, and I was never lonely even when I was alone. From the house and the place I would take a large part of my mature identity, and woe be to the suitor who failed to understand that.

#

But I would not understand for years that this was essentially a matriarchal domain, having come down through the women most generations and still in the present being under the control of me and my daughter Chase, all to the exclusion of Murray.

Maybe the whole *parish* was essentially a matriarchy, founded as St. Francisville was by the Capuchin monks from across the river (is there a more feminine order than these sexless long-skirted silent souls?), who ferried their dead over for burial atop the bluffs safe from Mississippi River floodwaters. Come to think of it, our first settlers were all dead, and some of the subsequent ones weren't a whole lot livelier.

The early Indians here, the peaceful Houmas, were driven out by the fierce Tunica tribe and the whole area is rich in Indian artifacts bespeaking a thriving trade with European adventurers traversing the river and visiting its shores, for the Felicianas attracted Spanish and French explorers as early as the 16th century.

The large planters who harvested immense acreages of cotton, sugar cane and indigo along the Great River Road from New Orleans to Natchez in the mid-1800's comprised more than two-thirds of America's known millionaires of that period, but the devastation of Civil War and disruption of the cotton kingdom brought about some lean years for the area. During the Civil War years in particular, the men were mostly dead or gone, but *somebody* was still running the old plantations and doing a really commendable job of holding things together—the women. There may not have been much cold cash, but

UTL

there was always that gentility, that haunting beauty, that femininity, that *strength*.

Turn-of-the-century writer-historian Louise Butler of The Cottage consistently referred to her homeland in the feminine gender, lamenting, "As to *her* (sic) physical features, no touch is lacking to her perfect picturesqueness, for *she* (sic) possesses lakes and streams of surprising beauty, marshes and swamps, hills and rich valleys where everything grows except, perhaps (and alas!) one's income."

Aghast at what she perceived even then as the weakened moral fiber of the country, this genteel lady nonetheless expressed undying faith in the fortitude of her parish and its peoples: "These are but poor words to describe West Feliciana Many of her daughters have married and live elsewhere. Her sons have wandered far in search of a wealth she cannot give them, but always she draws them back to her by the very sweetness of her charm. In this age of upheaval, of broken faiths and traditions, of discarded ideals, where money alone is supreme, the American Dollar being the standard toward which the eyes of the world are gazing and for which the pockets of the world are gaping, she is quiescent and ignored, dreaming of a day that is seemingly dead, but in her immobile body a soul lives, and the message of that soul is told in two lost words—Poetry and Beauty. Some day it will be spoken to the world in ringing accents."

But not everybody could understand the language.

#

Without negatively impacting the plantation, I had taken advantage of the year-round tourism in the Felicianas and had developed one of the area's most popular Bed & Breakfast operations, and I had done it primarily on my own—with a lot of help from Burnett, for years my real partner in the restoration. Together, using funds I borrowed in my own name for that purpose from the local bank, we constructed the private cottages for overnight stays.

"Restoration carpenter Burnett Carraway confers with
Anne Butler on renovations to the Cook's Cottage B&B"

My husband Murray liked to take a little more credit for the business than he deserved. I had all the ideas, did all the planning and

39

designing and decorating, and I did almost all of the work with the housekeeping staff, including a lot of the cleaning on busy days. He most often sat on the back porch, long legs stuck out in the way of everyone trying to get to and from the laundry room, periodically blowing his nose so loudly that the sound reverberated throughout the wood-floored rooms like the mating call of a lovelorn bull moose.

It's funny how little things can bother you. I hated to be in the middle of a house tour and hear him blowing his nose, just as I hated hearing him operating the microwave, intrusive noises which hardly enhanced the antebellum experience the tourists were paying to have in the house. I must admit, however, that he would occasionally open the gift shop or give a house tour when I was especially busy, and when he was in Baton Rouge on business he was good about picking up B&B supplies on the way home. But actually being part of the business? No way.

When we first opened a small gift shop where he planned to do picture framing, which he never learned to do, he thought he was being helpful by ordering at retail prices a few tacky items from some cheap mail-order catalog; he then wanted to raise the price even more for re-sale (some of these are still sitting in the shop). Later he had six large wooden grandfather and grandmother clocks charged to me and shipped from the clock manufacturer in his Tennessee hometown, thinking they'd enhance the gift shop inventory. He also ordered some rather peculiar hairy trolls made in the Tennessee mountains, which might have been popular there but were decidedly out of place in south Louisiana.

My market consisted mostly of tourists and other travelers who wanted items reminiscent of their southern cultural experience in the area and certainly did not want to be encumbered by a giant six-foot clock, no matter how well made, on a trip. I gave away one clock for a Christmas present, sold one at greatly reduced price, still have all the rest sitting around gathering dust. No, Murray was *not* the one who ran the business or knew what was appropriate for the place, regardless of what he would claim.

"Murray Henderson (left, with hand raised) and Burnett
Carraway listen to gospel music at a church supper on the
grounds of Butler Greenwood, with Anne visible between
them"

He had done the same with the two criminal justice books on
which we had collaborated, acting as if he'd actually written them,
when in fact he had no writing ability whatsoever. He used to dictate
letters for me to type—long verbose pomposities which I would totally change before typing—and then he would admire what a good
job he'd done. Not long after we married, when he first began his job
working for a home health agency as a social worker initially and then
calling on doctors and hospitals to push their services, he would get
me to fill out all his forms for him, and this took hours every night. For

awhile I didn't mind, because I thought it pretty amazing that he was working at all at his age. Actually, he really enjoyed working, especially the constant interaction with other people; he had told me how much it had bored him when he had first retired and just hated sitting around all day.

It would be hard to say just when I began to be bothered so much by these seemingly insignificant actions of his, especially such innocuous things as blowing his nose, but it did not take long for me to feel relieved when he left the house to go to work, or to hate seeing his car speeding up the driveway to come home. He left for work later and later each morning, and came home earlier and earlier, and each day it bothered me more and more.

Like most writers, I never quite know what I think until I see what I write, and sometimes it's a big surprise. At one point I was playing around with writing song lyrics and began a not-very-good country plaint about my four husbands. The verse about Murray which came out was something I had not consciously recognized until I saw it in print:

"Then came the fine gentleman
In his three-piece suit of gray
But everything I wanted
He knew a better way . . ."

"Called a real clothes horse by all who knew him, Murray
Henderson always liked to be properly and formally
dressed"

Early in our relationship I began trying to explain to him my need
for a little space from him, and the more I tried to explain, the closer
he crowded. And so I began to manufacture my own space. *He* might
be present, but I wasn't; even when my body was physically there, my
mind was a million miles away and the door to it was slammed shut
and bolted. Indifference was my weapon of choice—indifference and
inattention. It took him years to notice.

43

CHAPTER 3

On that August Sunday morning, the travel agents who toured the facilities loved Butler Greenwood. I didn't notice my husband Murray drive into the long oak-lined gravel driveway from the highway but the local tour agent did. She also saw him turn around and leave when he noticed all the cars, peeling out and ignoring her husband who waved to him. As the tour group was leaving after their tour, she saw him pulling into the driveway again; this time, there were no cars parked in the parking area by the main house. The two housekeepers who had come in unusually early to get the outlying cottages ready for the tour do not drive and had been dropped off by a friend, so Murray had no way of knowing they were even on the premises.

Even though we were separated at the time, there was nothing that unusual in his showing up. We had often separated during the seven years of our marriage, sometimes over trivial matters, frequently with little build-up. I would notice him carrying clothes out to his car, and he would be gone, sometimes sending back for all his things; and then he'd begin visiting again, visiting, visiting, until one day his things were being carried back in. At first I missed him when he was gone and encouraged his return, especially when he'd begin calling and appealing to my sympathy, saying I had such a soothing influence on his high blood pressure and all. But lately I'd been relieved by his absence and hoped he'd stay away.

Weep For The Living

Somehow our relations in the past had always been cordial and respectful, even during our frequent separations. We had nothing bad to say about each other to outsiders and kept our problems to ourselves, not wanting to cause undue hurt or embarrassment to the other. We had, after all, based our relationship on friendship and what I thought was mutual respect to begin with, and that had so far endured—even when we didn't want to be together.

During our separations, he would usually return to free room and board at his ex-wife's home, though they had parted company on not-so-cordial terms. Why she continued to take him in I don't know, except that he had told me she had angrily threatened him that I would be sure to throw him out at some point and she would magnanimously promise to always provide "a room" for him when that happened. Of course, I can't say why *I* made it so easy for him to shuttle back and forth between households, either.

My writer friend Abby Padgett would later wonder why Murray and I had not simply settled for an affair of passion, asking herself what it was that drove us into what she called the "traditional cage that would later run with blood." I thought of the little antique child's chair which sat next to my armoire in our bedroom, a tiny tufted armchair which had always been in my room when I was a child and in which I often sat when I was small. Now there was a little needlepoint cushion on the chair, flowers and leaves surrounding the central motto, "Every Age Has Its Pleasures." I had thought it most appropriate for an old home open for historic tours, especially one upon which every generation had left its mark. But more than one tourist, noticing the pillow as we toured the bedroom, remarked that the green leaves curling around the "A" in "Age" made it look more like "Cage." And perhaps it was just as true that every cage had its pleasures as well.

Throughout our marriage, Murray always exhibited great concern for his health, almost to the point of obsession, testing his blood pressure every few minutes on a home finger monitor I'd given him, taking enormous amounts of prescription and over-the-counter medications and vitamins for an erratic heartbeat, high blood pressure and bone and joint stiffness, seeing some physician or another almost weekly.

My robust good health must have been a real irritant to him, as I think my youth became; it had at first invigorated him (or so he said) but later probably frustrated him in the comparison, and his supply of what he jokingly referred to as "rooster" pills grew. I didn't know until after he'd left how boastful he was with the carpenters and others working at Butler Greenwood, crowing about his sexual prowess. As my interest in physical contact with him diminished, he would comment to Burnett, as they stood in the back yard and laughed at the amorous springtime activities of the mating ducks, that he was going to make me drink a big glass of that duck pond water.

#

Murray and I were always good friends but we lived together dismally, being total opposites in nearly every way. I was quiet and solitary, always pretty much a loner. He loved to socialize and to talk (mostly I think to hear what he had to say, though he could be quite interesting). He thoroughly enjoyed parties and group meetings and was a convivial host; I rarely attended parties if I could help it and *never* hosted any. We had almost no friends in common, and just as few interests. In the beginning of our relationship, in the excitement of newness, we didn't think it mattered.

And then there was the 24-year age difference, a difficult gap to surmount. We married when he had just turned 70 and I was 46. Now I had reached the point where, in spite of recognizing how significant the period had been in his own life and career, I would have thrown up if I'd been forced to watch another World War II documentary covering a time when I was a mere infant. When we first married, I think I made him feel young. Toward the end, he was making me feel very, very old.

My children were another source of discord. It had been many, many years since Murray had lived in a household with children, and I think he'd forgotten the accompanying noise and constant activity that entailed, not to mention the bickering. He recalled his own children's youth as idyllic and them as model children, always interacting intelligently and always perfectly behaved; perhaps his were, but mine were not. Murray really did make an attempt to adjust to them, and with Stewart especially he tried to establish a relationship; they went fishing once or twice, but Murray's idea of quality time was watching *Crossfire* or the *McNeil-Lehrer Report* on TV together.

Did I ever make him happy? He said so, and he also said that my quietness and calmness had a soothing influence on him. That may surprise some people, who know how outspoken I can be—and sure, I can get incensed at injustices or stupidities in the rest of society. But I never directed any animosity toward him, and we rarely if ever argued overtly.

Did he ever make *me* happy? There must have been some times, but the question reminds me of a fine sculptor from Baton Rouge who came on a tour of the house not long after Murray and I married. After completing his tour, this sculptor took me aside and said in an excited voice, "I *must* sculpt you. Would you let me?" When I asked why on earth he would want to sculpt me, he replied, "It's your face. It's so elegant, but it has such sadness, such sorrow in it." And I had not known. Perhaps it was that, as a sensitive intuitive artist he was seeing into the future rather than being restricted solely to the present.

Looking back now, I see the only photograph taken at our wedding ceremony, performed by the local judge at Greenwood. One of us looks happy. One of us does not.

Anne Butler

"The only wedding day photograph of Anne Butler and
Murray Henderson, on the front gallery at Butler
Greenwood, 1990"

#

After all that has happened between us, it is hard for me to dredge
up any early feelings of excitement and closeness—but I know they
must have been there. Murray and I began as professional colleagues,
traveling together to research the prison books we were writing. The
distances we had to travel to reach the necessary sources required
overnight stays after long days spent researching tiresome legal documents in sterile courthouse file rooms or interviewing subjects for
hours on end.

For the first few trips, there was no question but that we would
have separate motel rooms and after dinner discussing our day's work,
we retired separately to those rooms. I called him Mr. Henderson. He

called me Anne, and kept trying to get me to call him Murray, but it just wouldn't come.

And then on one trip, he was driving as he always did and my hand happened to be resting on the car seat between us when his own giant, carefully manicured hand approached and brushed mine, setting off unexpected sparks. After dinner, we retired to our individual rooms but there was no rest for either of us that night, and by the next night, the second room was empty.

Ironically, the stress of the moment and the sheer excitement combined with his age so that nothing physical took place that night either, but on subsequent trips I would find him to be a very considerate and sensual partner. He explained his prowess by saying that his wife was very cold and inhibited, and he had read dozens of sex books trying to find some way to please her, to warm their relationship; he never could, he said, but the things he had learned would enhance our relationship immeasurably. Nobody ever called *me* cold or inhibited.

We had known each other slightly for years, both attending the same church, and he often told me that he used to watch me walk down the aisle to communion and wonder what I looked like under the long loose dresses I wore (he called them my "Pentecostal dresses.") He said he had always admired my writing skills, and he asked me to visit him at the state forensic facility which he ran. This facility housed the state's criminally insane as they awaited psychiatric evaluation and trial, and gave Murray the close relationship with many of the state's psychiatrists which would later prove so helpful to him.

I thought he wanted me to write something about it; what he really wanted to do was start a relationship. He had planned, he said, to show me around the facility then take me to lunch in Baton Rouge and make his move. I showed up with my husband so all we got was the tour and a quick lunch. Later when he invited me to his retirement party, I didn't even go, which frustrated him even more. But he didn't give up.

49

Anne Butler

#

His "move" would not come until a few years later when we collaborated on the two books dealing with the state prisons and Louisiana's dismal correctional record. I did all the research and writing; he provided expert commentary and picked out just which legal cases would best illustrate various facets and failings within the criminal justice system. After several years of in-depth research in court records and prisons, including a number of personal interviews with incarcerated inmates, the only interview subject who really scared me during the writing process was a drunken retired judge from the Acadiana area—and I should have paid more attention to the discrepancy.

Collaborating on the books had been my idea as I searched for meaningful writing projects and couldn't help but notice the giant state penitentiary so nearby, with a compelling story behind every barred door and Murray able to provide access and in-depth interpretation of all of them.

"Publicity photo for prison book written by Anne Butler
and Murray Henderson"

50

As it turned out, the books also served the purpose of providing a justification for Murray's entire career, highlighting the progressive and humanitarian reforms he instigated—or tried to—in a very backward system. They helped explain to his satisfaction for the first time why there had been so many negative reports about his tenure as Louisiana prison warden, primarily because of changes being implemented before funding provided a safety net, causing many unnecessary deaths.

Inmates slept with Sears Roebuck catalogs strapped to their chests to ward off knives in the night, and the first correctional officer in modern history was killed during Murray's stretch at Angola, prompting him to leave for Tennessee. Angola was so bad and the state proved so unable or unwilling to improve conditions that the federal courts would assume control of it and other state prisons, continuing to monitor conditions at Angola for several decades.

"Murray Henderson, Warden of Louisiana State Penitentiary at Angola, in May 1979"

UTL

In Tennessee, Murray served from 1975 to 1980 as state Commissioner of Correction, until the influence-peddling scandals written up in the book *Marie, A True Story*, by Peter Maas with pardon board head Marie Ragghianti, sent him back to Louisiana to run the forensic hospital for the state so he could finish out his Louisiana retirement coverage.

As *Marie* details, the Tennessee governor, Ray Blanton, and his chief counsel were sent to prison, but Murray took pride in the fact that the feds could never pin anything on him. He was described in the book as a hard-drinking old-line bureaucrat who'd been through the political mill and never forgot which side his bread was buttered on, but about the worst thing whistle-blower Marie Ragghianti had to say about him—other than being falling-down drunk at some official functions—was that he didn't want to make waves and was a loyal team player who worked hard to maintain the status quo. Even today, Marie Ragghianti, now Vice Chair of the U.S. Parole Commission, says she never truthfully thought Murray was involved in illegalities, just "was on the wrong side of the fence."

He'd always told me that the FBI had tried to set him up in Nashville while he headed the corrections department for the state, but still hadn't been able to find any criminal wrong-doings on his part despite exhaustive investigations. There was plenty of talk, though, just as there would be later at Forensic when a sexual harassment suit was filed against him, but he would emerge unscathed. His version was that he always tried to help the female employees under him, encouraging them to further their careers by continuing their educations and taking advantage of opportunities for advancement.

Others whispered aspersions about casting-couch auditions, though not to me. So I had no reason to doubt his story and only much later would begin to hear the other versions of it. Of all the people who worked for and with Murray, there were certainly many who had great respect and admiration for him; there were also a lot who hated his guts, who said he was mean as hell, who insisted he'd come close to being fired from Angola when a high state official arrived during a crisis and found him, the prison warden, passed out.

Now, I think he was probably neither as great as he thought he was nor as awful as some others thought he was, but most likely somewhere in between. But back then, I had heard few of these derogatory stories and had no reason to question his version of what an outstanding career he'd had. I was one of those who had great respect and admiration for him. That he left nearly every high-profile job under a cloud of suspicion should not be allowed to detract from the undeniable good that he did in those jobs and the improvements he made in the corrections system.

When we first began working on the Angola books in 1990, I knew very little about prisons or criminal justice. The only version I had of his career came from him and I believed it. He had undeniably made some lasting improvements in a rotten system, especially in Louisiana, and I thought a lot of him for having made the attempt. In the early years of our marriage, no one ever told me the other side of the story.

#

During the course of the production of the first of the two Angola books, Murray left his wife of forty years for me and I left my third husband for him. Murray really could be very entertaining and had a marvelous mind, seeming to remember nearly everything he'd ever learned; his mother was like that, memorizing a poem daily well into her 90s to keep her mind sharp. He had a good sense of humor and could make me laugh. This was important. I like to laugh.

When he asked me to marry him, I was hesitant at first. I just couldn't quite accept the image of the two of us as a couple, given the tremendous age difference. I shrank from personal inquiries when we traveled, embarrassed for anyone to think we were together. Strangers usually assumed I was his daughter and I never corrected them, though he was quick to set them straight.

It took months for me to accept the idea of marriage, and my children never did accept it. When I told my husband at the time about our relationship, Murray's and mine, he angrily shouted that all Murray wanted was to have me write his autobiography and make him look good. Maybe he had something after all, but at the time I didn't think that could possibly be all there was to it.

Looking back, I think that maybe Murray and his first wife, a really lovely woman he married during the war years (she being from Luxembourg working in Germany while Murray was in the military government there) were well suited. She was bright and attractive but he always insisted she had a well controlled and carefully disguised mean streak, and she certainly could be harsh to him if half his stories about home life were true. Only later would I see he had the same personality trait in spades, just a little more tightly controlled. I never heard the public stories of dysfunction in that marriage until way, way too late, but there were some. At least once, in fact, the police were called and Murray was picked up for commitment to the nearby state alcohol treatment facility, though the commitment was stopped at the doorway.

I was the great love of his life, he would tell me. He had never loved another woman as much as he loved me, he would say. "My little baby doll," he would call me. But there was always something skewed about our relationship, and we spent nearly as much time apart as we did together. It was not that I was a trophy wife; it was not that I was a child bride—I was neither young enough nor flashy enough. But the relationship was never quite normal, if there is such a thing, never quite on even terrain, and certainly never anything that anyone else ever understood; I'm not sure either of *us* ever did either. He was usually proud to introduce me as his wife. I avoided introducing him at all if I could.

#

Murray exhibited jealousy of every facet of my life that did not center around him. He was jealous of my children. He was jealous of my close relationship with Burnett. He was jealous of the time I spent with Rose Pate (head housekeeper and longtime friend—whose ample and imposing stature led Burnett to call her Big Rose) exercising to Richard Simmons' *Sweatin' to the Oldies* aerobics tapes in our constant struggle to lose weight. He resented the time I devoted to operating the B & B. Having run prisons for his entire career, he was used to absolute control—and there were many facets of my life over which I saw to it that he had none.

He was also used to violence. Cocke County, where he grew up in Tennessee in the Smoky Mountains, was about as rough as it gets. Peter Maas, author of *Serpico* and expert on law enforcement corruption, in one book refers to the area as big moonshine territory where the law was considered an alien force and the per capita murder rate was said to be the highest in the country. It wasn't an ordinary Saturday night in Cocke County, Maas insisted—and he was not exaggerating—unless there were a couple of shoot-outs.

Murray subscribed to the bi-weekly newspaper from his mother's hometown of Newport, county seat of Cocke County, and it looked like things hadn't changed one bit since Maas' early eighties description. Every front page had several murders, the gorier the better, and assorted other acts of violence described in vivid detail. In Murray's younger years there, at least according to his stories, everybody in the county either made moonshine, ran it, sold it, or bought and drank it—many of them all of the above.

The only child of a father who was gassed in World War I and returned to this country just long enough to marry and conceive a child before succumbing to the sickness in his lungs, Murray was raised primarily by his mother's elderly parents and their equally elderly siblings, since he didn't seem to think much of the succession of stepfathers who would leave his kindly mother widowed over and over again.

As a child Murray would spend endless chilly evenings in front of the dying fire, enthralled with tales of his family's early pioneering days among the first settlers of the Del Rio area, tales told in fascinating detail by great-uncles and great-aunts who personally recalled Indian scalpings and Civil War raids.

Growing up in the unmatched beauty of the Great Smoky Mountains of east Tennessee, Murray lived with his grandparents before he went off to military school, and he thought the world of them, as they did of him. His childhood playmates were the offspring of tenants on his grandfather's farm, dependent on his family for their livelihood and homes—and there is no question who was the leader in control of even the simplest of childhood pursuits. Still broad-shouldered and as an adult well over six feet tall, he must have been a large child as well, and I would wonder if he might not have been somewhat of a bully, not physically, but maybe intellectually.

It would seem that he never really had a childhood and was always around aged relatives who must have doted on him and enjoyed indulging him, keeping him always in the center of attention and perhaps inadvertently beginning the lifetime of control he would become more and more adept at exerting, all against the backdrop of violence, violence, violence.

In general I would have to say I considered him a gentle and humane person. I never heard him raise his voice, never saw him raise his hand in anger; but I always recognized that he had a tightly controlled mean streak, and I should have known that no one can be around violence for half a century in the brutal world of caged criminals and frequently sadistic guards without at least absorbing some acceptance of violence as a quick solution to certain social problems. Abuse of power has always been a potential problem among those in law enforcement and corrections, and the abuse is rarely confined to the job but often infects domestic relationships as well.

"Murray Henderson at the peak of a distinguished career
in corrections"

#

Murray had spent nearly a decade running Angola, Louisiana's
sprawling prison near St. Francisville, the country's largest maximum
security penitentiary, where more than 5,000 of the state's most dangerous criminals are housed in camps scattered across 18,000 acres
bordered by the Mississippi River and the rugged Tunica Hills.

Angola began as an antebellum cotton plantation whose owner
leased convicts from the state to make a fortune on their forced
and very cheap labor. Their lives came just as cheap, and the stag-
gering mortality rate was considered inconsequential as these poor
wretches struggled through swampy quagmires to build levees along

ıUTL

the Mississippi River and succumbed as often to yellow fever as to brutal beatings and inhumane living conditions.

Just after the turn of the century, the state wised up and decided it should be profiting from those labors so it purchased several neighboring plantation properties and began a feudal system that unfortunately continued well into the present century. The warden was the all-powerful master, with inter-generational families of overseers in the guise of prison guards profiting from the forced labors of inmates under their control.

Slavery had from the beginning been a cancer poisoning southern culture, starting with the earliest settlers. Even my family, some of them Quakers emigrating from Pennsylvania, had brought with them slaves to clear the wilderness, plant the crops, help construct the homes and provide personal care for the family. The earliest wills from my homeplace, including that of Samuel Flower in 1813, leave slaves by name to designated heirs as casually as any other treasured possessions.

Family journals and records carefully penned in spidery script show that the plantation mistress through most of the 1800s, Harriett Flower Mathews, knew each of several hundred slaves by name, clothing size, medical and personal needs so I trust there was not the mistreatment here as elsewhere; and further evidence of this is provided by the fact that many of the slave families stayed on as sharecroppers and paid farmers after the Civil War, and in fact were still living on the place into the 1960s.

But long after slavery had been eliminated from other segments of southern life, this insidious disease eating at the heart of society was in effect continuing at Angola, the very name of the place coming from the African country from which many of the original slaves there had been stolen. Inmates waited hand and foot on the "free" families—the guards and their wives and children, who lived in cheap state housing provided on prison property.

The inmates in their baggy "big stripe" uniforms did housework—cooking, cleaning, gardening—cared for personal livestock, chauffeured, babysat, whatever the families desired. There was at least one officer's wife running a florist business with inmates planting flowers on prison time and on prison property while she made the profits; and there were always, always the rumors of sexual favors given and taken.

It is no wonder that even the free folks from the prison were rarely readily accepted into "polite society" in St. Francisville, where polite society was made up of the cultural elite, the planter aristocracy whose families had carved from the wilderness the great cotton plantations and whose family pedigrees reached back to Anglo-Saxon royalty. And this exclusion included the highest of them all at Angola, the all-powerful warden, the chief, the king.

Until Murray, there hadn't ever been a warden who really gave a damn about social acceptance, but he did. Coming from the Tennessee mountains where his family had been pioneers, he had expected to be welcomed with open arms into the upper echelons of southern culture here in spite of the fact that comparisons were not entirely favorable: his family heirlooms, for example, looked rustic and crude compared to fine New Orleans-made antiques of this area; some of his speech patterns rang rough on the soft southern ear; and the mountain pioneers of his ancestry seemed lacking in a certain degree of culture and refinement expected here.

This was all insignificant at Angola where he was in absolute control, for there was certainly no one there to challenge his social standing. To say that the early officers lacked professional training would be an understatement; underpaid and isolated, the staff positions at Angola attracted a few dedicated lawmen but also a lot of power abusers with little education and less empathy. Stories of the old days abound, including one about the unlettered officer who could keep track of the number of inmates checked out of cellblocks under his command only by picking up a rock for each prisoner and placing it in his pocket, then removing a rock for each prisoner as he checked them back into the cells. Abuse and brutality were rife in the early part of the century, and things were not much better by the middle of it.

Murray had undeniably tried to make some improvements in

BUTL

conditions at Angola, fighting the entrenched staff as well as the tight state legislature to do what he could, but it was an uphill battle. Inmate trusties had for years performed armed guard duty, giving them the power to settle scores and rub out enemies among the convict population, besides tempting them with bonuses paid for every escapee killed. When the state corrected this abuse by outlawing it without providing funding to hire professional correctional officers to take the place of the inmate guards, many unnecessary deaths would occur in the prison before sufficient staff was eventually mandated.

Murray had to run the place with an iron fist and he was used to doing so, having previously run prisons in Iowa and his home state of Tennessee, but the number of escapes and the escalating violence during his regime made St. Francisville's old families wary of granting him full social acceptance, though he would come closer to gaining admittance to Feliciana genteel society, certainly, than any other Angola warden before or after him.

"Anne Butler and Murray Henderson at Louisiana State Prison, visiting with inmate Douglas Dennis, *Angolite* prison newsmagazine writer and subject of one chapter in their prison book, *Angola*."

CHAPTER 4

Given his background, it was understandable that Murray would be a forceful authoritarian figure, as demanded by his career field. But his controlling behavior hardly went over well with me. From a long line of strong, maybe even domineering women, I have hated since infancy the very idea of being told what to do and have in fact been known to do exactly the opposite out of spite. As I recall from earliest childhood, my mother's favorite oft-repeated nursery rhyme was the one about the little girl who had a little curl, right down the middle of her forehead, and when she was good, she was very *very* good, but when she was bad she was horrid!

And there were undeniably times when I was horrid. There was something really frustrating about growing up female in the south, even the new south. My mother was a pampered southern belle who had never even washed her own hair until she married (there was a servant who did it for her), and she was sorely disappointed that I much preferred my father's company to hers and had little or no interest in domestic graces or feminine wiles. "Charlie Butler in skirts" she used to call me, my father's name being Charlie, and I guess I did take after him, not in masculinity but in a strong sense of independence considered *unfittin'* for a girl.

My grandmother harped in vain about how ladies don't cross their legs (as I sprawled with legs crossed not just at the knee but ankle upon opposite knee), ladies don't let the sun even *see* their delicate

BUTL

facial complexions (as I freckled and peeled from constant summer sunburn), ladies stand erect and don't slump (the book she balanced on my head never stayed there for long), ladies don't raise their voices or cuss or smoke in public or chew gum or drink too much or any of the other fun things boys could get by with and I would eventually take such pride in doing.

There was something about Murray—nothing *overt*, but something underneath—that reminded me of all that, of the place women had in southern society, of the days when women were awfully close to slaves themselves, when they too were considered mere chattel.

In 1970 when I had first moved back from northern California, where I earned a Master's degree in English at Humboldt State to augment my BA in English from Sweet Briar College in Virginia, part of the culture shock was in realizing that women were still excluded, as were all blacks, from service on the grand jury as well as most petit juries for court trials unless they specifically requested inclusion. When I went to purchase my first car with money I earned working at the local welfare office and was told that my husband would have to sign for it, I pitched such a fit that the car dealer still closes his door and hides behind his desk when he sees me coming 25 years later.

Women and blacks were the downtrodden minorities in the south even a few decades ago. Isn't it strange, then, that some of the strongest people I know here are black women, persevering through abusive relationships and economic deprivation with a courage and determination which should put most men to shame. Through adversity comes strength, I guess, and just maybe that's why you find so few strong males in some parts of the south but a whole lot of very strong females.

One of my local heroines, now deceased, was a colorful two-fisted drinker who singlehandedly on horseback drove a herd of cattle 30 or 40 miles to the LSU campus in Baton Rouge to pay her college tuition during the Depression. After a series of rather brief marital encounters, she retired to the isolated family plantation sporting a black eye patch and taking no guff from anybody—much less some mere man—unless maybe it was her elderly father with whom she lived.

Not so many strong women in modern times wanted to pay the price and stick it out in the south; it was a whole lot easier to move away to more progressive areas where acceptance came at not quite such a high price. I would see this battle being waged in family matters when the male cousins who were lawyers automatically tried to assume control, infuriating a female cousin who's a very tough attorney with the Justice Department in Washington and could run rings around the others in court.

As a writer, I had been foolish to have ever changed my name with successive marriages and had vowed never to do it again. Murray resented my use of my own name instead of his after our marriage, though he wouldn't come right out and say so in public, fancying himself a progressive thinker and all. Once at a book signing he was introduced as Mr. Butler, and made a joke of it, saying I had graciously allowed him to retain his own name—but he never let me forget it.

He did not like the idea that I was running my own business without him, and he especially resented the fact that I consulted much more closely with Burnett than with him about future plans and projects, but Burnett, as my restoration carpenter, had shared for nearly twenty years my dreams and goals for the place. It was Burnett who did all the difficult preservation work as well as built all the new structures, and he had a much firmer grasp of what was appropriate. Coming as he did from the Tennessee mountains, Murray's taste was very different from mine, and he never quite understood what I was trying to develop here. But he was jealous about being excluded from power. All of this, of course, contributed to our frequent need to be apart from each other.

#

As in our previous separations, I hadn't actually asked Murray to leave. When he decided to go, however, I just made it clear that I

UTL

didn't exactly want him to *stay*. But this week-long separation had somehow been different, and I hadn't been paying close enough attention to the danger signals because I was so relieved to have him out of my house. He'd made veiled threats this time, which had never happened before. "You'll be sorry you ever heard my name," he had angrily said, and he'd yanked the new computer out of the wall to take with him in spite of the fact that he didn't even know how to turn it on, much less use it. I needed the Internet connections to my business home-page and e-mail, so I had to write him a $2,000 check on the spot to keep the computer.

Neither of us ever had much money to spare: I made plenty, but immediately plowed it all back into the business in improvements, not to mention having two minor children to support, one in college. He had a full-time job—admirable for his advanced age—and quite substantial retirement income from the states of Louisiana and Tennessee, plus Social Security; but he kept nearly all of his money for his own needs, mostly medical and an extensive wardrobe. He always liked to be well dressed. I must say, though, he was also generous in buying gifts for us all.

Murray loved to shop, especially for bargains, and we eventually had to build an entire new closet-room to accommodate all his many suits and dress shirts and sport coats and slacks and ties. At six feet two inches and slim, with silver hair sprayed in place, he did look good in well-tailored clothes and, in spite of having a rather large nose, he fancied himself quite handsome.

His own two children were grown, married (one divorced and remarried) and well off, certainly needing no financial aid from him. Mine were both still totally dependent on me: Chase was in school at expensive Emory University in Atlanta (with insulin-dependent juvenile diabetes and very costly continuing medical needs); Stewart was just entering junior high school. Murray and I shared no financial arrangements—no bank accounts, no charge accounts, no credit cards, *nothing*. If he went to the drugstore to pick up a prescription for himself, he might pick up something there for me as well, but he would charge my purchase on my separate account, not his.

When his mother, in her late 90's, died in Tennessee after exhausting her funds for years of round-the-clock nursing care at home, Murray sold her house and paid off what he had borrowed against it to provide good care for her, then paid off his credit cards and bought himself a Cadillac with the balance, using my ten-year-old Plymouth Voyager mini-van as a trade-in. He just took my car one day and came home without it, giving me instead his old car, which was newer than mine (he'd bought five cars for himself during our marriage, I'd bought none) but had over 100,000 miles on it while mine had about 30,000.

When I wasn't thrilled about the deal, he took his old car and traded it in on a used Mustang convertible for me, something he knew I'd always wanted and something I now see as his last effort to buy me (the years of lavishing me with racy lingerie and Godiva chocolates I finally had to see for what they were).

He'd arrived in our marriage driving a 1981 Toyota, which he sold (not *gave*) to me at Blue Book value as a first car for Chase, who was in high school. He would later buy her a Saturn on time as a generous graduation gift. In their divorce settlement, Murray's ex-wife had kept their Cadillac (and their home and a rental house), and apparently Murray would not be satisfied until he had another Cadillac of his own.

Usually it worked out that we each took care of our own expenses, sharing whatever surplus there might occasionally be. But during this separation, he'd talked incessantly of money, wanting back everything he'd spent on my place. I figured whatever he had spent balanced out in the long run, since he paid only for an occasional appliance or fixture and I paid for all of the construction and furnishing costs; also, I paid not only all the business expenses but also all of our living expenses through the business—the utilities, phone, cable, water, garbage and other bills—not to mention providing the house itself. When I pointed that out to him, he replied that he didn't use much electricity.

#

He called only twice during the week of separation, once when I thought he was feeling me out about returning to the marriage and, when he got no encouragement, once more to order me to repay him for a Jacuzzi I'd just purchased with his credit card for our bathroom. I did not have the funds at that time, having just given him $2,000 for the computer, but promised I would try to get the additional money he wanted.

He said he needed it before the first of September, as he hoped to take a trip to Singapore with his daughter Jeanne, who lived there but was in St. Francisville visiting her mother. It would be with those two that he would spend the week, in what must have been an atmosphere of escalating tension, and I can't help but envision the constant goading which must surely have nudged him along the pathway to tragedy.

Murray's daughter was a very bright and attractive woman who seemed almost obsessive in her desire to have everything exactly right, just perfect, and she always made Murray rather nervous, though he loved her very much as he did his son Jerry.

Jerry was more like his father. Jeanne seemed to be more like her mother, and neither of the women had ever accepted our marriage. The week of Murray's August 21 birthday, they had all taken him to a celebratory dinner at The Cottage Plantation.

Besides observing his 77th birthday, they seemed also to be celebrating his return to the family, others in the restaurant said. It was, coincidentally, the week of our seventh wedding anniversary—a lot of sevens. In the midst of this jubilant party, the waitress commented on Murray's uncharacteristic quietness.

One day during that week, he stopped by the local Council on Aging where Big Rose worked weekdays providing transportation and other services to the indigent elderly; I had been the founding director there and had in fact hired Rose. Murray donated some clothes in return for a charitable tax deduction and chatted with Rose for a few minutes, telling her he had moved out, was happier than he'd ever been, and was going to get on with his life. He would bitterly say to her that I had asked for space and that he'd see I got plenty of it.

On the day he moved out, I had helped him get all his things together to move, including one box I found in the bathroom armoire containing a small black pistol I had never seen before. I simply put it in a pile of his possessions and thought nothing more of it until the day I looked up to see it pointed at me. I had always thought my obituary would read, "Died of lead poisoning from cutting off her tongue licking the top of a can of condensed milk." Instead it damn near said, "Shot six times with a .38."

UTL

CHAPTER 5

When he arrived that Sunday morning, I let him come in and fixed him a cup of coffee. We sat on the back porch just where we always did, me in my wicker rocker just in front of the outside door, Murray in his wicker armchair on the other side of the sofa, both facing out through the glass to the back yard. He talked in the same well-modulated voice as usual; I listened awhile, then stopped paying much attention. He had said it all before—how much he had loved me, how I was the only woman he had ever truly loved, how he had tried to make me happy. It was too sad to hear again and again. I didn't want to listen and get drawn back down into a relationship that was no good for either of us, a relationship that needed to be over.

He recaptured my attention when he said, still without ever raising his voice, "Space? You wanted space? How's this for space?" And I looked up to see him standing over me, less than a foot away, arms extended straight out, holding in both hands the black .38 Taurus Special pistol, pointed directly at me.

The first bullet hit me in the abdomen and hurt, hurt a lot. I marveled at how quickly the bullet traveled; I could almost watch it leave the gun and feel its impact instantaneously, a sharp painful intrusion, and only then hear the noise. With the first bullet, I half rose from my chair, facing him, and said, outraged, "Stop! What are you *doing*? You *know* I've got children to raise."

Calm and coldly calculating, Murray took his time, aiming carefully from his vantage point of a mere foot or so away from where I still sat upright in the rocking chair. Three or four bullets pierced my stomach area in rapid succession, rupturing the intestines, hitting the kidney, missing the spinal column by less than an inch. Then two hit my right arm. The bullet that shattered my elbow into hundreds of fragments flung my arm out onto the arm of the chair, and the one that hit my shoulder shattered that as well, tearing the flesh and causing extensive bleeding, bouncing into the chest wall and damaging the lymphatic system as it went.

At that point, the pain from the elbow was unbelievable and my entire focus was on that area from then on. My lap filled with a pool of blood; the chair was soaked with blood, and the rug beneath it as well. There was a telephone on my check-in desk a few feet away from my chair, but I doubt that I could have moved that far because of the pain in my arm.

I could feel the dark rich red blood spreading across my body as I sat in the chair, still upright, and I could see my husband standing over me with the gun, which at some point he reloaded. I knew he would shoot me again if I moved, and I knew he was standing there waiting for me to die, standing there impeccably dressed in immaculate oxford cloth shirt, precisely creased trousers and a richly patterned Victorian tie that I had bought for him, hair combed and sprayed ever so neatly, totally in control as always.

And so I decided the smartest thing for me to do was *die*—or at least make him think I had. I let my eyes close and my head slump over to one side, and I tried to breathe as shallowly as possible. When he took his eyes off me for a moment or when he went into the house for brief periods, I would try to fill my lungs with air.

Later I was told that this helped to keep me from bleeding to death by somehow slowing my metabolism down. I can't quite say why I did this, but it is amazing to look back and realize that I never panicked, never struggled, never fought back, never screamed, never cried, but remained completely calm and rational throughout the

69

entire ordeal. I guess it must have been at this point that I began being carried by angels, for I felt a comforting presence I can't explain. And I felt absolutely no fear.

The marvelous Scandinavian actress and director Liv Ullmann, asked in a *Vanity Fair* piece how she would like to die, answered, "Serene and with curiosity over 'How will it be now.'" That's a good description of what I was—*serene*. Don't ask me why, but that's exactly what I was. Perhaps that's the state customarily achieved in the arms of angels.

Burnett, good Baptist that he was, had always teased me about hardly being the perfect upstanding southern lady, and I would later say to him that I bet he was surprised that God had seen fit to save me. "Honey," he would reply, "*Everyone* is worth saving." And he would remind me of the "*Footprints in the Sand*" posters about the doubter who, promised that God would be with him in troubled times, feels abandoned when he sees just one set of footprints in the sand, only to be reassured that those are the very times when God is *carrying* him. God was certainly carrying me, or at least carrying my burdens, for I carried none, felt no fear or worry, and was calm and strangely at peace.

I spoke to Murray only once more, and the fact that I did so shows that I had not yet adjusted my view of him as decent and honorable, had not yet fully absorbed the impact that he was actually trying to kill me. My 12-year-old son Stewart was flying into the Baton Rouge airport at 12:55, returning from Atlanta where he'd driven the day before with Chase to help unload her multitude of possessions into her dorm room at Emory University for the last semester of her senior year. I was supposed to meet Stewart at the airport, and I was tremendously concerned that he might arrive alone and find no one there to meet him.

I said to Murray that he would have to make sure someone picked up Stewart so he wouldn't be frightened. At this point I still had no reason to consider him a danger to Stewart, and it never occurred to me that he might harbor any animosity toward a child, against anyone but me; it was hard enough to grasp how much hatred he obviously had for *me*.

He did go outside long enough to use the pay phone, the only phone on the place outside the main house and so out of my hearing. After calmly getting her phone number from one of the housekeepers who was walking between cottages on the grounds, he called Big Rose. When Rose said she had to go to church but would ask her daughter Carol Lynn to meet Stewart at the airport, Murray said he'd pay Carol Lynn $25 to do so. I must have been in and out of consciousness, because I don't remember Murray being gone, and apparently he didn't stay outside long.

I do, however, have very clear recollections of Murray at one point going into the dining room through the open French doors just to the rear of where I was sitting, and I heard a *glug-glug-glug* noise. What I thought he was doing was pouring gasoline on the floor and getting ready to burn the house down around me since he'd always hated the house and been so jealous of my love for it.

#

What Murray really was doing when I heard the *glugging* noise behind me as I sat bleeding to death on the back porch was pouring a fifth of red vermouth into his system so that he would be legally drunk when the police came. A recovering alcoholic, he did not drink at all during our marriage. In fact, I had never seen him take a drink, although he had been a notorious drinker during much of his corrections career, to the point of dysfunction in the workplace and abuse in the home. Somebody eventually told me that at one crisis point before Murray left Angola, the governor had sent a high state official by helicopter from the capital to check on conditions, and at the penitentiary a disgusted employee had angrily pointed down, saying, "*There*, there's the warden of your state prison,"—and there was Murray, passed out on the ground.

He had very carefully purchased the bottle of vermouth and a single drink, a cognac and soda, that same Sunday morning at the St. Francisville Inn, a wonderful Victorian hostelry and restaurant operated by friends of mine who'd be sure to remember his being there. Had he bought it at the grocery store, no one would have noticed and he'd have had no witnesses to his purchase of the alcohol he was no doubt already planning to make part of his defense.

He didn't even pay for it. The dining room waitress, Donna Price, had to go and ask the owners if he could charge it or come back later to pay for it, since they usually sell by the drink and no one was sure of the price of a bottle. Since he always had plenty of cash and credit cards, he surely could have paid whatever price was asked so this must have been just another way to assure that they would remember his purchase. It was not that he didn't have the means to pay; later, when the police would empty his pockets, they found $25, which he had apparently gotten out of his wallet to pay Carol Lynn for picking up Stewart.

#

I would also later learn that he had spent the early part of that same morning, while I was in church, down along the banks of the Mississippi River just below St. Francisville, target shooting with the pistol in the area known as Bayou Sara.

This desolate riverbank area under the bluffs of St. Francisville had been a thriving river port in the mid-1800s, with extensive commercial and residential neighborhoods and a mile of warehouses to store cotton being shipped by steamboat to New Orleans and thence around the world, but floodwaters and devastating fires had wiped out the entire town of Bayou Sara. Now there was nothing left but cottonwoods and weeping willows and the rusting hulks of abandoned machinery, and the river waters reclaimed much of the area with every spring rise.

As a child, I often went down there picking dewberries with Cap'n Johnny Ard. I was never quite sure why he was called Cap'n Johnny, but it was never "John" or "Mr. Ard," always Cap'n Johnny. He knew where to find the ripest, plumpest dewberries for making jellies and jam cakes, and he knew the history of the whole area, a lot of it first-hand.

Cap'n Johnny knew all about Scotsman John Mills establishing this early trading post right on the Mississippi River where Bayou Sara emptied its waters, a sheltered spot where flatboaters had long sought safe harbor. Around this post, a rowdy shanty settlement sprang up, taking its name from the bayou. Early written accounts attriibute the name of the stream to an old woman named Sara who lived at its mouth and washed her clothes in its waters. At least the name Bayou Sara blessedly took precedence over previous designations for the stream on early French maps as "*La Riviere de la Pucelle Juine*" (River of the Jewish Virgin) and as "*Baiouc a la Chaudepisse.*" Not even Cap'n Johnny could vouch for whether old Sara was Jewish, but for sure she wouldn't have long remained a virgin hanging around the rough riverside shantytown, and the English translation of Bayou Gonor-rhea was hardly as melodic as the French.

Bayou Sara in its heyday attracted heavy flatboat traffic as well as cargo barges and steamboats plying the Mississippi River from St. Louis to New Orleans along that era's most significant and well-traveled highway, the river channel. Shipping point for the cotton and produce from the rich surrounding plantation country, arrival point for the fine furnishings and other finished goods the wealthy planters imported to beautify their homes and lives, Bayou Sara became an important river port.

There were fortunes to be made in the thriving settlement, and the determination of its residents saw Bayou Sara rebuilt after several devastating fires (one in the 1850's destroyed more than fifty structures, the very heart of commerce in the town) and even more destructive shelling and torching by Union forces during the Civil War.

From its early-day rowdiness as a port filled with barrooms and

73

gambling saloons catering to the rough riverboat crews, Bayou Sara by the turn of the century had settled down into a thriving commercial center with an extensive residential area as well. Social life may have centered around St. Francisville up the hill, but trade teemed and activity bustled around Bayou Sara's China Grove Hotel and its boarding houses, drugstores and apothecaries, saw mills and lumber yards, livestock exchanges, butcher shops, fish markets, fairgrounds, baseball fields, liveries and stables, grocery and dry goods emporiums, post and express offices, clothing stores, railroad stations, ice houses, banks and other business establishments.

In 1850 Bayou Sara was the largest port between New Orleans and Memphis. Packet steamers and cargo vessels laden with the produce of the entire Mississippi Valley docked at Bayou Sara's wharves, and a regular fleet of luxurious steamboats picked up and discharged Feliciana folk bound for New Orleans and thence the world.

The West Feliciana Railroad, America's first standard gauge line, transported cotton from the plantations between Woodville, Mississippi, and St. Francisville to the port for shipment to factors in New Orleans for sale. But the coming of the railroad, ironically, signaled the beginning of Bayou Sara's demise, for it brought an accompanying decrease in river traffic. Cotton, too, fell into a decline due to the ravages of disease and the boll weevil as well as repeated crop failures, and devastating fires and floods finished off what was left of Bayou Sara. Its residents sought safety on higher ground atop the bluffs at St. Francisville, and even some of its structures were saved by laboriously hauling them up the hill on rolling logs pulled by teams of sturdy straining oxen.

Today proliferating swamp growth obscures the site of this commercial settlement that drew its life blood, and eventually its death as well, from the waters of the mighty Mississippi.

Popular at nighttime with teenagers seeking privacy, the desolate area serves as an approach to the ferry landing for crossing the Mississippi during the day, and it's perfect for target practice. In his years in corrections, Murray had taken many firearms courses and had also done a lot of hunting after World War II when he was in military government in Germany, so he was a pretty good shot in spite of being a little rusty. Later, he would tell Rose about target shooting along the river that morning, and several witnesses had seen him there and heard gunshots.

UTL

CHAPTER 6

The shooting occurred between 10:30 and 11 a.m. I knew that one of my cleaning staff, Patrice Nelson, was scheduled to come into the main house by noon so I could give her the house keys; she and the other housekeeper, Rosemary Blakes, needed the keys to have access to the laundry facilities at the end of the back porch to continue the Bed and Breakfast washing while I went to the airport to meet Stewart,

I think I had sat in the chair playing dead and slowly bleeding for at least an hour before I heard the back door open to the porch and secretly looked up to see Rosemary coming in with her arms full of sheets and towels.

And I thought to myself, oh shit! It *would* be Rosemary. If ever there were an example of the Good Lord punishing someone for speaking ill of another, this was it. Poor good-hearted Rosemary, who meant so well but who was so oblivious to everything that I had literally commented a hundred times that there could be a dead body on the floor of one of the Bed and Breakfast cottages and Rosemary would carefully sweep around it and never notice a thing.

In came Rosemary, loaded down with dirty laundry, a foot from the chair where I sat bleeding to death, Murray calmly sitting in his own chair at the other end of the wicker sofa. She turned and went into the laundry room at the end of the porch, started the washer, walked back past my chair and out the door, never saying a word.

Only later, when questioned by incredulous police, would she admit thinking fleetingly that it was odd I had changed from a yellow blouse to a red one. And even later, upon reflection, she would remark that she had never seen me taking a nap before.

Rosemary had even heard several of the gunshots as she walked from one cottage to another behind the main house, but thought they were the sounds of someone striking a piece of metal or tin, she said. When it finally dawned on her that the red color of my clothing and the noises she had heard might be connected, she began looking for Patrice, but didn't find her and went about cleaning the Treehouse cottage.

Patrice, thank God, was a little more observant. When she came through the back door right at noon as scheduled, she immediately took in what was going on and had the presence of mind to remain completely calm as she said to Murray, still standing over me, "What happened? Miss Anne needs a doctor right away!" "No," he answered her, "she's already gone. This doesn't involve you. You go on back outside. I won't hurt you." And Patrice, still calm, carefully backed away, down the outside stairs and along the sidewalk leading away from the house, never turning her back on him, until she rounded the corner of the Old Kitchen where he could no longer see her.

Pausing awhile to make sure Murray was not following her, Patrice found Rosemary and together they went, in hysterics, to the pay phone to call Big Rose, the head of my cleaning staff who serves as a mentor/mother-figure for the younger staff members. Big Rose, Patrice figured, would know just what to do, and the fact that Rose was at home dressing for church some 15 miles distant did not enter her mind.

Nor, apparently, did it bother a frantic Big Rose, who later said Patrice was crying so much that she didn't even recognize her voice and had to ask who was calling. "It's Patrice, and Mr. Henderson has shot Miss Anne," was the hysterical reply. "Oh, my God," answered Rose, "ya'll get in a cabin and lock up, and I'll be right there."

Rose covered those 15 miles in her pickup truck in about 10 minutes, stopping only long enough to pick up her equally large son

77

Carl. We have all said since then that it was the Lord's mercy Big Rose was not working here that Sunday (as she often was), because she would surely have charged right in through the back door and either been killed herself or killed Murray with her bare hands.

But even Rose wanted to be sure of doing the right thing at this crucial time, and so instead of turning into my driveway, she let Carl out to protect Patrice and Rosemary and continued a mile down the highway to turn in at the home of my cousin Bob, a young attorney whose wife Liz and three small daughters were there with him.

Rose burst through the doors in hysterics; Bob gathered the gist of what was going on and ran into the bathroom to tell Liz, soaking in bubblebath after a morning walk, then rushed out to his Bronco. He was going to use the car phone to call for help out of hearing range of the children, but Liz was sure he was going to get his gun and rush over here so she ran out naked, screaming "Stop him! Stop him!"

And Rose jumped into her truck and returned to Butler Greenwood in spite of Bob's admonition not to. "I told him I had to go back because Carol Lynn was on her way with Stewart and I couldn't let her come in on this so I had to get back over there and stop her from going to the house."

And so it was at precisely 1:02 p.m. that the first call was made to 911, several hours after the shooting. It was Liz who called 911, simultaneously as Bob called the sheriff's office from his car phone. Luckily Deputy Randy Metz was having Sunday dinner with his parents five or six miles up the road from here and, as soon as the call came in, he jumped into his squad car with partner Randy Holden, calling for backup assistance from young Jamie Daniel. Randy Metz and Randy Holden were two of the finest deputies in the parish; poor Jamie was in only his second week with the department.

I had known them all for years; Randy Metz's mother Lily is a close friend who worked for me when I was director of the local Council on

Aging, and I had ghostwritten the autobiography of his amazing grandfather James Imahara, second-generation California Japanese-Ameri-
can who overcame internment and ensuing bankruptcy during World
War II to found a million-dollar nursery business in Louisiana and
send all ten of his children to college. Ironically, Randy Holden had
been one of the policemen ordered to pick up Murray some fifteen
or sixteen years back when his first wife began commitment proceedings due to his drinking.

Opening my eyes just barely, I could look out from the glassed
porch into the back yard, Spanish moss swaying in the live oaks and
ducks waddling around the pond banks. I could see entering this
bucolic scene Randy Metz in his sheriff's department uniform, stealth-
ily coming up the walkway to the back door. Randy Holden, who'd
been behind the wooden lower half of the back door where I couldn't
see him, lunged in and grabbed me by the legs to try to drag me to
safety and was taken aback by their coldness; he told me later that I
was still and gray and that there was absolutely no blood circulating in
my legs at all, but at his touch I moved just enough that he could tell
I was alive.

Until then, they'd thought I was already dead. Realizing I was
alive, they immediately decided they had to get me out of there,
especially when they heard Murray walking and saw him in the kitchen.
The two Randys rushed in with guns drawn. Jamie stayed outside with
a shotgun, looking through the glass.

I heard the two deputies at the door yelling, "Drop the gun! Drop
the gun!" Their attention was focused just behind me where Murray
still stood, first in the kitchen and then backing into the dining room.
"You're too late," he told them. He was trying to get his pistol out of
his pocket, but the hammer hung up on the pocket lining.

His finger was on the trigger when Randy Holden lunged again,
and through Murray's pants pocket grabbed the gun and held the
cylinder so that it couldn't fire as Murray kept clicking the trigger.
Whether he was trying to shoot the deputies or simply trying to get
them to shoot him, it was a highly dangerous situation for everyone

79

involved, a situation these two young deputies handled with calm professionalism.

Murray wouldn't remove his hands from his pockets or get down on the floor as ordered, and the deputies had to rush him as he backed up saying, "No, no." Later, Randy Holden would describe the frantic activity: "He started looking like he was trying to come out of his pocket with something. At that time he was having trouble with it and I saw the butt of a pistol, the handle of a pistol. At this time as he hesitated, I rushed him, grabbed the pistol—with his hand still in the pocket; Deputy Metz came to assist me, we put him in a secure position and disarmed him. I was pretty much holding on to the pistol until I could get him in a position away from Miss Anne to disarm him. I disarmed him at the foot of the steps. We kinda pulled him outside, and then I retrieved the pistol from his right pocket." The gun removed from Murray's pocket was fully loaded with lead-nosed bullets, and there were more bullets loose in his pocket.

Murray was furious, telling them, "You didn't have to handle *me* so rough!" He would later complain to the Sanity Commission that he'd been treated "like a desperado or something." The deputies noticed a distinct odor of alcohol on his breath, but other than his anger at having been handled roughly, they noted that he was calm, not agitated, not crying; and he never once inquired about my condition.

. And then poor Randy Metz came to me, incredulously asking, "Miss Anne, are you still *alive*?" He said later that he had been sure I was dead, that I hadn't moved a muscle until Murray was handcuffed, but then I opened my eyes and spoke. "Kinda startled me," Randy admitted, "and I said, 'Just stay still, we got an ambulance coming' and she nodded."

I remember begging the deputies to see that someone picked up Stewart at the airport, not knowing that when Murray had called Big Rose, she had sent her daughter Carol Lynn to meet him. No reason had been given for why I could not pick him up myself, but Rose was used to my getting involved with tour groups and being unable to get out of the house on time. Not until Patrice called her had she known

anything was wrong. By then Carol Lynn had already left for the airport, and in fact she arrived back at my house soon after the police
did. Thank God she did not beat them there; if Murray had intended
to pay Carol Lynn for picking up Stewart, as evidenced by the $25 he
had loose in his pocket, just what exactly was he planning on doing
with poor Stewart?

#

I felt that my personally knowing all three of the deputies who
arrived to help me was no coincidence; it was the Lord's way of giving
me something to hold onto, a familiar face, a well-known voice, something I *knew*. And that blessing continued with the arrival of the ambulance. I don't know very many of the paramedics who staff the local
hospital's ambulance, but I knew both of the people in the ambulance crew that particular afternoon—the EMT Steve Moreau, who
calls himself a coonass from Opelousas, and aide Albert Jean Webb,
whose family I had known for three generations—so again I had something familiar to hang onto. I had met the paramedic several months
earlier when I'd taken Murray to the hospital with chest pains which
turned out to be from a hiatal hernia rather than his heart as he had
thought, and so I felt I was in the hands of friends, besides being in
the arms of angels.

Steve would later tell me he thought sure I was already dead when
he ran up the back steps and saw me drenched in blood. He said he
could hardly believe it when I opened my eyes and started talking to
him, still worrying about someone meeting Stewart at the airport.
Assessing the situation as extremely critical, not sure of the angle of
entrance of the bullets and so not sure if the cardiopulmonary area
was affected, he immediately started IVs and began pumping fluids,
stabilizing the wounds, strapping me onto a spine board because of
the possibility of spinal cord involvement, rushing me out to the waiting ambulance.

He was not sure, and even the doctors would later not be able to determine, exactly how many times I had really been shot—somewhere between five and seven, as the gun had been reloaded. At any rate, the state police ended up with four whole bullets and broken fragments which seemed to have come from two others. Additional bullet fragments remained in my body.

"Miss Anne," Steve Moreau would tell me later, "I thought you were gonna croak at any minute. I've seen a lot of murder scenes and killings in my 15 years as a paramedic, and you were about the worst I've seen. Somebody wanted to cause you a lot of suffering and pain, because you were gut-shot like you'd do a dog in the dump, and somebody wanted you to hurt a lot before you died. That was no crime of passion. In a crime of passion, he'd have killed you quick and then shot himself. What this was, was just plain *mean*, the meanest thing I've seen. But I'd have to say you're the strongest person I've ever seen with a gunshot wound, and I couldn't believe you talked and were responsive the whole way down to the hospital."

As I was carried out to the ambulance, leaving a trail of blood along the way, Big Rose rushed over from the pool house where Carl had made her wait, sobbing, asking what she should do about Stewart and about the main house. "Take Stewart to his dad's," I calmly told her, "and watch the house." She said I was speaking just as matter-of-factly as ever. I have no recollection of speaking to her at all.

When Stewart arrived soon after the ambulance left, Rose would gently explain to him what had happened, and Stewart, weeping with helplessness and frustration, would say he never *had* liked Papa, as he called Murray. Nearly everyone else involved would eventually voice similar sentiments.

#

I don't remember the IVs being started, but I know several were. I do remember being sure I was riding on the floor of the ambulance because it was so rough, (actually I was on a cot), and I distinctly recall hearing Steve shout to the driver, "Hit 100!" I could feel my clothes being cut off of my body, thinking with regret that I had on a new long linen skirt of cream and blue flowers and a butter-colored t-shirt that I would never see again, and I could feel Albert Jean yanking off my sandals.

I clearly remember thinking as we sped along that I was having an experience few people ever live to tell about and that it would make a fabulous book. In my mind I organized and wrote it, in minute detail. At least I thought I was doing it in my mind; I may have been saying at least some of my thoughts out loud because I also remember Steve frantically saying to me, "Keep talking to me, Miss Anne! *Please* don't stop talking!"

All I really remember doing though, was to complain about the excruciating pain in my arm, which must have been tied down but which I kept thinking was flopping around with every bump in the road. "My arm, Steve! My arm!" I remember saying, to which he frantically replied, "Fuck your arm, Miss Anne! We've got more to worry about than your arm!"

The little local hospital in St. Francisville, which did no surgery and at that time could not even admit any in-patients because the roof was leaking, would later question Steve's competence for not stopping at its emergency room first before transporting me to the nearest full-size facility, but if he had stopped, I would surely not have made it.

Somehow Steve with consummate skill managed to keep me alive until we got to Lane Memorial Hospital in Zachary, 20 miles away, with Jamie Daniel in his sheriff's patrol car providing escort. Before we'd left the house, Chief Deputy Albert Bryant had told everyone with regret that there was no way I could possibly live and that my funeral arrangements should be made. Poor Bob, frantically following the ambulance to the hospital, was already making plans for the care of my children.

CHAPTER 7

As I was transported to the hospital, there was total chaos at my home. Most of the sheriff's department had arrived, including W. M. "Bill" Daniel, the sheriff himself, as well as state police detectives and the crime lab staff. Just about the only deputy who wasn't there was the sheriff's son Glenn, to whom I had been married briefly in the 80s and who remained a close friend; fortunately he was not on duty that day, for he would later remark that had he walked into the house and seen me sitting there bleeding and Murray trying to pull his gun out of his pocket, he'd have shot the son of a bitch. He really wouldn't have, being too professional, but it sure was a comforting thought.

The house was cordoned off and a search warrant executed. The cleaning staff was kept outside and interviewed collectively by the deputies and then individually by detectives. Not having been much of a drinker or carouser in my old age—I disliked parties, hated crowds and mostly stayed at home minding my own business—I had always had cordial relations with the local law enforcement agencies, especially the sheriff's department. But the state police detectives came from Baton Rouge and didn't know me from Adam, so they had to start from scratch in trying to figure out what had happened and what might have precipitated it.

The intense search of the house turned up nothing belonging to Murray, which they found odd until it was explained that we had separated. They did, however, find some puzzling things. First they thought I must be a crackpot, having carefully concealed torn strips of paper behind every sofa cushion; only later would they learn that I always tore the sample perfume strips from magazines and stuck them around for the pleasant scent.

Then they found syringes in the refrigerator, suspicious until it was explained that my daughter Chase has been an insulin-dependent diabetic since the age of nine. They even questioned the prescription medication labeled for Hilda, who had not been mentioned in the brief family history hastily given to detectives; upon closer inspection, it was determined that the prescribing physician was a vet and Hildegarde was Murray's big black German shepherd.

They questioned whether in fact I was more of a drinker than anyone knew since there was a well-stocked liquor cabinet in the dining room, but some of the bottles were covered in dust and had been there since the time of my grandmother's death in 1962, while the Ballantine scotch was left over from my mother's time, and she died in 1982. An inveterate recycler, I've never been one to throw out something which might prove useful later, and we often had guests who wanted a drink so I just kept everything, even unopened bottles of beer left in B&B cottages after guests departed. The only thing that was mine, I later explained to the detectives, was the bottle of Bailey's Irish Creme in the refrigerator, and that was hardly a drinker's drink.

#

Interviewing the staff, the detectives probed for answers and explanations. Had they ever heard me yell at my husband? Had they ever seen the two of us argue? Had they ever seen me strike him, or him strike me? The answers were always, truthfully, no. Had they ever heard me use bad language? Here my loyal staff may have fudged just a bit, but any cussing I used was never directed toward Murray and was usually forthcoming only after a visitation by the occasional "house guest from hell" which every B&B experiences periodically.

The detectives were particularly interested in Rosemary. How in

Anne Butler

the world, they wondered, could anyone be so unobservant as to walk past a dying woman covered in blood and notice nothing. But the more they talked to Rosemary, the more they understood that that was just Rosemary and that there had been no malice or intent involved. She simply did not notice much and when she did notice, she simply did not make the connection between what she saw and doing something about it.

Big Rose, a formidable force not to be trifled with, was still so upset she made the detectives keep a respectful distance. She didn't want "*no* mens" near her, she told them, and she damn well meant it. But one of the detectives, Steve Dewey, turned out to be an old Mississippi boy from close to Rose's childhood home on the Mississippi River, and he was so kind to her that he eventually even drove her home that evening, calming her with discussions of the Bible and old friends from their mutual old stomping grounds. He was the same detective who would gently take a deposition from me, weak voiced but clear of mind, in the intensive care unit so that there would be a record of the crime in case I died.

The search of the house and staff interviews took all day, and not until nighttime could Big Rose get into the house to straighten up after all the investigations. She took her responsibilities so seriously that she stayed through the night, watching the house as I had asked her to do.

Unfortunately she had not yet been allowed in when poor Chase began calling from Emory to let me know her dorm room phone number. Since the dorm phones were not yet activated, she was calling collect from the lobby and got a sheriff's deputy who took a while to figure out how to handle her call. He eventually accepted the charges and told her to call Bob for information, scaring her to death.

Finally reaching Bob's wife Liz, Chase was told only that there had been an accident, Stewart was all right, I was in the hospital, and Bob would call with details as soon as he knew something. And so Chase began an all-night vigil by the dorm lobby pay phone until she could get a flight out of Atlanta to Baton Rouge the next morning.

Weep For The Living

#

My closest relative besides my children is a sister, Mary Minor Hebert, who lives in Austin, Texas, and she and her husband Mike, an attorney and professor at the University of Texas Law School, caught the first plane out that Sunday afternoon. By the time they reached Lane Hospital, the emergency waiting room had filled up with what must have seemed like half of St. Francisville: Bob; longtime friend and working partner Burnett Carraway and his sweet wife Ruby, who for years had managed to take care of me and my children during times of crisis; gentle loving Stewart, who said he wanted to get a gun and shoot Murray; assorted good friends and cousins; and the Grace Church ministers Ken Dimmick and Matt Rowe, who would administer the rites of extreme unction and insist that Stewart be allowed in to see me no matter how awful I looked. Bob sat through the entire five hours of abdominal surgery; the others straggled in and stayed as long as they could.

Again that divine intervention seems to have assured that I would hit absolutely marvelous surgeons on call that particular shift. Dr. Lisa Mazoch, strapping lady surgeon with as much human compassion as she has pure medical skill, did five full hours of surgery in the abdominal area, performing a colostomy where the intestines had been severed, removing the gallbladder, sewing up the damage to the kidney (I lost about a third of it), removing those bullets and fragments she could locate. In the Emergency Room and in surgery, I needed five transfusions, having lost so much of my own blood, and had three more in the next few days.

State Police detective Steve Dewey was waiting right there to preserve the evidence after surgery. Four intact bullets were accounted for, three in me and one that had penetrated the elbow and chair; only later would the final bullet make its way to the skin surface in my back just to the rear of the colostomy, and it would be removed in the fourth surgery in November.

It was decided by orthopedic surgeon Dr. Donald Fonte, who confessed to almost walking away in horror when he counted the number

87

UTL

of fragments the elbow had been blown into, that the arm surgery would have to wait until the end of the week—so my right arm was simply stabilized and packed in ice.

As I was taken to recovery and then to Intensive Care where I would remain for almost two weeks, Dr. Mazock informed the waiting friends and family members that I should indeed make it. Actually, in spite of at least five bullet entrance holes, one exit hole and several more drainage holes emptying profuse internal blood seepage, tubes everywhere and looking like a virtual ghost, my vital signs had remained so stable that I had not once even been put on the critical list.

Back in St. Francisville, Murray had been taken in handcuffs to the jail and booked. He was only charged with second-degree attempted murder. For *first* degree, even attempted, there must be mitigating circumstances—the victim must be very young, or very old, or rape must be involved. Only once, the chief deputy would later recall, during the nine-hour period of time he was with the defendant, did Murray ever ask how I was, and that was just in passing, the deputy testified later. To the sheriff and chief deputy he would confide, "My friends, I've screwed up," and he would lead the chief deputy to consider him suicidal and at risk of a heart attack. The sheriff calmly had him examined by the parish coroner then transported to the hospital in Baton Rouge for cardiac tests and a psychiatric evaluation, and neither examining physician found evidence of any pressing physical or mental concern.

A local attorney was retained for him, the lawyer-son of his close friend, St. Francisville mayor Billy D'Aquilla. A former attorney of Murray's was also quickly on the scene, a rotund assistant district attorney whose questionable involvement and rifling through the sheriff's confidential crime statements would later lead, at least in part, to the local DA's recusal from the case. The district attorney for our parish, the 20th Judicial District, would cite friendship and political ties with

Murray as the cause for recusing himself and his office. Murray had indeed helped his candidacy quite a lot, introducing him to friends and associates, but it was on *my* property, not Murray's, that the first campaign sign was displayed on white-owned property for his candidacy as the first black DA in the state.

Murray's children and ex-wife quickly posted $100,000 property and cash bond for him. He didn't spend even 24 hours in jail.

CHAPTER 8

The intensive care unit at Lane Memorial Hospital is a respite for acutely ill patients needing special individualized attention—and I certainly qualified. I spent about two weeks in the unit on such strong pain medication, including morphine, that I remember very little of the experience. I do clearly recall hallucinating as I lay in the bed, watching strange black bugs crawling all over the ceiling and seeing frost forming along the walls.

The frost bothered me the most because it kept covering the large clock hanging on the wall, which I was trying very hard to watch to assure myself that time was indeed passing, that this terrible period of pain and suffering would not last forever. (Later, as I struggled through excruciating physical therapy, I would make sure I was positioned so that I could see the clock there too, a visible assurance that there was a time limit on the torture.)

It wasn't that I was particularly scared by these delusions; I just remember watching them with interest rather than terror. On subsequent hospital stays I would in more lucid moments note that the ceiling tiles did indeed have black specks in them and there was a wallpaper border around the tops of the walls that I must have fuzzily seen as frost forming.

I had been told by visiting family members that Murray had been released from jail and was free, and that I needed to be cautious as there was some reason to think he might try again to kill me. I was registered into the hospital under another name, Anne Jones which someone pulled out of the blue, and the nurses and other hospital staff were diligent in their efforts to keep unapproved visitors away from me. There was a photograph of Murray posted at each nurse's station.

This security was put into effect after Murray's son Jerry, an assistant district attorney in another parish, had come into my room in intensive care and spoken with me when there were no family members at the hospital. I had always liked Jerry and had good relations with him; he and his fiancee often stayed in my B&B for weekends, and his son came up from New Orleans in the summers to visit Stewart and enjoy the swimming pool and country living.

Because of the strong medications I was taking, I have absolutely no recollection of this visit from Jerry but it made my family increasingly concerned for my welfare, especially since the day after the shooting Jerry had climbed over a locked gate across my driveway and with his fiancee and sister had driven his father's car out through the lawns, removing without police permission what could have been important evidence.

There was some suggestion of business files being tampered with and records rifled at some time during my absence. I was not there and have no way of knowing what exactly went on. I *do* know that confidential Bed & Breakfast financial reports would be in the hands of the defense attorney by the time of trial preparation, and I certainly had not given them to him or to anyone else, but I have no way of knowing exactly when or by whom they were removed from my home office.

#

As my mind slowly cleared, it was filled with worries. What effect was this having on my poor children? Would Murray come to the hospital and try to finish the job? Could I trust any of the hospital personnel, when many of them could well have worked for him at one of the several nearby state institutions and hospitals he had run? What was happening to my business at home without me to run it? Would I be bankrupt and lose everything with my income shut off? I was also beginning to have some dim understanding of my physical condition and what long-term permanent handicaps I would have.

I had a very vivid nightmare of being sent home and being there alone in a hospital bed with an overhead trapeze arrangement so I could try to pull myself up with my one good arm since I couldn't strain all the staples in my abdomen by using my stomach muscles to sit up. Unable to get out of bed and increasingly frustrated with having to wait for someone to help me, I kept hearing in my head a voice saying, "Help yourself. Help your *own* self."

I also remembered my will, a handwritten one sitting on a shelf in my home office. I had revised it as recently as May 1997, just a few months before all this happened. I left everything I had to my two children, naturally, but without Murray's knowledge I had added a codicil stipulating that my husband, should he survive me, was to have the right to live in whichever of the Bed & Breakfast cottages he might choose, until the end of his own life. Wouldn't *that* have been interesting?

One particularly bad night in intensive care, delusive on morphine, I interpreted loud noises nearby as being a party. When my nurse Ken came into the room, I let him know how furious I was at being neglected (which couldn't have been farther from the truth). Mad, scared, I was certainly an awful patient, but Ken sat by the side of my bed, holding my hand and looking into my eyes as he spent hours reassuring me and giving me strength. I know the other nurses were just as caring and competent, but for some reason it was Ken who penetrated the fog and gave me the courage to carry on.

After I was released into a private room and was a little clearer mentally, I sent for Ken to apologize for being so mean, and he assured me that most ICU patients are just as screwy. The fact that my new mental clarity showed him to have a long bleached blonde ponytail and an earring in one ear endeared him none the less to me. Of all the excellent nurses I would have over the course of the next two years, Ken was always my favorite, his wife Goldie a close second.

#

While the first ten days of hospitalization passed in a blur for me, poor Chase and the rest of my family were struggling to get the B&B business functional again. My sister and cousins were all for shutting it down, but fortunately Chase understood the absolute necessity of continuing to bring in some income, and stood up to the older family members, insisting that Butler Greenwood would re-open within four or five days of the shooting.

The cleaning staff knew their jobs well and immediately assumed additional responsibilities—the 70-year-old groundskeeper Johnny Harris needed no one to tell him how to continue to keep the lawns in immaculate condition as he always did—but *no one* knew my job, the heavy burden I alone shouldered, and it was extremely difficult for them to figure things out in my absence.

Chase knew the most about running the business. She assumed most of the responsibility for handling cancellations and reservations, finding volunteers to man the phones and check-in desk. All the while, she was also running back and forth to the hospital, perform-ing the tasks most needed by me, struggling to re-orient me to time and place and reality.

Friends and family members volunteered to stay at the house in the evenings, but Chase would not stay there and neither would my sister. Even Burnett, who usually loves this place, having invested so many years and so much effort in it, would say that once my children and I were no longer in residence, it was the darkest, loneliest place he'd ever been.

So poor distraught Chase farmed herself out to other houses at night, returning home only in the daytime and running the B&B in between flying trips to the hospital, during which she performed the helpful necessary tasks like bringing toiletries and bathrobes; I hadn't

UTL

exactly arrived prepared for a long stay. She thoughtfully made a big monthly calendar to tape to my hospital room wall so I could begin to figure out what day it was. I had come into the hospital in the dead of summer and wouldn't leave until well into the fall. Even during the day, she couldn't bring herself to enter our house except in dire emergencies; she moved the B&B office into the pool pavilion.

We had guests scheduled to check in that Sunday and also scheduled for arrival almost daily thereafter. In fact, the guests who were in the Dovecote the night before the shooting agonized over the possibility of whether they might have prevented it, for when they saw how busy I was early that Sunday morning getting ready for the group tour, they'd offered to come back later, but I had gone ahead and hurriedly checked them out before the tour began; had they waited until our normal check-out time of 10:30, they wondered aloud to me the next time they stayed, might they have stopped Murray from taking action? I doubt it.

For the first four days, guests with reservations at Butler Greenwood were shifted to other good B&Bs in the area: The Cottage, Barrow House, Lake Rosemound Inn, St. Francisville Inn, Shadetree—all of whose owners were most cooperative in providing assistance, friends that they were. By that Friday, however, Chase had organized things sufficiently that the B&B began operation once again, and it has managed to limp along ever since in spite of initial cancellations for concerns over security.

It has been difficult to surmount the rumor mill. Every time the newspaper ran an article about what happened—not only right at first but also over the course of the next six or seven months—reservations would be canceled and phone calls would be made by potential guests worried about safety. One guest who was already staying here was absolutely flabbergasted to be told at the tourist information center in St. Francisville all about what had happened—in inflammatory and inaccurate detail—and was also told that Murray was still on the loose and could just as easily come gunning for guests here the next time. With friends like that. . . .

Rose and Patrice helped with reservations and phone queries in between cleaning chores, and good friends Ann Weller and Eleanor Beattie answered the phones a couple of days each week. Out of the past emerged my father's retired secretary Mary Lea Dyer from Baton Rouge. We had not seen her for nearly thirty years since his death, but she was just as capable as ever and looking for a challenge to bring her back to involvement with life since her own husband's recent death and her subsequent withdrawal. She volunteered her time and skill on a daily basis for many weeks.

#

The B&B would limp along in my absence, but the house was closed for tours because there was no one who could do them but me. We're one of seven plantations locally which conduct daily historic tours for visitors, and these tours form the backbone of the tourist industry that has become so vital to the well-being of the area.

The economy here has not been what you could call robust since the Civil War and the boll weevil ruined the cotton empire, and it has most recently been in a state of transition over which there is considerable disagreement locally.

The tourist industry, non-polluting and helpful in providing the means and motivation for preserving some of our historic structures, has in recent years become a major employment source, supporting not only the plantations open for tours but also the spill-over related businesses—gift shops, restaurants, service stations and the like.

Tourists are attracted to the area because the history here, with its emphasis on English and Spanish influences, is fascinating and far different from any other part of south Louisiana. This is in marked contrast to the French influence of the rest of the southern part of the state, the well-promoted Acadian or *Cajun* Louisiana.

St. Francisville, skirting along a narrow, undulating loessial finger ridge high above the Mississippi floodwaters, was laid out in the early 1800's. The first lots were sold in 1807 and the first hotel had been

UTL

erected by 1809 to serve as legislative chamber of the Republic of West Florida the following year. The third newspaper in the Louisiana Territory was established here, and its editor became America's first war correspondent during the War of 1812. That same year, the state's second library was begun in St. Francisville, the Masonic Lodge was chartered in 1817, and by 1828 the state's first Episcopal congregation outside New Orleans had joined together in worship at Grace.

Long the social, cultural and religious center for the cotton-rich plantation country which surrounded it, St. Francisville became the commercial hub as well upon the decline and then destruction of the river port of Bayou Sara, just under the bluff, after continual fires and floods. St. Francisville's high concentration of quaint 19th-century structures, both residential and commercial, have been preserved and protected as a National Register Historic District, and tourists on the walking tour love to peer over white picket fences and across gingerbread-trimmed galleries into the lace-curtained lifestyles of another century.

It's rather unfortunate that the tourists who come here from all over the world are assumed (I hope mistakenly) to prefer hype and histrionics to authentic history. The plantation tours emphasizing accuracy (like this one, or Oakley where bird painter John James Audubon lived, and The Cottage Plantation with its complete collection of original outside dependencies) get a whole lot fewer visitors than the widely promoted Greek Revival Greenwood, magnificent massive columned mansion that burned to the ground after being struck by lightning and was resurrected for use in filming such made-for-TV movies as "North and South," or The Myrtles, now billed as the most haunted house in America since a prior owner from California took the perfectly natural deaths which occurred there as in every old house and spiced them up with tales of vindictive slaves—their turbans hiding ears cut off for eavesdropping and their tempers inflamed by ejection from the master's bed—putting poisonous oleander leaves in the children's birthday cake (actually, the mother and both babies died of yellow fever, not nearly so exciting, but a whole lot more common).

My house is just up the road from The Myrtles, and I get so many questions from tourists about whether this house has ghosts that I've hung a large *papier mache* Christmas angel over the empire four-poster baby bed in the back bedroom, and I say, "No, we've got *angels* in this house." I'm sorry to say that once, when I had been questioned a few times too many about why the 19th-century lace curtains in the formal parlor here don't overlap onto the Brussels carpet the way the rich folks at the Myrtles supposedly "puddled" their drapes onto the floor to show off how wealthy they were, I answered rather peevishly that in *this* house the residents were secure enough in their social position not to have to try to impress visitors with something as phony as how much fabric they could afford to waste.

"Barely visible in the righthand corner of the bedroom at Butler Greenwood is the angel hanging over the 19th-century four-poster child's bed"

UTL

That ingrained ability to distinguish substance from mere style used to be characteristic of the whole parish, but I'm not so sure it is today. The old ladies' book club and the old men's poker club still accept "appropriate" new members only when a sitting member dies (not that aspiring newcomers actually wish the aging members *ill*, but they sometimes do get rather impatient waiting their chance to review romantic literary treasures or play cards). But as a whole our community has been awfully quick to accept new money coming in— not that there's anything wrong with money if it's backed up by something more substantial. Maybe too many of us are getting a little too impressed by the "puddling."

And so instead of magnificent Rosedown Plantation, where aging genteel ladies endured postbellum poverty and helped the few remaining servants haul manure to fertilize the 28-acre formal gardens, our spring pilgrimage now promotes the *nouveaux parterres* of Hemingbough.

The pilgrims probably don't even notice that everything so very grand at Hemingbough is also so very, very new, for it is lovely as the sun sets over the carp in the old swimming pool and darkens the little pseudo-Greek Revival temple at the side of the lake. Hemingbough is without doubt a marvelous setting for the summer outdoor concert series of the Baton Rouge Symphony, and everyone in the parish enjoys spreading out a quilt under the stars to enjoy this rare cultural experience as the peacocks call from atop the concrete cherubs. And now that a comprehensive museum of Audubon's works has been added there, it actually seems not too out of place on the historic spring tour.

#

Even with the differences of opinion over presentation, the area does have a fascinating history and a remarkable amount of scenic beauty preserved almost untouched, and tourism has definitely become a major economic factor. The most wonderful thing about the new economic base is that it is no longer male-dominated the way agriculture was, leading to some power shifts which have been hard for a few people (notably most men) to swallow in the Felicianas today.

The formidable ladies of the parish historical society—called behind their backs (way behind their backs) the *hysterical* society, but positively a force to be reckoned with—have done a commendable job fostering preservation of significant historic structures, protecting all of St. Francisville's 19th-century downtown district through listing on the National Register of Historic Places, and actually making some of the less sensitive and more complacent locals sit back and appreciate the fragile beauty which surrounds them on a daily basis. We've come a long way since an early pilgrimage weekend when one local wag let rampant weeds and crabgrass overgrow his littered lawn on the main street of town and put up a sign for the tourists solemnly proclaiming it "I-SO (*eyesore*) Plantation."

But there are some folks moving into the area as well as some old-timers lacking much appreciation of the historic or scenic beauties, who would never be satisfied until we had a McDonald's and a bunch of industries. *Economic development*, they call it. It wouldn't take long for that to spoil what our tourists come for in the first place. It very nearly happened downtown, where century-old live oaks and a magnificent crumbling Victorian mansion were replaced with paved parking lots and a Junior Food Mart convenience store before zoning regulations were enacted and an advisory commission named to regulate growth in the historic part of town.

Our tourist commission spends much of its time and tax money promoting the local Arnold Palmer golf course instead of the historic sites or the B&Bs that form its tax base, and we have our golden arches now, too. It grieves me to say that my son joined the rejoicing when St. Francisville's McDonald's opened (even *I* sneak in occasionally for fries). Still, our town meetings often turn into free-for-alls when the debates and disagreements get hot over future planning.

Often the disagreements over St. Francisville's future spill over

UTL

into the home; they certainly did in mine. Murray served on the economic development commission for the parish while I was a member of the tourist commission. He was all for four-laning busy U.S. Highway 61 which borders the front of my place; I thought two lanes quite sufficient and didn't want any further impact on my property or any of the other historic sites bordering the road. He also was all in favor of a bridge spanning the Mississippi River here instead of the ferry we currently have as part of the highway system, thinking it would increase visitors and ease access; I cringed at the impact bridge approaches would have on the historic district of St. Francisville: concrete highway spans running right along the edge of peaceful Grace Church cemetery.

The ferry is part of the highway system and tourists love to ride it across the Mississippi River. There's no better way to view the sunset than across the muddy Mississippi waters, and not many people mind waiting ten or fifteen minutes to make the crossing. The only drawback is that most maps don't actually show the ferry so visitors unfamiliar with the area think there's a bridge or causeway crossing the river.

One unfortunate elderly couple driving too fast at night actually sped down the approach ramp and drove right across the ferry dock and off the other side into the river, the ferry itself being at the time at the opposite bank of the Mississippi. Their frantic efforts to open the windows proved unsuccessful as the car was swept away by the river's fierce currents and gradually sank.

And there is the occasional overloaded gravel truck which loses its brakes making the steep descent to the ferry and drives right through the boat and off the far side with a mighty splash, sinking like the ton of rocks that it is and joining the rusting hulks of sunken steamboats that exploded with regularity when the boilers were stoked too high in the rush to get to New Orleans or the struggle to go against the strong current upriver. But in general the ferry is an asset enjoyed by visitors and locals alike.

#

But the tourists don't know anything about the local disagreements over the proper balance between preservation and progress, and so they come, and they stay, and our Bed & Breakfast is certainly one of the most successful in town. Chase and friends had their hands full trying to keep up with it while I was still hospitalized. Even after I returned home, there was a lot that I couldn't do at first—and some things I will never be able to do again.

It's a good thing we were blessed with helpful friends and family because running a Bed & Breakfast is no small task. There's an endless amount of manual labor—cleaning, changing linens, washing dishes, scrubbing jacuzzis and toilets, replenishing breakfast foods—and there's a lot of advance work, public relations, reservations, advertising, networking and the like, not to mention being on call 24 hours a day and dealing with the traveling public, often but not always entirely a pleasure. I'm reminded of a little plaque at another area Bed & Breakfast, which reads, "All of our guests bring us pleasure . . . some by coming, and some by going."

When people ask me what it's like operating a B&B, I describe for them the one night when we had as a guest in the Old Kitchen B&B the first genuine, card-carrying whore we've had to my knowledge—a young woman with bleached orange hair, a tight blue spandex dress which came nearly but not quite to mid-thigh, three-inch heels and a very outgoing personality. She worked the casino circuit, she cheerfully said, and was on her way from the Jersey shore to New Orleans.

Behind her cottage in the Gazebo B&B with its three nine-foot-tall antique stained glass church windows, we had two charming gentlemen-partners from New Orleans, accompanied by their twin pampered pets Hunter and Mignon—slender trembling whippets who were always welcomed here, being much better behaved than most of the two-legged children and considerably quieter and more considerate than a good many of the adult guests as well.

In a third cottage, the three-story, slope-sided, shingled Dovecote, we had two Pentecostal couples, whose dip in the swimming pool clad in full-length skirts, pants and long sleeves caused considerable interest among the other guests. The whippets were soon being walked around the pool and the young lady in the Old Kitchen felt challenged to emerge from her cottage in a purple bikini about as wide as a gummi-worm and nearly as tasteful. And all of this in a single evening!

We often had guests just as colorful, but thankfully not usually all at once. Just this spring for several nights all of our cottages were filled to overflowing with forty ladies bicycling from California to Florida, 3,135 miles, as a fund-raiser for breast cancer awareness. Think of the jocks who were your worst nightmare on the opposing team in high school PE and these ladies of WOMANTOURS were *not* them; they were fit, of course, but decidedly feminine, vital, fascinating, and determined to brave not only inclement weather but vicious dogs, unskilled drivers, treacherous fire ant mounds, wolf-whistling truckers and terrible, terrible roads to reach their goal.

Besides that, they seemed to be doing it with good humor and gusto—in spite of one having been knocked off her bike by a passing truck and another having to endure rabies shots due to a dog bite. Perhaps that's why I felt such an affinity with them, these ladies, all over 50, some even 70, and many of them cancer survivors themselves; we are *all* survivors, strong ladies all. They loved it here and promised to return yearly with a different group.

#

And in fact, through the years many of the B&B guests have returned repeatedly, becoming almost like family. We watched as they married and celebrated anniversaries and their families grew; we met their friends and relatives as they recommended our accommodations; we shared in their turmoils and troubles when reservations were canceled due to death, divorce or dread disease.

WEEP FOR THE LIVING

And they shared in ours. Once news went out about the shooting, I had cards and letters and phone calls from former guests across the country and around the world.

A guest from the New Orleans area said she and her husband were driving through heavy city traffic when a report came on the radio news about it and her husband nearly ran off the road, shouting, "That's our Anne! That's *our* Anne!"

A frequent corporate guest who worked for Entergy was at a business meeting in Mississippi when another employee mentioned that I had been shot and killed. He jumped up from the conference table to call his wife, an artist who'd made me a beautiful pottery bead necklace in which she embedded bits of the broken blue Spode china which surfaces all over our lawn with every rainfall. She immediately called here and, reaching Chase, tried to delicately phrase the urgent question, "Chase, is your mother . . . *uh* . . . is your mother . . . *uh*?" No, Chase would answer, not dead.

Guests put me on prayer lists, sent prayer cloths, said rosaries. Letters and cards told of shared woes. One distant older cousin wrote three pages on the dispensability of men in general and husbands in particular; she'd had one only briefly in her youth, she said, and finding she could do very well without him had stuck to less formal arrangements since.

Even the nurses began telling me tales of their own stalkings and beatings by abusive husbands once I got clear-minded enough to listen; and they confided their worries about controlling boyfriends. I was not, it seemed, alone in my situation, and the shared stories and concern of others were extremely helpful in the healing process.

I received literally hundreds of wonderful cards, many inspirational in nature, filled with messages of hope and faith and love, carefully selected to offer encouragement. But the most appropriate one was a colorful picture of a solicitous servant in black and white French maid's regalia bending over her Victorian-era mistress, resplendent in lavender and lace and wilting in misery upon her dressing table.

"Does *Madame* not feel perky today?" asks the retainer. "No, *Fifi*," comes the testy reply, "*Madame* feels like shit!"

But the cards and heartfelt handwritten notes were a great help in my recovery. So were the flowers that soon filled my hospital room with color and delightful scent. The first huge bouquet of roses came, much to my family's horror, from Wilbert Rideau, inmate editor of Angola's prison newsmagazine. I put Wilbert's flowers right next to the ones from the retired sheriff, and those and all the others that arrived gave me great pleasure and went a long way toward making a dismal hospital room seem brighter. My compulsive sister ranted and raved about staph infection from water in the vases, but I clung to each arrangement and plant.

When I was first transferred to a private room, with my right arm totally immobilized in a cast, an IV in my left arm and my stomach full of staples and drainage holes, I definitely needed a lot of help, so my family hired sitters through the hospital to stay with me during the long dreary nights and busy days. These were aides who were from the area around Lane Hospital or retired ladies looking to make a few extra dollars; some of them were extremely helpful, especially the ones who worked as nurses' aides and were quite competent in helping me to bathe, eat, and make it through the long sleepless nights.

Some were not the least bit competent and would come in for their evening shift of eight hours, go immediately to sleep and not get up again until their shift was over. One told me in great detail about how her former husband had attacked her with a baseball bat, leaving her with lasting disabilities and scarring her children for life. I knew none of these sitters, so they were no help in my struggle to regain my identity.

I was still on very heavy pain medication, which affected my thinking ability and my memory. I couldn't remember *anything* from one minute to the next. After being released from ICU, the first night in a private room was very disorienting. When the sitter shift changed at 11 p.m. I must have been drowsing, for I awoke to find a strange young woman coming into my room in the dark and immediately starting to whisper on my telephone. I struggled to hear what she was saying; I had some hearing loss from the bullet noise and from surgical procedures so it was hard to hear. But I thought I heard her say someone had been caught on the roof.

I had been lying there all day concerned, as my mind cleared, about how helpless I was and how easy it would be for Murray to get to me to finish the job. By this point, he had voluntarily admitted himself to the psychiatric unit of a Baton Rouge hospital, where the director had worked closely with him at the forensic facility Murray ran for ten years. After a week or two, he checked himself out and drove off in his own car, free to go where he pleased, having established a basis for an insanity plea later if necessary—and, according to subterranean reports we were getting, having expressed absolutely no regret or remorse for his act; the nurses there thought him so mean, in fact, that we were told they surreptitiously called him "the old bastard."

So I knew that he was out there somewhere as I lay helpless in the hospital bed, heavily medicated, unable to walk or help myself at all, and lying—as I noticed the minute I was transferred to my private room—directly beneath a very large air conditioning grill that seemed to lead to some sort of sub-floor or crawl-space above my ceiling. A perfect entrance for a hired assassin, I figured. And now there was a total stranger whispering on my telephone to someone about an associate being captured on the roof.

I asked the woman who she was and what she was doing with my telephone, and she said she was just calling the time. Even in my drugged state I recognized that most people do not usually actually converse with the time recording, even in whispers, and so I rang for the nurse, who came and rang for the security chief, who called in the security guard from the grounds.

The hospital security officer on duty that night was a very large, no-nonsense woman. When I pointed out the questionable air conditioning grill right above my bed, which seemed to me so easy to remove or shoot through and a good place by which to enter the room from above, she explained that it could not possibly be entered. Well, I pointed out with absolutely no tact, maybe *you* couldn't, but someone smaller . . . The sitter, who finally admitted she'd been talking to her boyfriend on the phone, left in a huff, glad to be relieved of having to care for a lunatic, and Bob's sister Virginia, who had flown in from Washington, D.C., came to stay with me for the rest of the night.

As I came to realize later, the hospital actually had a very good security system and had taken great pains to assure my anonymity and my safety, moving me periodically to other rooms, denying visitors access, never confirming on the phone that there was any such inpatient as Anne Butler, spiriting me down service elevators and back corridors to other areas of the hospital for tests or therapy.

This attentiveness may well have saved my life. At the same time, it also denied me visits and calls from friends that in time would have proven helpful, though in my early state of drugged confusion, it was just as well I did not receive them. As I got clearer in my thinking, the nurses would ask if I wanted to see visitors and then admit them, but in the initial restrictive period, my cousin Murrell would get swept away in the security net when he innocently arrived to bring me a bar of Dial soap and couldn't make the hard-of-hearing receptionist understand his name. Other visitors would be standing outside my door, sure they could hear my voice, as the floor nurse emphatically denied there was an Anne Butler in the hospital.

Only once did anyone get past the security, fortunately not Murray. It was Miss Eudora, a wonderful little old lady with whom I had worked in the welfare office several decades earlier. Somehow she managed to elude all clearance checks and burst through the door into my room, saying she just had to see me with her own eyes to be sure I was all right.

I would quickly request sitters from St. Francisville, hometown people I knew, and would find their presence much more comforting than that of total strangers, especially Belle Jones, who had nursed me after Chase was born, her sister Katie Hilliard, and Belle's daughter Gail, who was one of Chase's favorite babysitters when she was small— all of whom had solid medical backgrounds. Belle and Katie had worked at the St. Francisville hospital for 30 years, ever since it opened, and I would trust them more than nearly any doctor I know. They would make time for me in their busy work schedules every single day for nearly six months.

UTL

CHAPTER 9

I remember very little of the people around me while I was in intensive care. I know Chase was there every day, and Stewart as often as he could come, plus my sister, Bob and Burnett—but I really don't recall much of their visits. The only clear memories I have are of looking up one time to see Burnett laying his hands on my forehead in blessing (he's a Baptist minister but is usually not too preachy with me, though this circumstance was certainly extreme enough to excuse anything) and of seeing my yardman Johnny Harris in the distance trying to get in to visit me, all dressed up in a purplish suit and tie and hat.

I remember being deeply touched by both visits, and I also clearly remember that just about the first lucid comment I made to Burnett was that I had been carried in the arms of angels. "I believe you," he would reply, and he meant it sincerely. Chase would tell me later that I talked to her and everyone else who came in, already beginning to urge her to get on back to school.

My own minister, Father Ken Dimmick of Grace Church, would inadvertently antagonize my family by the dilemma he found himself in, with both Murray and me being communicants of his church. For awhile he would try to visit us both in his attempt to understand, until the Bishop finally told him that he should stop trying to find a justification, that there *was* no justification for attempted murder and that he should just visit one of us. I was pleased that he chose to continue visiting me, though my family was furious when he tried to remind them that there were two victims, two grieving families.

When Murray's name continued to appear on the Grace Church prayer list, Chase would loudly whisper to Stewart one Sunday during the Prayers of the People, "Well, *we* don't have to pray for *him*." And that was the last time she would go to church there. I continued to go after I was released from the hospital, but would begin getting more and more spiritual guidance from Burnett and indeed would find that his whole church was much more concerned and considerate during my hospitalization and recovery than my own was.

Although Father Dimmick has worked hard to make Grace more inclusive and more open to the entire community, it remains a very conservative and closed congregation that, without his firm guidance, would still be clinging to the old 1928 prayer book for its traditional services and the unparalleled beauty of its language.

It reminded me of the days when I worked in the local welfare office and tried to get some of the Boy Scouts from wealthier neighborhoods to come and interact with some of the deprived children, singing carols, sharing refreshments, and giving gifts these children might not otherwise receive at Christmas time. But the scouts wanted only to *pay* for the presents, not to see or hear or touch the poor kids, so the exercise in Christian charity lost much of its meaning. It was this arm's-length concern I got from Grace.

Burnett said it was like the story of the Passover in the Bible, where the most puzzling aspect is the command that the chosen people in bondage in Egypt select a perfect lamb from their flocks and bring it into their homes for four whole days and nights before smearing its blood on their door posts that the Angel of Death might pass over their homes and spare their firstborn children while slaying all others.

Why was the lamb to be so intimately part of each family for four days and nights, the little children petting it, the parents feeding it? Because they would come to know and love it, precious little baby lamb that it was, and thenceforth for them the sacrifice would have

UTL

deep meaning, would be personal and heartfelt. Without that close contact and personal love, the sacrifice is meaningless—and so is generosity or charity.

And it was this impersonal expression of concern that came from those members of my own church who expressed any concern at all, though there were notable exceptions. I would be included on the prayer list, and that was close enough for most of the church members. I would be the first to admit that, not having been involved in many of the church activities myself except for the Sunday services, I deserved no more.

But nearly everyone in Burnett's warm and welcoming backwoods Mississippi Baptist church showed great concern with visits and calls and flowers and food. One sweet little child, Mandi Tynes, decided on her own to make me her personal prayer project, praying for me daily with the special heartfelt childhood innocence which must surely touch the heart of God. I lay in my hospital bed and thought of all the sad occasions when I should have sent cards or flowers to others in need—and I had meant to but had never quite gotten around to doing anything at all—and I was ashamed.

#

Once I was in a private hospital room, an attempt had to be made to stabilize my arm so that the horrors of therapy could begin. Lisa Young, the highly skilled occupational therapist in the hospital's in-house therapy unit, had worked with Dr. Fonte from the initial surgery, and she would be enlisted to make a special open split-cast of molded plastic so that the right arm could be removed from the cast for therapy.

This was an agonizing process with all the pins and rods and stitches, and it took several attempts before the cast fit right because of all the swelling. There were about 15 or 20 internal metal pins of varying size holding the elbow fragments in place, some right at the surface of the skin, so that area had to be well padded, and there was a large rod running down from my shoulder joint to hold that area in place, so no extra weight could be supported by the shoulder.

Lisa devised a cradle-type device, open on top and held closed with velcro straps crossing the top surface of my arm, bent to hold the arm at a right angle, supported by a detachable sling over the opposite shoulder. The cast was shiny hot pink plastic with royal blue velcro closures and looked for all the world like I was cradling a plump little baby piglet.

The day Lisa made the cast in my hospital room, some vital piece of equipment was not working and she had to melt the plastic in an electric skillet filled with boiling water, then mold it to my arm and dry it with a hair dryer. Every single movement was excruciating, but she finally got it right and gave me the first few almost pain-free moments I'd had in weeks.

This only meant the freedom to inflict pain in a new and exciting way—therapy. Two weeks spent flat on my back and barely conscious meant that I had lost all motor ability. I couldn't even walk and, when the therapist came to drag me out of bed, after the excruciating pain of sitting up with a stomach full of staples, I could move erect only with the aid of a walker—weak, bent over, shuffling like a little old woman. I could barely manage to make it to the door of my tiny room and then back to the bed, but by the next day I had progressed to walking a bit in the hall.

I know I was a sight to behold—hair matted to my head (because of all the staples and stitches and cast which could not get wet, it would be several weeks before I was permitted to shower), dressed in hospital gown and flapping bathrobe, one arm in a cast, the other attached to the IV pole—but I knew I was making progress if I could move. All those years my children laughed at me for sweating to the oldies with Richard Simmons had actually paid off. Big Rose and I always did aerobics in the pool pavilion every night—she in voluminous sweatpants, me in colorful flannel men's boxers left in the bottoms of B&B beds (I had a never-ending supply)—so I had plenty of strength in my legs at least.

III

When the physical therapist first took me to the workout gym and laid me down on an exercise mat and uncovered my legs, I heard her say in amazement, "My God! She's got fit legs!" I would soon swap the walker for a cane and in a few days managed to walk on my own. By the end of the week I was climbing the stairs of the hospital for therapy and, after the danger of strange visitors diminished with the end of visiting hours, roaming the darkened hospital halls at night.

#

But the worst of the therapy was not re-learning walking skills but trying to restore some mobility to my arm. There was nothing that Lisa could do to it that did not hurt, hurt a *lot*. The first few times I went to the therapy gym, I was wheeled down in a wheelchair and rolled up to a table so Lisa could lay my arm out on the flat surface and give me simple tasks to perform. I could do none of them. I could curl my fingers under but could not open my fist. I could not bend my elbow at all. I could not move my shoulder. And trying to do any of it was excruciating.

I was given a small square of sponge to squeeze and a few simple exercises to do on the tabletop like placing my arm atop a folded towel and trying to slide it along the smooth surface. As I struggled, exhausted and full of frustration, a wheelchair came through the door with a young bearded man in it. With a warm smile, he pulled right up to the therapy table and introduced himself as Gary Carpenter.

I didn't know who he was—and I didn't care. For all I knew, he could be a spy for Murray. He was, in fact, simply volunteering there as he considered the possibility of going into therapy as a career, having seen the miracles therapists could work when he was paralyzed from the chest down in a teenage motorcycle accident. I was not very friendly, in fact hardly spoke to him the first few days I saw him.

But he persevered, continuing to join me when I arrived for therapy. My whole focus was on my own misery, but he remained warm and friendly and outgoing. Finally, through the fog of my self-absorption, I began to realize that I should be ashamed of myself for sitting there whining and crying when someone like Gary had obviously been through far worse and would continue to have more to face on a daily basis than I ever would.

And I began to come out of myself and enter back into the world a bit and, as I looked around me in the therapy gym, I saw little old ladies with broken hips, and feeble old men who'd had strokes, and middle-aged ladies overcoming mastectomies, and strapping young football players with sprains or broken bones, and even tiny children struggling with cerebral palsy—and finally I began to work a little harder and complain a little less.

When the therapy unit began raising funds to surprise Gary with a desperately needed new wheelchair for Christmas, I would donate a free overnight at Butler Greenwood B&B as the prize for the winner of the drawing. In the presentation ceremony, I told Gary what an inspiration he had been to me, and he in turn wrote me a thank you note saying that I was the one who had been an inspiration to him.

He and all the patients I saw struggling in therapy showed me the potential we all possess if we build on what we *do* have, regardless of our limitations and losses. Later, after I had returned home and resumed a nearly normal life, Burnett would make some casual comment about the hatefulness of Murray's crippling me, and I would furiously reply, "Don't you *ever* call me crippled! Don't you ever even *think* that!"

Truthfully, I never did really feel sorry for myself or get all that depressed in the hospital. The surgeon, Dr. Mazoch, was one of those rare physicians who sees not just her own area of specialty but the patient as a whole, and she was concerned that I was showing no anger or sorrow. As I related the tale of the shooting, I was matter-of-fact in the telling, not showing the emotion she thought should be coming out by then.

So Dr. Mazoch had a therapist visit me several times, and it was helpful to tell someone the whole story from start to finish—but even then I showed little emotion. I really never did get angry, never did feel vindictive or vengeful. It seemed to me then and it still does today that Murray hurt himself much more than I could ever do by ruining the reputation which was so important to him.

As I struggled to understand not only what had happened but *why* it had happened, I kept hearing from others how he was trying to shift the responsibility onto me. I knew that he had been furious at me, I knew that I had certainly contributed to our problems, but I could find nothing that would warrant killing. That's the infuriating part of most domestic violence cases: the attempt to make the victim shoulder the blame, to make the violent action a *deserved* punishment. I would not take the responsibility for his horrible act. It was *not* my fault—but it would take me months of soul-searching to accept this.

And the sorrow that was in me would not come out until much later, and then it would descend upon me without notice so that I cried for weeks, overcome with the horror and sorrow of having someone hate me enough to try to kill me. I cried alone and in front of others too. I cried at therapy; Lisa joked that she had been trying to make me cry for months, but she clearly recognized and encouraged the necessity of venting the sorrow, and over the course of the next year, she would serve many functions for me, rehabilitating not only my body but my mind as well, becoming not only therapist but also psychiatrist, confessor, counselor, friend.

In private I agonized over the motive for the shooting. Was it because he loved me so much he could not, would not, give me up to an independent life without him? Or was it, as the ambulance paramedic insisted, an act not of love but of hate, of pure sheer meanness, meant to cause as much pain and suffering as possible and then a long, agonizing death. Did he feel I had *embarrassed* him, made him look like a fool, he who thought himself so great? Could it possibly be mere resentment at having spent some of his money during our marriage, with no consideration for how much of my own money had been spent? Had he expected me to beg for mercy—and would he have been receptive to such pleas? He knew I wouldn't beg. In fact it never even entered my mind, and I don't think he'd have been swayed from his purpose for anything.

All of this, mind you, from someone like Murray, who always professed not to believe in the death penalty—even for those convicted of heinous crimes. I don't believe in it myself. Besides being morally reprehensible, it solves no problems other than the removal of one offending individual from society. It certainly doesn't deter anyone else. Today's criminals far too often are spaced out on drugs and have such diminished mental capacity that there is no way they can make the connection between crime and consequence. Most of them do not recognize the value of human life or the humanity of others, perhaps because of dysfunctional early examples and the dearth of love or kindness in their own homes. How can we expect hardened criminals to, when someone like Murray, with his years of psychological study and his distinguished half-century career in upholding the law, could disregard it so blatantly when *he* felt like it?

Murray had graduated from Carson-Newman College in Tennessee with a major in Sociology, studied for his law degree at John R. Neal College (never quite finished because of changing course requirements during World War II, never took the bar), received a Masters degree in Psychiatric Social Work from the University of Tennessee, and worked toward a doctorate in Sociology at Vanderbilt (never quite completed it).

He worked in military government in Germany after World War II and ran prisons in three states, establishing a national reputation as a liberal prison reformer. This was certainly someone with the mental capacity for connecting crime and consequence. To hear him tell it, his whole career had been a struggle to gain the recognition and acceptance of everyone's humanity and human rights, including those of prisoners under his control. How then could he discount *my* rights so readily?

UTL

Anne Butler

I was reminded of a Bed & Breakfast guest, a writer for *Esquire* working on a story about Angola. A large man of White Russian ancestry, masculine and urbane New Yorker to the core, he returned from the prison one day in tears. When I asked him what on earth was wrong, he replied that he had been arguing with Douglas Dennis, one of the *Angolite* writers who had been convicted of two separate murders, one essentially self-defense and the other essentially senseless. Dennis had insisted that within *everyone* is at least the capacity for murderous rage, and the writer had insisted that he was dead wrong. Only in the car driving back to the B&B, he said, had he realized that Dennis was probably right, and that his denial of the possibility in himself just might account for the many years he had spent in therapy.

#

More therapeutic than my anguished private psychoanalysis were the visits with family members who'd come in from far-flung locations to help me and who were functioning for once as a family unit. We are not a close family, especially on my mother's side, and we had horrible examples set for us in the way of functional familial closeness.

My mother absolutely loathed and despised several of her own brothers and sisters, not even speaking to them for years. In her later years, she could not remember what furnishings were in her own childhood room but could remember distinctly what her sisters had in theirs, clearly caring nothing for what was hers but coveting what everyone else had instead. My brother-in-law to this day makes snide references to the dreaded *furniture gene*.

When we were children, my mother pitted my sister and me against each other ("Anne may have gotten all the looks, but precious little Mary Minor got all the personality."), setting us up for a lifetime of competition and resentment and hidden jealousy.

Bob and Virginia, the children of my mother's sister and my father's brother, thus double first cousins to me, now competed in a more civilized way as two adult lawyers; when they were small, Virginia—slightly older and a whole lot more aggressive—used to sit on Bob's stomach and spit in his face, and I believe could do so still.

But here were family members from all over the country pulling together and positively interacting to accomplish some very difficult tasks: Bob and my brother-in-law Mike taking care of compelling legal matters; Virginia helping me through therapy as I had helped her through her awful double mastectomy and reconstructive surgery a few years earlier in Washington (her very own version of tough love, "You want a sip of water? Then get up and get it for yourself, you're not helpless."); Mary Minor organizing sitters and helping normalize life for my children; Chase as always bearing responsibilities well beyond her years; cousins Pat and Lucie and Murrell watching over the house and providing food for other workers there.

This lasted as long as it needed to and then began deteriorating, slipping back to normal—arguments and bickering going on across my hospital bed which I would have to rise up from the dead to settle. But while it lasted it was wonderful to behold: male cousins taking Stewart fishing and hunting; delicious meals being prepared for those who'd come in from out of town; tempting treats sent to me in the hospital.

Once it fell apart, I was relieved when they all had to go back home to their own lives, but I was grateful that they had given me so much time from those lives to help rebuild my own.

#

Most of what I needed to do at this point I needed to do alone, and that was to work through the whole matter in my head. I must, at some point, leave the hospital and go home, go back to the place where I had been shot and where I had very nearly lost my life. The driveway to the house goes around to the rear, not the front, so everyone always comes in through the back porch. I would have to enter my house right at the point where I nearly bled to death.

UTL

I knew enough about post-traumatic stress disorder to realize that I could expect to have some very real continuing mental problems. The state police detective had cautioned me that gunshot victims are different from any others, often suffering long-lasting consequences, and that just the sound of a shot can return them to their own prior personal traumas.

One of the chapters of my last Angola book, *Dying To Tell*, had been about Wayne Felde, a Vietnam vet who killed two people and was Louisiana's first capital case to use post-traumatic stress disorder as a defense. He blamed his killings on terrifying flashbacks that in post-war years returned him to the nightmare of Southeast Asian jungles where he'd had that most awful job of all as tunnel rat, sneaking silently and soaked with sweat in the dead of night into enemy under-ground bunkers to blow them to smithereens.

The defense did not prove successful, the jury not quite grasping the psychological implications or at least not buying them, and Wayne Felde was executed by the state of Louisiana in its infamous electric chair. One of his defense lawyers, J. Michael Small, would later repre-sent my husband Murray, and I hoped he would meet with as little success in my case.

I began my own mental therapy, during those long, long, long sleepless nights in the hospital as I went over things endlessly in my head. The human mind is a wonderful thing, and it protects itself when it needs to. In my case, it admitted to my awareness only as much as I was capable of coping with at that time, and then would gradually increase the awareness as I became stronger and able to handle more'.

I was slowly beginning to piece together in my head what had happened and with each passing day a few more pieces were added to the puzzle. Family members and visiting staff would tell me things which had happened while I was unconscious or absent, and that little bit of information would somehow help something else finally make sense

I had not watched television at all, not wanting to see anything about my case on the news. The first day I felt strong enough to turn it on was right after poor Princess Diana was killed, and the news reports were so heartbreaking I soon turned the TV off. I didn't turn it on again for days, and by then saintly little Mother Theresa had died and her seemingly endless cortege through the streets of Calcutta was equally depressing; off went the TV again.

It would be weeks before I read any of the newspaper accounts of the shooting, and only then did I learn that Murray was described as legally drunk at the time of arrest. This would bring to mind the *glug-glug-glug* I had heard as I sat in the chair bleeding, and I would realize the implications of the noise and the importance of my clear awareness that he was not the least bit drunk when he arrived that morning.

#

In my head, as I lay aching and sleepless in the dark hospital room every night, in those rare moments of peace between vital sign taking and pain medication and the other necessities of hospital life, I went over and over my homecoming plans. Would I have a flashback and immediately be transported back in time to the actual event when I had to face the porch on which I sat, the chair, the blood-stained rug? Would I relive the shooting, over and over again, feeling fresh pain each time and renewed sorrow?

Maybe, I thought, I should get Big Rose and Burnett, the two strongest people I knew, the two I trusted most in the world, to meet me upon my arrival home from the hospital and enfold me in their arms and carry me like a sobbing baby up the back steps, past the chair where I had sat bleeding, into the house. I considered that a workable plan for a number of nights, then moved on to a new idea.

I would have a good Episcopal house blessing upon my homecoming. Father Dimmick could say a prayer, blessing the house and proclaiming it once again a house of love, not hate. Then I would deliver a few well-chosen words to the assembled loved ones, thanking them for their help and concern. After that, we would all move together up the front steps and across the broad gallery into one of

119

the front doors, thus bypassing altogether the back porch where I'd been shot. Perhaps we might even enjoy light refreshments in the formal dining room, nothing too fancy.

A few more nights, and this rather elaborate ritual began to seem a bit much. It was *my* house, damn it, and no one was going to take away from me my enjoyment of it. I would march right up the back steps, directly confront the crime scene, and then reclaim my home, relishing the absence of my oppressor. My most effective way of dealing with problems always had been head-on confrontations (collisions, sometimes).

This was by far the most sensible plan—practical and courageous—and it was this which I followed when the time came. Rose and Burnett and Bob and Liz were standing by, just in case, and I was glad they were there and that they had cleaned the rug and removed the bloody chair, replacing it with another.

But most of all it had helped me to have relived the scene so many times in my head so that when I actually had to face it, I had no problem. Later, I would even insist upon having my same chair back, slightly stained but still just as comfortable. I had to prove to myself that I could deal with it, and I left it in place for more than a year before I finally felt I could replace it. Having faced the horrible scene, I could then, and only then, obliterate it and move on.

CHAPTER 10

After I was released from intensive care and put in my own private hospital room, the state police detectives arrived to take a deposition. I was exhausted. My days consisted of doctor visits, both occupational and physical therapy sessions, family visits, and a continual round of student and visiting nurses referred to me because of the high level of medical interest in my case.

These young students were often quite helpful in providing extra hands and thoughtful services, but also sometimes tiresome in their continual requests for lengthy family medical histories and endless "head-to-toe assessments": Does this hurt? Does *this* hurt? Toward the end of my hospital stay, I even had visits from the accreditation team inspecting the facility, referred to me because I was about the only coherent one on my hall where the other patients were mostly comatose nursing home residents, and I was certainly glad to fill them in on what a wonderful hospital Lane Memorial is.

State Police detectives Steve Dewey and William Davis would be gentle and courteous as they explained the necessity of recording another statement from me—the first one taken in intensive care being necessarily rather brief and to the point. I should tell only what I had seen and what I knew, Steve cautioned me, not anything I had later heard from someone else. And so I told him exactly the same thing I had told a few weeks earlier, and in great detail. I knew what I had seen, and I remembered it explicitly.

"I can't wait to put you on the stand," Steve would tell me, "you've got the most amazing eye for detail." I explained about being a writer, and how attentive to the little things that makes you. Whatever I'm writing, I always like to use a whole lot of detail, which I think adds tremendous interest and credibility, and even in ordinary situations, I usually find myself assuming the role of watchful observer rather than participant. My ancestors always sat on the first pew in Grace Church to be closer to the altar and to God, to be able to see the presiding rector better; me, I sit on the next-to-last pew so I can watch everyone else.

What, Detective Steve Dewey would ask me, did I think had been the major issue of contention between Murray and me? "Control," I would answer without hesitation. I had already figured it out. I thought that then, and I think it still. He wanted to be in complete control, and when he wasn't, he hated it. And he hated *me*.

Perhaps I was the first one, it occurred to me—in all his many years of dealing with prisoners and politicians and just plain people— who had aroused in him feelings so strong that they could not *be* controlled, feelings both good and bad. And in some instances that was good. And in some instances that was very, very bad.

Both detectives seemed to take a real interest in my case and were very supportive. But when I asked if their agency could provide any protection for me once I went home, the answer was, necessarily, no.

#

I could barely walk, my stomach was still full of staples and my arm full of stitches in several different incisions; I could not change the colostomy on the left side of my waist because my right arm, the only one that could reach the area, did not bend or otherwise function and my hand did not work. Yet after several weeks the insurance company began to suggest to the hospital that it was time for me to go home, that my hospital coverage was about to run out.

There was no way I could return home alone, twenty miles from the hospital and doctors. The main thing I needed was more therapy in order to learn to function as best I could with the limitations I had, and so the hospital worked out a plan with the insurance company allowing me to transfer to the skilled nursing part of the facility, less expensive because doctor visits were not included there. This was a unit mainly for nursing home patients or other elderly people who were simply not quite well enough to function on their own but who didn't require daily physician visits.

After more than two weeks in the hospital in ICU and a private room, I was transferred to this skilled nursing wing for another ten days, allowing me to continue the all-important daily therapy. Dr. Mazoch would no longer be paid for seeing me there, but she didn't miss a day. She would remove the staples from my abdominal incision there and, since Dr. Fonte was out of the country on a humanitarian medical mission, she would also remove his stitches from my arm; she estimated that she took out about 100 stitches/staples from the two areas.

\#

While I struggled with physical recovery, Bob and my sister's husband Mike Hebert were struggling with the judicial system, fighting against an entrenched insider who knew all the tricks. Murray had had dealings with most lawyers and judges throughout the state during his many years at Angola, and his son, an assistant district attorney in Rapides Parish, knew even more of them. When Murray was head of Feliciana Forensic Facility for the criminally insane, he had developed close relationships with many of the state's psychiatrists and certainly learned all the tricks of insanity defenses. All of this he would now put to good use.

Murray's family hired as his defense attorney Mike Small from Alexandria. A friend of mine mentioned this to someone who lived in that area and was told, "Oh, yes, Mike Small. That's the lawyer you get when you're guilty and want to get off." That was him, all right. One New Orleans prosecutor who stayed in the B&B said he'd been amazed when he walked into Small's office and found every square inch of wall space covered by diplomas and various testimonials to his prowess—not the office of a small ego by any means, he said.

It wouldn't take long for the games to begin. After our 20th Judicial District DA recused himself, the case was shuffled around the state judicial hierarchy, going to the Louisiana Attorney General's office and eventually ending up dumped in the lap of the District Attorney in St. Tammany Parish, the 22nd Judicial District, along the north shore of Lake Pontchartrain near the Gulf Coast, a good two-hour drive from here. That meant that the assistant DA from St. Tammany who was assigned the case would have to drive several hours just to get here to take care of anything; plus he would carry a full load of cases in Covington.

Young Scott Gardner was the attorney assigned to the case; he was highly professional, well trained, and anxious to see that justice was served. His youthful and innocent demeanor gave no hint of the down-and-dirty training he'd had for years as a prosecutor under DA Harry Connick in New Orleans.

Attorney Gardner hadn't reckoned on having to fight for even the simplest things that should have been taken for granted. We would continue the case under the same local judge who had let Murray out of jail on $100,000 property bond within 24 hours of the shooting when there was absolutely no question of his guilt. While Judge Wilson Ramshur did sign a restraining order prohibiting Murray from contacting me, Murray had free run of the parish, driving himself wherever he wanted to go.

My family considered this a highly dangerous situation, especially once Murray began calling Big Rose to inquire about my condition: whether I could walk, whether anyone was staying with me at night, and other questions which seemed to indicate an unhealthy interest rather than any genuine concern. Rose has Caller ID on her telephone and could always tell when he was calling and where he was calling from. If she didn't pick up the phone right away, he would call back over and over again until she would answer, sometimes as often as six or seven times.

The initial court hearing was the first week in November 1997. Murray and his attorney entered a plea of "not guilty at this time." They also agreed to amend the restraining bond to require him to give the local sheriff 24 hours notice before he came into West Feliciana, and the state attorney stipulated that Murray was to reside outside of the parish. No one appeared at this hearing except the two attorneys and the defendant. Even though for some reason Mike Small had subpoenaed me and several of the cleaning staff, we were notified at the last minute that we would not be needed.

Mike Small released a statement to the press that his client had no interest in remaining in this parish and would certainly be glad to get out of it. Before the ink was dry on the agreement, he would send the sheriff a fax that his client could not possibly leave the parish for a number of days because of pressing medical needs, and subsequent visits by Murray to the parish would begin before the sheriff's office was even notified of his impending arrival.

The amended bond allowed him to return here from his son Jerry's home in Alexandria for legal, medical or family reasons, so he would be in and out of town frequently over the next few months. Once I was released from the hospital, this caused great concern, so a night watchman was required for my security and also to assure the safety of the B&B guests. My sister joked that I could have a security patrol made up entirely of ex-husbands since they had all been extremely solicitous and wanted to help in any way possible, Chase's father even offering to come over from Florida.

We settled more practically upon Rose's gentle-giant son Carl, an experienced security guard who patrolled the grounds here at night while a nurse stayed inside with me. We worried over whether to arm Carl with a gun of some sort. The sheriff's office discussed the matter with us and told Carl that if he *did* have to shoot someone, for God's sake not to kill them. We armed instead Carl with a cellphone and

Stewart's baseball bat, and he was hell on the armadillos that dig up the grounds at night rooting for bugs.

#

Even when I was released from the hospital the end of September, I remained quite weak and unable to do much for myself. The abdominal incision was still draining and required special disinfecting daily, and the colostomy had to be changed several times a day. I could not even bathe myself with just one hand since I could not get the colostomy under water in the tub and instead had to stand under a hand-held shower, holding which occupied my only functional arm.

My right arm was in a cast and would require additional surgery within a few weeks for the removal of the rod in my shoulder and some of the pins in my elbow. My body was rejecting these foreign substances, pushing the rod up out of the shoulder and causing intense pain to radiate all through my back, taking my breath away. And a few of the metal pins in my elbow had worked to the surface of the skin, causing a lot of pain in that area.

Dr. Fonte scheduled me for day surgery, saying I could come in to the hospital early one morning and go home by that evening. He hadn't counted on complications, but when the anesthesia tube was inserted into my lungs—and this apparently had to be attempted several times—it dislodged a large clot of blood and started a hemorrhage, raising concern that additional clots might be forming and traveling through the bloodstream. I was dragged around unconscious for chest x-rays and scans and would not leave the hospital after all until the following afternoon, still feeling like I'd been run over by a Mack truck. My poor friend Lily Metz, who had driven me to the hospital, would remain with me all day.

When I got home from this hospitalization, a letter was waiting for me from a lawyer with the indigent defender's office in one of the north Louisiana parishes. He had stayed in the Bed & Breakfast several times while working on projects at Angola. He enclosed a newspaper review of a recently released book called *Intimate Enemies: The Two Worlds of the Baroness de Pontalba.*

Written by Tulane University professor Christina Vella, the book detailed in fascinating richness the life and times of Micaela Almonester de Pontalba, born in Louisiana in 1795, about the time my family was establishing the plantation where I now live. Daughter of a wealthy philanthropist who built many of New Orleans' most famous landmarks, she was married at age 15 to Celestin de Pontalba, only son of a controlling and possessive French nobleman who immediately began trying to wrest away her fortune.

French law of the time did not permit divorce and further decreed that any woman who refused to live with her husband forfeited all rights to her property, so the father-in-law began a campaign of terror designed to drive her away. This culminated in her husband's father actually shooting her four times in 1834, then turning the gun on himself. He died. *She* survived. She then reclaimed her property and built not only the Hotel Pontalba, which now serves as the American Embassy residence in Paris, but also the Pontalba Buildings in New Orleans, French Quarter landmarks.

In the short note accompanying the book review, the lawyer wrote, "I thought of you when I read this. You and the Baroness de Pontalba give new meaning to resilience and perseverance, not to mention survival. Hope your recovery is speedy."

#

The removal of the rod proved helpful to my shoulder area, but the abdominal drain continued to leak infection. I was scheduled to have the colostomy reversed on November 2 but after I had been put to sleep and cut open Dr. Mazoch found a large abscess that prevented her from doing anything more than just cleaning it out and sewing me back up again, still with the colostomy—which would have to stay in for another four months.

It was a great disappointment for me. I can cope with anything for a limited time. I was supposed to have the colostomy for just six weeks, then for a few months, and now it would be nearly six months. But I was fortunate not to have to make the adjustment to it on a permanent basis, and so after another week in the hospital, I returned home and began trying to build up my strength yet again.

A colostomy, need I explain, is absolutely the punishment from hell, a hole cut into the abdominal cavity at some point where the intestines have been severed, rerouting the bowels from rectum to the ostomy opening.

Instead of pooping into a pot, the ostomy patient's bowels move into a bag attached to the stomach by a flat wafer glued onto the skin. The plastic bag pops onto and off of the wafer like a tupperware top and can be emptied or changed as necessary several times daily, while the wafer is only changed a few times a week. It is like having a large whale-like blow-hole in one's side, from which periodically emerge odiferous gaseous clouds that are sometimes unfortunately accompanied by highly undesirable sound effects. There is no embarrassment like that suffered by a colostomy patient.

I know that some people live perfectly normal lives with colostomies. My own colostomy, on the other hand, submitted to control about as well as I myself did and seemed to have an uncanny ability to sense when it would cause the most embarrassment. There was absolutely no controlling its action as there is with rectal movements by the sphincter muscle; there seemed to be some perverse triggering mechanism which kept it still and quiet when alone but activated it the moment there was dead silence—in church, for example, or some other place where one wishes not to call attention to oneself.

My worst nightmare came true on Christmas Eve as I attended midnight services at Grace Church with family and friends, wearing a new dark green long velvet dress of which I was inordinately proud. It had taken hours of shopping to find a dress which could accommodate all of my handicaps: large enough to go over the bad arm, long-sleeved and high-necked enough to cover the elastic sleeve I had to wear to control the arm's swelling, loose enough to conceal the colostomy bag at my waist.

I had thought that, since the bowels don't continually move through the rectum, they shouldn't have to continually move through the colostomy, so I covered the whole thing up with control-top panty hose and hoped for a quiet, uninterrupted evening. But soon after returning home for carols around the Christmas tree, I found that the eruption which had not been able to move out into the colostomy bag had given up on that route and forged a new one, spewing out through the sides of the wafer and nearly ruining my new dress, not to mention the evening.

Most of my family members went back to their own homes and lives once I returned to my house, but even at home I was blessed with continuing attentions from Big Rose and Patrice on a daily basis, as well as Belle and Katie to provide nursing care for a few hours morning and night. For awhile, when I was really weak and helpless after successive surgeries, one or the other of them spent the evening with me as well. They called me Baby, called themselves "babysitting" when they stayed with me, and treated me like the wayward child. "You stop that, Baby, and get back into bed this minute! You know the doctor doesn't want you trying to do too much!" "Lord, would you look what Baby's trying to get away with. You quit that, Baby, or we're gonna call the doctor and tell on you!"

My cousin Virginia Marshall and her husband Sam came from Virginia to take me home from the hospital and stay with me. While in the hospital, I had received piles of get-well cards, all saying, "Call if we can help." I received *one* card that said, "When you are released from the hospital, we will be there, and we will stay as long as you need us." It was from Sam and Ginny.

Anne Butler

"Cousins Anne Butler and Virginia Bruns, shown on the
backyard swing at Butler Greenwood, were always close as
children and became even closer when Virginia and her
husband came to stay for three weeks when Anne was
released from the hospital"

They had planned on being here a week or ten days and ended up
staying for a full three weeks when they saw how helpless I was, driving
me to therapy, fixing meals, overseeing the operation of the B&B.

Sam, a graduate of Virginia Military Institute and newly retired
interceptor pilot and technology specialist, was the perfect one to
supervise the installation of a security system, not an easy job in a

rambling 200-year-old house full of floor-to-ceiling windows and French doors. The day I arrived home from the hospital, there were people hanging from the ceiling and hammering away in every room. All I wanted to do was get in bed; the half-hour ride had exhausted me, and I certainly didn't want to hear the complicated details of how to operate the system.

Sam attended to that and also installed the telephone Caller-ID system which would later prove so important. Ginny took charge of the kitchen. "Well," she complained, "this is the most *poorly* equipped kitchen I've ever in my life seen"—and it is. So she went to the store and bought a proper ice cream scoop and several gallons of Blue Bell ice cream, and we were in good condition ever after.

But besides the ice cream, always a necessity for gracious living in the heat of the South, what we sorely needed was some levity, and it would be up to Big Rose to provide it. She certainly proved equal to the task, she and her little blue man.

While I was confined to the bed and not able to get up or get dressed decently, Rose and Patrice would sit on my back porch waiting to check people in to the Bed & Breakfast cottages, and while they sat, they would thumb through the endless supply of mail-order catalogues which arrive in my rural mailbox daily.

I get every catalogue known to man, and then some: for clothes, for gifts, for household furnishings, for cookware, for toys, for gardening supplies and plants, for artwork and crafts, for books and videos—and a Victoria's Secret catalogue at least every other day. When I turned fifty, my sister had called to inquire whether I was wearing purple, and I was able to reply, "Yes, and it came from Victoria's Secret, too!" And it was the truth.

One of these catalogues happened to be full of ethnic crafts from around the world and there, begging to be brought home with her, Big Rose found her little blue man. He was actually a scaled-down replica of some African village gateknocker, his erect oversized wooden penis meant to be detached and rapped against the wooden fencing around the village so that the gate might be opened to admit a visitor.

131

He was about 12 inches tall, bright blue in color, with glowing gold teeth and eyes, a real knock-out.

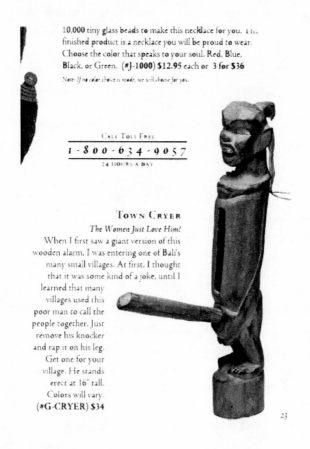

10,000 tiny glass beads to make this necklace for you. The finished product is a necklace you will be proud to wear. Choose the color that speaks to your soul. Red, Blue, Black, or Green. (#J-1000) $12.95 each or 3 for $36

Note: If no color choice is made, we will choose for you.

CALL TOLL FREE
1 - 8 0 0 - 6 3 4 - 9 0 5 7
24 HOURS A DAY

TOWN CRYER
The Women Just Love Him!
When I first saw a giant version of this wooden alarm, I was entering one of Bali's many small villages. At first, I thought that it was some kind of a joke, until I learned that many villages used this poor man to call the people together. Just remove his knocker and rap it on his leg. Get one for your village. He stands erect at 16" tall. Colors will vary.
(#G-CRYER) $34

"Rose Pate's little blue man, called the Town Cryer, advertised in the mail-order catalog which says 'women just love him.'"

Big Rose had gone through more than a year of deep mourning after the death of her aged husband Buck, a real elder statesman and the parish's first black deputy sheriff. She had faithfully nursed him for 12 years during his drawn-out bout with prostate cancer, and she had deeply missed him. But now she was just plain lonely at an age when decent single men are hard to come by. And so she began mooning over the little blue man, and Patrice and Belle and I began teasing her about him.

One day when Rose was not around, I picked up the phone and surreptitiously ordered the little blue man to give her for Christmas. Then I thought better of it—what if Rose innocently opened my nicely wrapped gift under the Christmas tree with her college-educated career-girl daughter Carol Lynn and son Carl? Carol Lynn would be mortified, and protective Carl would beat the little blue man to pieces with a baseball bat once he got a look at his outrageous outstretched pecker.

So instead of waiting for Christmas, I gave the blue man to Rose as soon as he came in the mail, and she fell out laughing and then began plotting the best way to introduce him to Belle and Patrice, so they might be properly impressed and not a little jealous of Rose's good fortune.

Belle was scheduled to come that evening to change my colostomy for me, so Rose arranged to arrive a little earlier so she could hide her truck behind one of the B&B cottages. She rushed into the house, ran a tub full of hot water in the jacuzzi in the bathroom connected to my bedroom, added enough bubblebath to practically reach the ceiling, lowered the overhead lights to a romantic dimness, stripped and climbed into the tub, balancing the little blue man on the edge of the tub.

Belle soon bustled in through the back door of the house and innocently walked into my bedroom, chatting cheerfully all the way. She hardly glanced toward the half-closed door into the bathroom and busied herself with preparing me for the colostomy change. From the darkened bathroom came the lovelorn strains of *"Let Me Wrap You In My Warm And Tender Arms."*

Belle, sure I had been alone in the house, had no idea what to think and ran to open the bathroom door, and there in the teal-colored jacuzzi sat a naked steaming Big Rose, Buddha-like in bubbles,

133

trying to keep a straight face as she sang tenderly to her man. You could hear Belle holler all the way to St. Francisville.

It was a fitting coming-out party for the little blue man, and he has proved a popular addition to many a social gathering since. Once, during a particularly slow period, he was even kidnapped and held for ransom ($3,000 or a big platter of home-cooked fried chicken) and was returned safely only after a furious Big Rose threatened to go directly to Bill Daniel, the sheriff himself.

"Rose Pate brought joy and humor to the task of taking
care of 'Baby,' as she called her recalcitrant patient at
Butler Greenwood"

CHAPTER 11

My days at home settled into a routine. Once Ginny and Sam went home to Virginia, I was at last alone in my own house. Funny how you miss having a few moments of privacy when you have none, and it's not funny how little modesty you leave a hospital with after weeks of being poked and prodded and stripped of what shred of dignity you struggle to retain in that environment.

I tried to take over as much of the daily running of the business as I could, but I would get awfully tired with the least little effort. I'm right-handed, naturally, and it was next to impossible to write legibly with my left hand, taking reservations over the telephone as prospective guests rattled off credit card and phone numbers a mile a minute and I struggled to hold the phone between chin and shoulder and write and turn calendar pages with my one operational hand. Some of the B&B reservation forms I filled out during this period are pathetically illegible.

135

Anne Butler

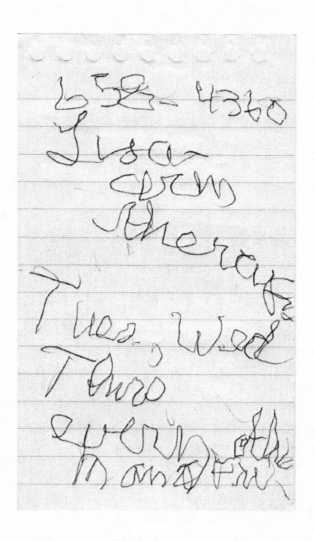

"Struggling to write left-handed, Anne's note about arm
therapy scheduled with Lisa Young is barely legible"

136

Because the bullet that hit my shoulder bounced into the chest wall and did a lot of lymphatic damage, I had problems with constant swelling in my arm, had to keep it elevated as much a possible, and was fitted with an elasticized compression sleeve that tightly wrapped my entire arm and was secured by elastic straps crossing my back and running under my armpit, not what you'd call comfortable and certainly not what you'd call attractive.

But Lisa and Dr. Fonte were quite concerned that the severe swelling would cause damage and inhibit therapy progress as well, so I gritted my teeth and wore the miserable contraption, taking it off only to bathe. It was supposed to push the swelling back into a healthier part of the body which could handle it more easily, and it did that fairly well, but it was awful to wear and impossible to get into and out of without assistance.

Each hospital stay knocked me backward, and in between I tried to walk a lot in the driveway and do other exercises to build up my strength. Before each hospitalization, I had to have CAT scans and barium x-rays, which meant I had to take Fleet's enemas and drink gallons of Go-Lightly, the nauseous purgative surely named by some sadistic pervert. Those are bad enough normally; with a colostomy, sheer hell.

Before each test, usually scheduled for the morning, I would have to take the laxatives the evening before, which meant emptying the colostomy bag every five minutes all night long, then struggling to make it to the hospital by car, once rushing through the hospital halls shouting to Belle, "It's too full, it's gonna *break!*" Poor Belle, who had taken vacation leave from her day job to go with me to the hospital and help with the colostomy, would rush me into the first ladies' room, where the colostomy bag did indeed pop off just as we made it through the door, and clear liquid gushed out all over the polished floor.

Three days a week I had to go to therapy at the hospital, half an hour's drive away, and for the first few months, unable to drive, I had to impose on the generosity of friends and family for rides. Soon after Thanksgiving, though, I began trying to drive myself, one armed, and managed to do pretty well.

137

I *had* to be able to do this because I wanted Stewart to move back home; he'd been staying with his dad until I could drive him to school, and he was anxious to get home. At first my bad arm was so useless that Stewart would have to shift for me since the gearshift on my Mustang convertible was on a console between the seats by my right arm. I could do fine as long as I didn't have to back up; I would tease Stewart that I would drive forward to take him to school, circle through the parking lot still going forward, and then have to run into a tree to stop when I got home.

Once Stewart moved back home, instead of settling into his own bedroom on the second floor of the house, he insisted on sleeping in my kingsized bed with me. "I need to sleep down here so I can protect you tonight, Mama," he would tell me, and he meant it sincerely. Since I had to sleep with my right arm propped up on several large pillows to elevate it enough to keep it from swelling during the night, it was like being in separate beds anyway, separated by a mountain of pillows, so I let him stay with me. It made him feel helpful, and I have no doubt that he would indeed have tried to protect me had the need arisen.

Fortunately, Stewart did not have to protect me, though we were constantly harassed by private investigators hired by Murray's defense attorney. They parked at the end of my driveway, then followed my staff to their homes and other jobs until they had to call their own attorneys to get any peace. Rose confronted one investigator in her home driveway and then had to ask Bob to meet her at the Council on Aging and tell the investigator who'd followed her to work to leave her alone, that she had nothing to say to him.

I had always felt secure in my own home, but began to wonder when certain "guests" started asking suspicious questions of the staff and conducting surveillance under the guise of being paying tourists.

Weep For The Living

Once, just out of the hospital and sick to death of being cooped up inside, I put on my bathrobe and struggled to walk with assistance over to the pool area so I could sit in the warm sun for a few minutes. I noticed a single male "guest" taking photos of me from his cottage porch. This sort of thing was unsettling as I struggled to get my strength back and should have been able to concentrate solely on my physical recovery—and it was infuriating.

Every time Murray was in the parish, I would get reports of where he had been and who had seen him. I was curious about the reaction of the community to him, as I had been about its reaction to me.

I had received many concerned calls and letters from relatives and friends and had so much good food delivered to the house that I didn't cook a meal for months. People who hadn't spoken to me in years made a point of expressing their concern. Other people crossed the street when they saw me coming and didn't speak at all—and said behind my back that they thought I had gotten just what I deserved.

Honesty is certainly a virtue, certainly one of mine. But honesty in my case is also one of my worst faults, especially given the great pleasure I have in past times taken in pointing out the failings of others (rarely behind their backs, more often right to their faces). So there were certainly some in the community who sympathized with Murray despite his criminal actions.

Big Rose was in line behind Murray's ex-wife in the grocery store one day and heard her telling some shopper that poor Murray was so anxious he just couldn't sleep at night; Rose had a ready retort, but thought better of offering it. Word around town was that Murray was telling everyone who would listen that I had spent all his money and then kicked him out of the house at his advanced age. I guess this made some people feel sorry for him. It would have made *me* feel sorry for him if it had been true—but it wasn't. *I* was the one with a couple of hundred thousand dollars' loans at the bank; he was debt-free.

139

#

We hadn't even gotten into court yet and already I was getting a good look at the unfortunate tendency of our criminal justice system to victimize the victim twice in its efforts to protect the rights of the defendant, permitting the defense to attempt to shift the blame—at least in public opinion—from criminal to hapless victim. I had to keep reminding myself that I wasn't the defendant, I wasn't the one who had committed a crime, *he* was.

When my friend Abby Padgett, a wonderful mystery writer from California, flew into Baton Rouge and tried to get a little gift for me at the airport shop, she was explaining to the clerk that it was for a friend who had lost the use of her right arm, and the clerk immediately replied, "Oh, is that for Anne Butler?" She told Abby that everyone in Baton Rouge said that Murray had Alzheimer's. That was a joke. As much pride as he took in his mental prowess, I could not imagine that he would ever resort to using *that* as a defense.

There were certainly some townspeople, mostly his old friends, who did feel sympathy for him but, as a general rule, I would have to say that the community reaction was one of pure horror that such an awful thing could happen here, and this gave way to outrage at a judicial system which continued to leave free and unpunished someone who'd obviously attempted to commit unprovoked murder. Even at Angola, that place of violence, the reaction among staff and inmates alike was shocked speechlessness.

The worst part of Murray's being free was the distinct possibility that my children or I would run into him in the only post office in town, the main grocery story, the same drugstore we both continued to use, nearly anywhere in this little 19th-century river-town that is called with not much exaggeration "the town that's two miles long and two yards wide," its one main street running atop a narrow ridge.

Stewart, I thought, would react in anger, striking out; Chase on the other hand would fall to pieces, I was afraid. She had returned home from college after graduating on the Emory honor roll in mid-December with nearly all A's in a semester that began two weeks late and was filled with anxiety and anguish. With every backfire or shot in the night—usually illegal deer hunters along the rural highway—she would run downstairs to see if I was all right. She had a recurring bad dream in which she rounded a corner in the grocery store and was confronted by Murray. In the nightmare, she said, the worst part was that she couldn't find anything to throw at him except heads of lettuce.

And if I had run into him, I'm not so sure how I would have reacted. I knew I'd eventually have to face him in court—but that would be a good while away, if ever. If I'd encountered him on the street or in town, I think I could have handled it and simply not reacted publicly at all. But then I had thought I could handle guns too, and that proved not to be quite accurate.

Burnett had insisted that I should have some sort of weapon in the house when I was alone, and he had given me a little rifle, showing me how to load and use it. But with a useless right arm, I could not raise the rifle to sight it, could not hold it to my shoulder to fire it. And so, in all innocence and trying desperately to help, he showed up one day with a .38 pistol, thinking I could shoot it more easily than the rifle, and I burst into tears at the sight of it and made him take it away.

CHAPTER 12

Ginny and Sam and their grown daughter and son-in-law came back for Thanksgiving with us, and then it was Christmas. It had taken months before I noticed one day that I was actually feeling almost cheerful, that I was experiencing how delightful the day was and how pleasant the weather, and I was suddenly aware that I had for the first time had a few moments completely free of worries and thoughts of my ordeal. It had been so long since my mind had been able to concentrate on anything else, and it was a distinct pleasure to be feeling almost myself mentally. I had always taken such pleasure in the simple small beauties of country living: the first daffodils of spring, the baby wrens tumbling out of their nest in my hanging flower basket and bumbling around until they learned to fly properly, and a myriad of other simple pleasures. Now maybe I would regain that enjoyment.

I struggled to keep the holidays as normal as possible for the sake of my children. When Chase tried to talk me into a tiny tabletop Christmas tree, which wouldn't be so much trouble, I insisted on our usual freshly cut 12-foot evergreen, fully decked out with the hundreds of ornaments we've made and collected over the years. Burnett and Ruby would kindly spend Christmas Eve with us and go to services at Grace Church; without them, Chase wouldn't have gone because she was afraid Murray, who was visiting in the parish, might be there.

This was the year that everybody gave me angels for Christmas—angel earrings, stained-glass angels, angel candleholders, angel soaps, angel statues, kneeling angels, flying angels, trumpeting angels, praying angels—and I put a lot of them on the window ledge overlooking my bedroom so that they could continue to keep an eye on me. With their help, I had come a long, long way.

The December court hearing date came and went with no hearing. The two attorneys had hammered out an agreement over the phone that Murray would come into the parish only for "essential" medical or legal reasons. But who would decide what was essential? I didn't think this was much of an advance. Murray was still calling Big Rose at her home—asking questions about my state of health, whether I could walk, who stayed with me at night. He admitted having shot me, told Rose he couldn't remember doing it, and then turned right around and described every action in great detail; and he called her telephone number over and over again until she answered.

We had hoped the judge might agree that this sudden obsessive interest was unhealthy and unsafe, particularly with both of my children being back in my home at the time, but he did nothing about Murray's holiday plans to come into the area for two full weeks at Christmas.

The trial date was supposed to have been set at this hearing; instead, it would now be set in mid-March at another hearing, which would make us miss the spring session of criminal court and throw the trial into the following fall, if that soon. And Murray's attorney was allowed by the judge to change his plea from "not guilty" to "not guilty by reason of insanity," even though there was a ten-day limit on changing pleas, a time period long expired.

Drowning in debt, I was frustrated with the court system and beginning to give up ever getting any help. My hospital bill was astronomical, and the insurance coverage I had through Murray's state retirement policy began denying all claims because there had been an "intentional act" that necessitated the treatment. After my first few weeks at home, the insurance denied payment for home health care, so I had to pay Belle and Katie to come twice a day to bathe me and change the colostomy, since my arm was still too nonfunctional for me to be able to manage.

Winter is the slow time for B&Bs here, the weather being so unpredictable and dreary, so my income dwindled just as my bills escalated, and at one point I was $16,000 overdrawn in my checking account. While a big-city financial institution would have been carting off the furniture, I was blessed with supportive friends at the Bank of St. Francisville. Banker Conville Lemoine said he knew I would eventually get things under control again, and I hoped his faith was justified.

The best news I got was from the insurance company, where I found a wonderful friend in the clerk who looked into my claim, indignantly took the denial letters to the legal department and insisted that the claims be paid, mailed out the checks herself to the hospital and doctors, and called to ask me if "the perpetrator" was their insured. When I answered yes, she said she hoped I wouldn't mind if she told me that she wished "the perpetrator" had saved a bullet for himself!

In fact a lot of people expressed that same sentiment. Murray himself tried to tell the police that he had intended to take his own life. He certainly had two uninterrupted hours to have done so if he'd really wanted to. When he'd been taken into custody, a note had been found in his pocket, saying to call his son Jerry at Murray's ex-wife's phone number in St. Francisville. Much was made by the defense team about this "suicide note." I think it was my sister who, hearing this, snorted, "Sounds more like a 'call my lawyer, I've done something bad and am in trouble,' note to me." Verbal as Murray is, even I think that if he had meant this to be a real suicide note, his last opportunity at communication, he'd have tried to offer some explanation for his actions, some justification, some *something*.

#

I was greatly relieved to have the insurance coverage straightened out before my next scheduled round of surgery set for the beginning of March when Dr. Mazoch returned from six weeks of maternity leave.

She was to remove the colostomy and repair the abdomen, and Dr. Fonte was to remove bone from the opposite hip for a bone graft into the elbow, where he would also put steel plates to try to hold the bone in place.

There was still a large part of my arm that had not healed, and bone which should have been running straight up and down the arm from elbow to shoulder had instead splintered and was partly sticking out the front of my arm, causing pain and swelling just above the elbow. This prevented my doing much meaningful therapy. I worked hard on maintaining and improving mobility in the shoulder and hand, but the elbow was freezing up and would be a real long-term problem even after the bone was stabilized.

Four weeks before this last surgery was to take place, Dr. Mazoch expressed reservations at the large number of separate procedures scheduled for the same time and said that because of the danger of infection or contamination, she was particularly hesitant to have Dr. Fonte removing bone from the hip area so close to the abdominal incision for the colostomy reversal. She suggested I have the colostomy surgery first in March and after I recovered from that have the arm surgery. But that would take the entire spring. My business and my income were dependent on the tourist traffic, which was heaviest in spring. I could not afford to miss so much time from doing house tours.

In desperation, I called Dr. Fonte to express my frustrations. He replied, "Well, let's see. I'm busy today. Come in on Tuesday and we'll do your arm surgery then." That gave me three days to prepare myself for major surgery, and Murray would know I was going into the hospital almost before I would, so good was his information pipeline.

If Dr. Fonte performed the arm surgery first, the second week in February, that would give me a couple of weeks to recover before the other surgery March 2. I did not want two separate hospitalizations, two different anesthesias, two totally separate recoveries. But it was the best we could do.

#

While I was awaiting these last two surgeries, I had a long visit from Lloyd Hoyle and his wife Jo. Lloyd had worked with Murray for years, first in his home state of Iowa and later, after Murray became warden at Angola, he served as associate warden in charge of all budgeting and purchasing, construction and just about everything else.

During that time, in the racial tensions of the seventies, when a young white correctional officer was killed by prison Black Panthers, some of the entrenched Angola guard families tried to blame the much-resented new administration of the penitentiary. Lloyd became the sacrificial lamb; he was pushed through a plate glass window by the grieving brother of the dead boy and nearly killed. Murray left soon afterward to become head of corrections in Tennessee, leaving Lloyd behind to take the heat, but the two continued to respect each other as professionals in their field.

When I opened Butler Greenwood as a Bed & Breakfast and began making money for the first time, Murray had suggested hiring Lloyd to set up a bookkeeping system, and he took my very feeble attempts at record keeping and turned them into a thoroughly professional accounting system. For several years he kept the books and did the taxes, taking on more and more responsibility as time went by and the business grew by leaps and bounds. His advice on new construction projects was always sound, and Burnett and I came to rely on Lloyd for more and more assistance in areas besides bookkeeping.

Lloyd also did our personal income taxes, and he soon became convinced that Murray was not carrying his weight here financially. When his suggestion that Murray pay a share of the utilities and other living expenses fell on deaf ears, eventually Lloyd suggested that Murray pay his salary as a fair and predictable share of the monthly expenses. This worked for awhile, then Murray began to balk at paying that much and soon began insisting that I replace Lloyd with someone who would keep the books for less money.

Of everyone in this area, Lloyd probably knew Murray better than anyone except his ex-wife, and Lloyd had seen him over many years, in good times and in bad. He did not think I was safe, even after nearly six months had elapsed since the shooting. He said that once Murray got an idea, he would never let it go. Lloyd had been the one who had filled in for Murray when he was drinking, and this had apparently been a fairly frequent occurrence during the bad years. Lloyd said that once a fixation got started with Murray, he would either act on it or start drinking. "If he's not drinking right now," Lloyd would tell me, "you're not safe." And if he was drinking? I wasn't safe then, either.

Lloyd had recently received a phone call from Murray, who acted as if nothing had happened and asked Lloyd if he would do his taxes; Lloyd said he didn't believe he would. If anyone knew our financial situation, it was Lloyd, and I was counting on him to back me up in court by showing that the money I had spent on my place had been my own and that I had in fact been pretty well supporting Murray once the business got going. Lloyd knew how much I had borrowed from the bank for construction of the B&Bs, and he would not lie for anybody, so I knew he'd be just what I needed if Murray tried to claim part of my business as I had heard he planned to do.

#

Lloyd was never one to pry into our business, but I knew he'd never quite understood the relationship between Murray and me, and he was certainly not alone. I don't know that even *we* understood it. How do you, after all, explain the attraction between two people? Often, it has as much to do with timing as anything else, and I had grown close to Murray, a real scholar and interesting conversationalist, right at a time when I was feeling increasingly isolated and confined in a marriage which left me feeling starved for intelligent conversation.

I'd been married three times before Murray, and each husband had some very appealing qualities, but never quite . . . *enough*. It would have been necessary to put them all together to come up with someone who could meet all of my needs, the perfect husband. Perhaps each met my needs at the time, but the nature of those needs changed as my life changed.

My first husband appealed to the wanderlust of post-college footloose hippie days, and we traveled extensively and enjoyed a life free from responsibility and care—great fun for a while, but eventually at least one of us had to settle down and think about a permanent job and roots, and this would be me, especially when Chase was born. My second husband answered the rebound need for normalcy, a settled life. He was a deputy sheriff in cowboy boots who handcuffed me to my desk and wouldn't let me go until I promised to marry him; and he was certainly thoughtful and re-sponsible, with the voice of an angel, but, well, maybe I wasn't ready for straight dull normality after all.

My third husband was someone I had admired for having sacri-ficed his college plans after his father died to take on the grueling responsibility of running the family dairy so his younger brothers and sisters could continue their own educations instead. He brought me fresh cream full of butter fat from the dairy when he thought I wasn't eating enough. I hoped his farm equipment and tractors would be helpful with the upkeep of my own place.

Murray and I began traveling together to research the Angola books, and the stimulation of writing something I regarded as mean-ingful combined with the stimulation of a new and rewarding rela-tionship to enhance his appeal. My husband at that time, the third, was a hard-working cattleman in blue jeans and battered cowboy hat with a million things claiming his attention besides me: fences down, cows sick, bulls out on the highway, calves coming, hay to bale, rye grass to sow. Burnett had in fact been so worried that I wouldn't make it to the hospital when Stewart was born that he and Ruby spent the last several weeks of my pregnancy here so that he could drive me himself if my husband was in the hayfield when I went into labor.

Along came a very attentive, solicitous soul, seductive and suave in well-tailored suit and tie, offering intellectual challenge and the opportunity to travel and to use my talents in creative and worthwhile ways, smelling of expensive aftershave instead of cow manure. The appeal was undeniable, and the return to writing something mean-ingful restored my neglected self-esteem.

As a husband, Murray was without question thoughtful and con-siderate—as long as things were going his way. But now—what was it he had said to me when he left, that I'd be sorry I'd ever heard his name? Is it any wonder I have a hard time recalling quite what that initial appeal was? As one of my dear departed ex-husbands had said to me at one point—for somebody so smart, I was pretty damn dumb; and that was especially true regarding my choice of men I guess.

Then I thought of what John Senette, rector of Grace Church when I first moved back to St. Francisville, said at the time of my unhappy parting from Chase's father: that there are some people who just shouldn't be confined by institutions, even institutions like marriage. I thought at the time he was talking about my departing husband. Now, I think maybe he was talking about me. And that was probably true, too.

#

It was fortunate that Dr. Mazock had had reservations about per-forming the colostomy closure along with Dr. Fonte's arm surgery. The arm surgery itself took six hours and was far more involved than anticipated. The elbow had essentially collapsed and would have to be shored up by two steel plates, the nerve to the hand had become impacted in all the other repair work and had to be pried loose, and the bone graft entailed two hours' work with hammer and chisel on my hip through an incision as long as a hand.

There was no way the two surgeries could have been done to-gether. As it was, Dr. Fonte, bless his heart, made a stand in the oper-ating room and told the extremely competent staff there that they'd better get ready for a long siege because nobody was stopping until they'd given me back my arm. My therapist Lisa sat in on the operation as well, consulting with Dr. Fonte as the surgery progressed, and he kept them working for six straight hours.

Dr. Fonte, latter-day renaissance man with scholarly enthusiasms for just about every subject under the sun, sometimes seemed like the proverbial absent-minded professor, but everyone involved with my case assured me he was an excellent surgeon. We used to joke about a movie being made about my ordeal, and Dr. Fonte felt that Alan Alda of "*MASH*" would be just right to play his part. The therapists thought hysterical, bumbling Dick Van Dyke would be better suited for it.

I would have to spend five days in the hospital and would leave with my arm in a sling and with a terrible limp from the graft, but the minute I came out of the anesthesia I was already moving my fingers more freely than I had in six months, and it soon became apparent that the arm could now begin to respond much better to therapy. At least there was not the added pain of broken bone grating against bone.

Two weeks later I was enroute back to the hospital for the colostomy closure. Dr. Mazock had returned from maternity leave as jolly as ever, and everyone in the hospital came by to wish me well the night before surgery. I awoke to see a giant poster decorating my wall from my friends in therapy, "Way To Go Anne!" It was signed by all of the therapists and everyone else who happened to pass by as creative, thoughtful Lisa worked on it. And Chase would add another poster, saying "Free at Last!"

After the last experience with the failed closure operation, I was almost afraid to ask questions or feel my side as I awoke, but I was soon assured by Chase and Burnett, who had sat through this whole surgery together as they had most of the others, that all had been successful.

What a tremendous feeling of freedom. Now I would not need nursing assistance every morning and every night; now I could appear in public without fear of embarrassment; now I could eventually even wear clothes that touched my waistline once the scars healed. I felt like I had been wearing garbage bags for six months. And I had looked like it too.

#

I had entered the hospital for this sixth surgery on Monday, March 2. Dr. Mazock had cautioned me to expect at least a week's stay since everything had to be fully functional for discharge. But with my strong legs I was up on my feet and walking within a day of surgery, so by Saturday she decided I could return home if I would be careful not to strain my stomach, full of sutures from the chest on down and all across the left side at the waist.

It was actually hard to leave the hospital. I guess it had become a sort of safe haven for me, and I had made good friends with staff from every department. Lord knows I saw enough of every department and knew staff members everywhere: medical staff, nurses, aides, cleaning staff, physical therapists, occupational therapists, respiratory therapists, operating room staff, anesthesiologists, intensive care staff, x-ray and cat scan technicians, student nurses, dietary staff, social services staff, admissions clerks, day surgery staff, in-patient surgery staff, recovery room staff, insurance representatives, pink ladies—you name it, and I had had contact with someone or everyone in that department.

In the hospital hallway I ran into one of the older doctors and introduced myself to him, thinking he'd probably forgotten me in the years since he'd so compassionately treated my favorite aunt, who died of cancer, and he replied that he'd seen plenty of me in the hospital, I just hadn't been conscious. I wanted to go home desperately, but I cried at leaving all these people who had been so kind and caring and who had taken such a personal interest in my recovery.

The last night I spent in the hospital, my therapist Lisa and her husband spent in my Bed & Breakfast celebrating their wedding anniversary. They had departed by the time I returned home but had left certain mementos of their visit—a bouquet of colorful sugar cookies and a warm welcome home card.

Lisa had also had the nerve to bring along the plastic clips which she used at home to keep her toddler from fishing in the toilet bowl, so after six months of not needing to use the toilet thanks to the colostomy, I found my toilet top clamped shut the first time I *did* need to use it.

Good old Lisa! I paid her back in full a few months later when she had some intimate female surgery requiring painful stitches and I arrived with the perfect present for her own homecoming—a very risque black and blue bustier that some racy guest had left in the B&B, the outfit complete with matching G-string, black thigh-high hose and even black net gloves!

CHAPTER 13

I got home on Saturday afternoon, March 7, full of sutures and requiring assistance to get in and out of bed because of the need not to strain my stomach incisions. By Monday, I was getting phone calls at my home from Murray. Apparently not satisfied with calling Big Rose, he became bolder and more arrogant, typical of stalking behavior.

Well aware that the terms of his bond and restraining order required him to have no contact whatsoever with me, he called twice on Monday. The calls registered on my Caller-ID as emanating from his place of employment, the Episcopal church book store in Alexandria, the town where he was supposed to be residing with his son.

The first time he called, he just hung up. The second time, I answered the phone, saying "Butler Greenwood." There was a pause, and then he said, with no effort to disguise his voice, "Oh, *excuse me*. I have the wrong number." I hung up.

If he had just wanted to find out if I was home from the hospital, he need not have spoken. He wanted me to know that he was calling and that he could call here with impunity and do anything else he wanted too. I called the sheriff and the prosecutor, both of whom had felt Murray belonged in jail the whole time.

It was essential that action be taken promptly, because this was a particularly dangerous time: not only was I at my most helpless and weakest, but I now also had two children in the house with me and

UTL

because of financial constraints we no longer had a guard on the grounds or a sitter inside with me.

Furthermore, the Alexandria TV station was devoting the entire week to coverage of the West Feliciana pilgrimage, and this house, unfortunately, was one of the featured homes. I could ill afford to open my home to 3,000 visitors to benefit the local historical society but had been reluctant to remove the house from the tour line-up after all the promotion had been done.

Murray was sure to see the coverage, and that would add fuel to the fire. As if that weren't enough, the following week on March 18, just two days before the pilgrimage began, a court hearing had been set to re-arraign him under his new plea in open court; so he would obviously have an excuse to be back in the parish.

The pilgrimage would be a security nightmare—1000 people a day for three days touring the house and grounds—and if he were trying to establish an insanity defense, what better place to do so than in front of 3000 witnesses. Burnett, who usually only worked a few days a week at my house, began appearing daily, sticking close; Bob and Rose began carrying guns; Chase and Belle would call frequently from work to see how I was doing.

The sheriff was so concerned he began posting a deputy near my driveway during the daytime, and at night as well whenever he could spare one, and he personally came to visit to reassure me that his office was doing everything it could to protect me and my children. I knew he meant it. He also suggested to the judge that we needed a speedy trial and was told May or June might be the next possible court date.

St. Tammany Parish Assistant DA Scott Gardner, who had been assigned to prosecute the case, had held off putting me on the stand for any of the previous hearings because he had not wanted to show Mike Small, Murray's attorney, what kind of witness I would make. Of course I had been physically weak throughout most of the previous court activities, but he felt I would make a pretty good witness, not easily intimidated, and he didn't want to play his best card too quickly in the case until it would count.

Feeling very apprehensive, I was led into the old courtroom with its dark beaded board walls, where my grandmother's father, Judge Samuel McCutcheon Lawrason, had been one of the earliest judges, as had my grandfather's grandfather, Judge Thomas Butler, before him.

Murray, a master of control, had no visible reaction to my presence, although Rose had passed near him in the hallway earlier and heard him frantically asking his attorney, "Where is she? I *know* she's in one of these rooms. Which room is she in? Where *is* she?" Mike Small cautioned him that he was to have no contact with me, but Rose said he continued asking. In the courtroom before the hearing began, he had nonchalantly chatted with everyone he knew in the jury pool and among the court personnel, working the crowd like the good politician that he was.

To be sworn in to testify, I had to raise my right hand, but my right arm raises only about a third as far as it should and that's as high as I can pick it up—just one lasting disability I must learn to live with. I took the stand and was asked by the prosecutor to describe the telephone contacts from Murray, including two to my home phone while I was in the hospital, which registered on the Caller-ID as from his place of employment, and two after I returned home from the hospital, including the one that I answered when I heard Murray's voice say, "Oh, excuse me, I have the wrong number."

Mike Small then began insisting that the earlier calls had been placed by some other employee of the bookstore who was trying to buy Angola books from me. These crime books would hardly be suitable for a church bookstore. Moreover, no reputable bookstore would attempt to purchase books directly from an author; the book jacket gives information on ordering from the publisher, one of the state university presses, the proper place to order.

Small also insisted that the call during which Murray actually spoke to me had been a mistake, that he had actually been trying to call his ex-wife to get some income tax information and had dialed the wrong number because some other employee had written my phone number on the desk blotter in front of him.

UTL

The prosecutor asked me if I had been forced to take security precautions at home and had me describe the security system and the Caller-ID. He wanted to hear why I no longer had a guard on the grounds; I was nearly bankrupt, I explained, and could no longer afford the extra expense. He asked if some of my employees were armed, and I said they were.

He asked if I carried a gun. I replied rather forcefully that I had never considered violence an acceptable solution to problems and I did not consider it one now. "I have never carried a gun in my life," I said, "and I'm certainly not going to start carrying one now."

When Scott Gardner tried to introduce evidence about other phone calls, mostly to Big Rose but also to another friend whom Murray had called just the night before to ask her to influence me not to try to revoke his bail, the judge sustained every objection Mike Small made about the introduction of this evidence. With each objection sustained, it began to look as if we were going to get nowhere.

Mike Small looked smug and arrogant as he proffered evidence to be entered into the record about the so-called accidental phone call, telling the court that the "poor elderly gentleman" had made an honest mistake in calling my home and speaking to me. He put Murray on the stand, and Murray made a big show of stumbling and describing how he was undergoing psychiatric care and taking medication (which turned out to be a mild anti-depressant, Zoloft).

It seemed pretty hopeless when all of a sudden the judge, the Honorable Wilson Ramshur, sat up straight in his chair and announced to the court that the explanation about someone else trying to buy books from me was totally unreasonable. Furthermore, he added, any time Murray called me, even if all he said was that he had the wrong number, what he *really* was saying was that he was out there and that he was going to get me again. Bond revoked! Put the defendant in jail!

Every mouth in the courtroom fell open. Bob hustled me out of the courthouse so we wouldn't have to walk too close to Murray, and my ex-ex Glenn Daniel was the deputy who drove Murray in his Cadillac to the parish jail around the corner. Murray turned to Glenn on the way and said, "I can't believe the judge did that to me." And Glenn answered, just as truthfully, "I can't believe it either."

UTL

CHAPTER 14

Two days later the pilgrimage began. The three-day house and garden tour commemorates the connection with flamboyant artist-naturalist John James Audubon, who in 1821 painted nearly a third of his *Birds of America* series in the parish. While he was here, he knew my family well, remembers them in his letters and diaries, and his wife Lucy, ever the more practical and stable of the two, tutored several of the daughters of the family.

Audubon painted perhaps the truest and most vivid picture of West Feliciana, with words rather than brushes, surprisingly, when he praised the richly blessed countryside as being where "Nature seems to have paused, as she passed over the Earth, and opening her stores, to have strewed with unsparing hand the diversified seeds from which have sprung all the beautiful and splendid forms which I should in vain attempt to describe . . ."

With paints and brushes he then proceeded to "describe" further these bounties, for no less than 80 of the artist's famed bird studies were painted in West Feliciana in the 1820s as he lived at Oakley Plantation and tutored the beautiful young daughter of the owners. These bird prints provide a permanent record of the lush and fertile wildlife habitat he so admired while here.

The artist himself must have cut a dashing figure in the pioneer woods, confessing in his journal, "It was one of my fancies to be ridiculously fond of dress; to hunt in black satin breeches, wear pumps when shooting, and dress in the finest ruffled shirts I could obtain from France." It is this dandy and his artistic appreciation of the area that we celebrate in the annual Audubon Pilgrimage the third week-end of March, re-creating the atmosphere he enjoyed here even to the extent of dressing in costumes duplicating the fashions of the years he and his wife were present in the Felicianas.

This year (1998) for the pilgrimage, the azaleas were in full bloom, the lawns and gardens of Butler Greenwood looked like a fairyland, the sun shone, the thousands of tourists enjoyed touring the property, and I in my 1820s costume felt a wonderful freedom I hadn't enjoyed in months.

"Historic Butler Greenwood Plantation is often a popular feature on West Feliciana's annual spring pilgrimage, but the 1998 tour was a special trial to prepare for, with Anne just out of the hospital after major surgery"

UTL

Murray's attorney had ten days to appeal the judge's ruling to a higher court and he would do so immediately. But for a little while at least, we no longer had to worry about his being out there and after me still. It was a great feeling.

We had nearly 3,000 visitors through the house on pilgrimage weekend. Those who knew me were pleased to see me taking an active role, those who didn't know me and the idly curious were discouraged in their inquiries when they got too personal, and one lady saw one of the Angola books in my working office and said to her companion, "There's that *murderer!*" Thank goodness Dr. Mazoch didn't appear—she'd made me promise I would stay in bed through the whole weekend, and there I was conducting tours.

Murray meanwhile remained in jail. His attorney appealed to the First Circuit Court of Appeals and then to the Louisiana Supreme Court, and both courts upheld the judge's ruling, denying the appeal. At no time was the "other employee" of the church book store produced, the one who supposedly called my house to order Angola books, the logical assumption being that this person wasn't produced because there was no such person and it was Murray making the calls.

The June 1,1998, court date would be continued due to prior commitments by one of the examining psychiatrists, who had to go to a convention in Canada, but we were hopeful that with Murray in jail his attorney would not try to delay the trial too long.

Exactly eight months after the shooting, the two attorneys had a telephone conference with the judge and set a new trial date of October 5 instead of June 1. Besides the psychiatrist having a June schedule conflict, Mike Small was tied up all of July, Scott Gardner couldn't make himself available in August, and September was always a notoriously crowded court docket after the summer recess here.

So another six months would pass. I think the current catch-word is *closure*, and we would have none of it for far too long to suit me. I was ready for it all to be over and behind me. The sheriff was concerned that the judge would amend the bond and let Murray out of jail; the defense attorney was already trying to get permission for Murray to leave the state and reside in his daughter's Texas home.

When he was supposed to be staying with his son, the assistant DA, Murray didn't do very well at staying *there* and leaving me alone, and I didn't know what guarantee we'd have that *this* would be any different as long as he had his car, his phone, his guns. Besides, his daughter spent most of her time in Singapore where her husband was employed by one of the big oil companies, so it's not as if he'd have had any supervision at her Texas home.

With the criminal proceedings pending, I was not at liberty to file a civil suit or publish any written accounts of the ordeal for fear of jeopardizing the court case. I had been writing this book in bits and pieces over the course of a year, beginning the second I could manage to wrench my aching hands onto the computer keyboard, arm propped on a pillow. I strongly felt that the story was worth telling, but I wanted to tell it like it *was*, not turn it into a contrived novel, and I wasn't anxious to keep working on it much more than a year. I felt that once I finished the book, I would be more capable of putting the whole miserable ordeal behind me.

But it was hard for me to get personal enough in the writing. I didn't *want* to go back to those feelings of love and kindness for Murray. Perhaps it was a protective mechanism which made those feelings seem so remote now. But everyone who read the manuscript in progress insisted that it needed more detail . . . more intimacy, more conversation, more *sex*. I resisted re-opening those old doors, but I knew that would be necessary for the book to have much of a market.

Did I want to preserve the privacy I had always valued so highly and put the manuscript aside once the trial was over and consider it as simply good therapy for me, mentally and physically? No. I wanted it *published*, I wanted people to read the real story, I wanted the lessons of this book to keep someone else from going through the same ordeal, and yes, certainly I wanted to make some money from a year's difficult struggle and hard labor. I was, after all, a writer. I would try to finish the story and find an agent or a publisher who would produce and promote the book.

Besides family and a very few trusted friends, I had the good fortune to have several professional authors read the manuscript and offer constructive criticism and suggestions, but Burnett, bless his heart, would surprise me by offering the best literary critique of them all. A longtime lover of old westerns with dozens of dog-eared Louis L'Amour books on his bookshelf, he would tell me, "If there's one thing I've learned from reading all those Louis L'Amours, it's that you've got to always have another Indian behind another rock on the next page. You've *got* to make the reader want to keep on reading, to keep on turning those pages." Tell it all, he would advise, and tell it honestly, even if it does make you feel stupid after the fact. I cried, and then I tried.

#

By this time, I was able to cut expenses in the business by taking over most of my old chores again. Maybe I couldn't do them quite as well as I had before, but I could do them myself and not have to pay someone else.

I just had to learn to accept the limitations of what my arm could and could not do, because by the end of May, I would finish with therapy, Dr. Fonte and Lisa concurring that what arm function had not been regained by then would never come back. After nine months of grueling therapy sessions at least three times a week, I had regained almost full use of my right hand, some use of my right shoulder and wrist, and very limited use of my right elbow.

My arm would never again straighten out completely or bend fully, mostly because of the steel plates. Besides having limited function, it would also certainly never *look* normal. I would never be able to lift or carry a very heavy load with that arm; I certainly could never clean up six B&B cottages between check-out and check-in times the way I had once been able to do. I could not quite reach the back of my head with my right arm, could not comb my hair, could not apply makeup; I don't wear much anyway, so that didn't make too much difference, but I also discovered that I could hardly use my camera since I couldn't get my hand up high enough to click the shutter while seeing through the viewfinder. That would be a loss for a photojournalist. I had learned, of necessity, how to put on stockings or tights with one arm, how to tie the laces of my tennis shoes, how to zip up a dress—if you think it's easy one-armed, just try it.

And to fold king-sized sheets, which I have to do all day every day, required holding the centerfold in my teeth because my arm would not extend fully. But I was finally able to get food into my mouth with my right hand if the fork was long enough; well, not peas or soup, maybe, but I could at least eat respectably enough to dine in public again. I had had nightmares in which I dreamed that Lisa told me I could never eat again until I could feed myself using only my right hand. Now I knew that at least I wouldn't starve.

The multitude of scars on my arm were healing nicely but the scars all up and down my stomach were awful looking, and the scar where the colostomy had been was simply folded over and would forever be unsightly. I was never without pain. And I never would be.

But the therapy staff hummed the standard old *Aida* graduation march to me, gave me flowers, and sent me out into the cruel world without them—as they *had* to do. I don't think they usually keep patients as long as I was with them, and I know it was awfully hard for me to leave them behind.

I had gotten deeply attached to each and every one of them, but now *I* would have to try to do the painful stretches and exercises, which wouldn't be nearly as effective without Lisa as stern taskmaster. It would be hard—but I knew I was fortunate that most of my lasting scars were more physical than emotional.

#

Big Rose in her travels for the Council on Aging often passed by the jail and once saw Murray out in the exercise yard in his orange jumpsuit. The other inmates were playing basketball. He was standing in the corner alone. Most of the time he didn't even go outside at all, and he associated as little as possible with the other inmates.

Word from the jail was that his major occupation was reading in the detox cell—where he was initially confined so the jailers could keep a close eye on him—and his major concern was for his Rolex watch. He had never had a Rolex watch that I knew of when we were married (actually, I'd never noticed what kind of watch he *did* have), so he must be trying to spend out all of his money—kind of aggravating as I struggled with bills I'd never have incurred had it not been for his actions.

According to insurance records, after my sixth surgery my hospital bills alone exceeded $105,000, not counting therapy or diagnostic lab work or all the other things that are billed separately. In preparation for the trial, I asked the bookkeeper to put together a list of medical-related expenses I would not otherwise have had and was astounded when the total reached over $75,000 from my own pocket, strictly for nurses, sitters, doctor and hospital bills not covered by insurance, guards, loans to cover payroll and keep the business afloat and pay bills, extra hours worked by the B&B staff doing tasks which I would normally have performed and which nearly doubled the payroll expenses for months. And this did *not* count the business losses due to security concerns of potential guests.

No *wonder* I never could quite catch up. I had to borrow from the bank and from my sister (who also *gave* me money to cover security and nursing expenses early on), and had to sell a little property just to try to keep up with the out-of-pocket expenses. Me, I have *no* Rolex.

#

But I have something more important. With help from Burnett and a few other friends with spiritual insight, it has actually become possible for me to see a beneficial side to the horror of my experiences. I've been told that God must have had big plans for the rest of my life to have spared it, and perhaps that is so. I hope so.

In June one longtime guest who had spent his honeymoon at the B&B and has come back for special occasions every few months in the ensuing years left for me upon his departure a tiny card in the shape of a Victorian angel with a note inside saying, "Anne, it surely must have been an angel that has watched over you. I see you look at life with different eyes, and you display an inner peace now. Clearly an aura of love surrounds you."

In July I would receive a card from someone I couldn't quite place, a nice sentimental card with a handwritten note saying, "May God bless you with Love and Happiness always. Anne Butler, I am so very happy you are alive. I have been wanting to tell you this for a very long time, but did not know how. Your will to live, your courage . . . God is not through with you, Anne Butler. Not yet. How wonderful."

Because I deal with so many people every day doing tours and running the B&B, I don't always remember them all, so I telephoned this dear lady in the nearby city where she lives to find out if she might be someone I had perhaps met briefly or taken on a house tour, but she said she was a total stranger who just wanted to tell me how much she admired my courage and strength. What a nice thing to do, sending such a message to someone you don't even know. I hope I won't be a disappointment to her when we *do* meet.

I know that I have emerged from the trauma a better person, certainly more concerned for other people, more willing to admit my need of help from others, more willing to offer my own help to others in need. Seeing firsthand how genuinely good some people are in times of trouble, how generous and sharing, and seeing also in the hospital as well as in therapy how many people are even worse off than I am—these experiences couldn't help but change me for the better.

"Gifts of growth," that's what one motivational speaker calls life's trials and tribulations, the painful struggles which can culminate, if we let them, in increased strength of character, increased strength of faith. If nothing else, I have certainly grown.

Just recently I was in the grocery store check-out line behind a lady who was having to put back some items because of insufficient cash. I've been in that position before, counting pennies from the bottom of my purse as impatient shoppers behind me glared irritably, and so I told the checker to put the lady's excess purchases on my ticket and I would pay for them.

I just did it to be helpful. The poor lady burst into tears and told me she had especially needed to have something good happen to her after a particularly trying day. She wanted my address to return the money but I told her just to help somebody else when she was able. Would I have done this before my experience? Yes, I hope so, but who knows? The point is that I'll certainly do it, or something similar, whenever I have a chance from now on. I've got a lot to pay back.

#

A near-death experience forever alters anyone, most especially those personalities needing to make some changes anyway, like mine.

I have a friend, Wilbert Rideau, who is the longtime editor of Angola's prison newsmagazine and an award-winning journalist. Wilbert and I are about the same age, only I've spent my last 30 years picking up bad habits and being self-indulgent in the outside world, and he's spent his last 30 years behind bars shedding bad habits and becoming a world-class writer. After committing a teenage murder and confessing, a scared young black boy, on live local television, he was sent to Angola's Death Row where he would absolutely hit bottom and plumb the depths of despair as he awaited execution.

Remember the book called *Been Down So Long It Looks Like Up To Me?* From the bottom, Wilbert had nowhere to go but up, and up he went, reading everything he could get his hands on, educating himself, absolutely *re-inventing* himself to the extent that when he speaks of his crime, which he does only rarely, it is in the third person: "Wilbert" did such and such; "he" did such and such; never "I," because the person who committed that regrettable crime is no longer even present.

Maybe that's a little bit like what happens to anyone who is so very close to death, physically or spiritually, and in the nearly dying there is a rebirth, a sense of being saved by a supreme sacrifice and of being given the opportunity to be born again. The slate is wiped clean, and another chance is given. I came out of the experience blessedly lacking some of the excess baggage I had been carting around and needing to shed for years: grudges, old animosities, petty resentments— all gone. In their place was a new openness to other people, a new tolerance for the failings of others (at least more than there had been before), and these were great improvements.

There is a lot of the old stubbornness and strength left, though, and this is not all bad. I've resisted encouragement to join victim's rights groups because I refuse to see myself as a victim. I'm too stubborn to be a victim—and too strong. Me, I'm a survivor. It would be nice if all victims were, but they're not. I've seen too many "professional" victims in the course of interviewing for the crime books, those who seem to thrive on misfortune, who see victim-hood as a claim to fame, who relish the attention even if it is mostly pity.

CHAPTER 15

I had Bob file for divorce for me in May, simply on the grounds of living separate and apart for more than six months. I had hoped it would be simple. I asked for no alimony. I asked for nothing but the legal status of being completely free from him. But then Murray began trying to claim part of my business, so we put off filing to wait until everything could be accomplished at once. In Louisiana, a community property state with laws based on the ancient Napoleonic Code, debt and gain incurred during a marriage must be shared—but not separate inherited property.

I was adamant about wanting to be totally finished with having to deal with him once the divorce was final, and I didn't want to have a claim hanging over my head for my separate property which he was trying to consider community property. We *had* no community property, we *had* no community debt. I was not trying to make him pay off my bank loan, and if anything was considered community, then that should have been as well, since it was used to build up my business that he was trying to claim as his. He knew my young children would need their inheritance from me; at his age, surely he didn't need to try to take it from them.

It would have been so simple for us to go our separate ways, wishing each other well in other lives. I may never understand why he could not let that happen or why he had to try to destroy not only me but my home, my family, my business, everything I had, in the most hurtful way possible and to do it in a totally controlled and well thought out way.

There is a fine line, I think, between deep passionate love and deep passionate hate, and I can't help but think that sometime during that week we were apart he crossed, or perhaps was *pushed*, over that line. In pre-trial interviews with legal and psychiatric professionals, he tried to disparage our relationship and make light of his feelings for me, but that was for public consumption. I know that he had a very strong love for me, a love that the issue of control perverted and twisted into a very strong and violent hate. What he did was not done because of madness but because of pure meanness. But I will always believe in my heart that he had some help getting to that point.

#

Both court-ordered psychiatric examinations found Murray competent to stand trial, capable of understanding the charges against him and clearly aware of the difference between right and wrong. To both doctors appointed by Judge Ramshur to a Sanity Commission, Murray mentioned having gone to the river target shooting that Sunday morning and then buying liquor, which he admitted he did not drink until after the shooting. He said he couldn't remember shooting me but embellished the aftermath by telling the doctors that as I sat dying in the chair, I said to him, "Kiss me, my darling," and he kissed me. That's the only crazy thing he said in his interviews.

Besides clinical interviews, behavioral observations and a review of available records provided by the attorneys involved, the court-appointed psychologist, Dr. Robert D. Davis of Baton Rouge Psychological Associates, administered certain standard tests: the Mattis Dementia Rating Scale, which provides a multidimensional assessment of cognitive functioning in the elderly (findings indicated no substantive evidence of mental defect); Shipley Institute of Living Scale, which is a measure of general intellectual functioning (Murray's scores were average); and the Minnesota Multiphasic Personality Inventory-2, which provides a formal objective assessment of the patient's personality and current emotional functioning (he was found to be depressed, somewhat frightened and distrustful of the motives of others toward him, besides likely having a substance abuse problem).

The psychologist's competency assessment found Murray fully capable of understanding the nature of the charges against him and of appreciating their seriousness, as well as capable of understanding the defenses available to him and the consequences of his plea, able to understand his legal rights and the roles of the participants in the trial procedures, and also able to understand the possible verdicts which might follow.

The Georgia Court Competency Test-Mississippi State Hospital—developed as a quantitative measure, administered orally, to sample a defendant's knowledge and skill in understanding courtroom procedures and knowledge of charges and possible penalties, as well as ability to communicate effectively with an attorney—accepts scores of 70 or above as competent to stand trial, those of 50 or below as incompetent. Murray's score was 96. He was determined to be capable of assisting in his defense and was found also *not* to meet the M'Naughton standard of insanity or the other two standard measures of criminal responsibility regarding inability to comprehend the nature of criminal behavior or to recognize the moral or legal wrongfulness of such behavior.

The court-appointed *psychologist* thus found the defendant, though depressed, to be suffering from no substantive mental defect on standardized neuro-psychological measures and perfectly competent to stand trial. The court *psychiatrist*, Dr. John W. Thompson, head of Forensic Neuro-psychiatry at Tulane University in New Orleans and Director of Forensic Services for the State of Louisiana, would build on these standard tests and expand the examination; both doctors interviewed Murray several times, and the psychiatrist also interviewed me.

The psychiatrist also found Murray competent to stand trial. After his interviews and testing, he found Murray's behavior on the day of the offense goal-directed (target shooting, reloading the gun and carrying extra shells, leaving when there was a tour in progress and returning when the tour was over and no one else was in the house) and found that other individuals who saw him on that morning observed no bizarre or irrational behavior.

The behavior he *did* exhibit, Dr. Thompson found, indicated a more logical approach than would be consistent with someone suffering from severe mental disorder. Further, Murray was by his own admission not intoxicated at the time of the shooting, having drunk the bottle of vermouth *afterward*, not before, so that his blood alcohol level on the Breathalizer test administered when he was taken to the local jail was .200, over twice the reading required to be considered legally drunk

The psychiatrist found him to be revengeful and resentful, ranting about money even when the police were transporting him to jail and not calling for assistance even though he was clearly aware that he had shot and severely injured me. When he told Patrice not to be afraid, to leave and not get involved, that I was already "gone," this also indicated to the psychiatrist Murray's understanding of the lethality of his actions and the recognition that Patrice had something to fear from him as well.

Capable of distinguishing right from wrong and competent to stand trial, both Sanity Commission examinations concluded. Of course there would be a different conclusion from the two psychiatrists/neurologists hired by the defense, but their testimony, for *pay*, could not be considered unbiased like that of the court-ordered evaluations. One of them was even flown in from Utah to testify. The defense must have cost a fortune.

CHAPTER 16

An odd quirk of fate very nearly brought us all together again just before the actual trial date. It involved a twenty-five-year-old murder case which shook Angola when it happened and was still causing problems today. It happened in April of 1972 amidst racial tension and strife nationwide; Angola was no different, a microcosm of the larger free global community, and there was a Black Panther group reportedly itching to make a statement. Earlier that year there had been bloody riots and street battles pitting out-of-state militant Black Muslims against local police in nearby Baton Rouge, leaving five dead and a television newsman savagely beaten to permanent paralysis.

Conditions at Angola were undeniably deplorable at this time, and the entire prison was still completely segregated. When the fourth anniversary of Dr. Martin Luther King's death was marked by peaceful memorial services in Baton Rouge, area black leaders called for renewed vigor in the push for minority rights. Angola's fledgling Black Panther party would choose more violent methods to leave their own bloody mark on history.

On April 16, a white correctional officer was firebombed in his guard shack and a letter addressed by inmates to the Baton Rouge newspaper promised other unspecified acts of violence aimed at bringing Angola to the attention of an unconcerned public that was just as guilty as "the racist pigs who hold us captive."

On April 17, the very next day, young Brent Miller, white correctional officer who'd grown up on Angola and had only recently graduated from high school and married, left the dubious protection of his own guard shack and went into one of the medium-security dormitories to have coffee with an elderly black inmate named Hezekiah Brown. The prison was terribly short of professional staff, and Miller was the only officer in an area that ideally should have been covered by five guards.

Within four minutes he would be dead, stabbed thirty-two times with at least two knives, the blows so brutal as to collapse the chest cavity completely. Hezekiah Brown ran wildly from the dormitory and tried to establish an alibi elsewhere but would eventually identify three black inmates as the killers. It wouldn't take long for Angola politics to get in the way, inserting an uninvolved fourth defendant into the case for devious reasons, and soon associate warden Lloyd Hoyle would be mistakenly blamed for releasing those inmates responsible for the killing and would be nearly killed himself by one of Brent Miller's anguished older brothers.

One of the original defendants named by Hezekiah Brown as the real ringleader was Albert Woodfox, a professed black militant from New Orleans, veteran of numerous gun battles with the police and a daring courthouse escape with a smuggled gun that left several prison guards and policemen handcuffed in the elevator. Woodfox was convicted on March 7, 1973, of the murder of Brent Miller; the other two defendants named by Brown would not be tried until the following year because a judge quashed their initial indictments due to the racial imbalance of the grand jury, and then they too were found guilty.

Nearly thirty years later another judge would finally examine the initial indictment of Albert Woodfox and would require that his case be resubmitted to another grand jury. One of the co-defendants was dead, other witnesses had dispersed, even the principals had pushed explicit details back into the far reaches of distant memory, but Hezekiah Brown was still alive and living in New Orleans, from whence he journeyed to testify before the grand jury, his chilling account helping to convince jurors to re-indict the defendant Albert Woodfox for the murder of young officer Miller.

I had written in great detail about this case in my book *Dying To Tell*. The chapter was called "Racist Pigs Who Hold Us Captive." The book was in great demand as the grand jury considered this case yet again, because with the passage of time nearly everybody had forgotten the little details that can be so important. The attorneys read the book; the witnesses read the book; even some of the jurors read the book. And who should be called for grand jury duty out of the 13,000 or so registered voters of the Parish of West Feliciana? Me.

I asked the assistant DA handling the case if he shouldn't excuse me from duty but he insisted that it was the right as well as the *responsibility* of every citizen to serve when called and furthermore insisted that the situation was different from the petit jury, in that it was not necessary to be ignorant of the facts of a case to serve on the grand jury. And so I served, I heard Hezekiah's testimony, I joined the unanimous vote for re-indictment. That was several years ago, and I had forgotten about the case.

Suddenly it was scheduled for prosecution by the state, the trial date set for late September, just a week before my own case was to go to court. Hezekiah Brown had died, so the state was really relying on the testimony of prison officials who had investigated the case—Murray and Lloyd in particular.

Murray of course was in jail, but the state prosecutor of the Woodfox case was trying to work out a deal with Murray's defense lawyer so that he could testify as an expert witness without any mention of "his current problem," that problem being that he was claiming insanity in the shooting of his wife and was currently incarcerated himself. Without his testimony the state would have a difficult time convicting; *with* his testimony, it would seem to me that the defendant would have a ready-made appeal if Murray's "current problem" were not made known to the jury assessing his credibility.

The prosecutor of my case was following these developments with rapt attention, relishing the possibility of Murray testifying as an obviously competent "expert" the week before he would be pleading insanity in my case. Woodfox's defense attorney insisted that Murray was not claiming to be incompetent or insane *now*, but just when he shot me, and so he announced his firm intention of issuing a subpoena for Murray to appear. One of the defense lawyers even went so far as to suggest that the state's case in the Woodfox matter had had some impact on my own case, that Murray's court trial had been purposely delayed so that the state's prize witness would not be a convicted felon at the time he appeared as an expert in this old murder case (the prosecutor insisted this was not the case).

I found it all kind of amusing until that same defense attorney called and suggested that he might have to subpoena *me* as well to join this odd cast of characters in what the attorney described as "the law case from hell." What he really wanted were my notes and tapes of interviews for this particular chapter of *Dying To Tell*; he said there were certain statements Murray had made in the book that he was afraid he might try to change on the stand, and he wanted the verification of the initial interview conclusions.

Needless to say, I was not anxious to get into a courtroom with Murray just a week before our own court confrontation, regardless of subject, and I planned to fight my inclusion in this other case every way I could. Right now I had enough to worry about preparing for my own ordeal in court, and I didn't feel I had much to add to this other case. As a writer, I wasn't convinced that the court—*either* side—should have access to my notes, but this was another distracting issue I didn't want to have to deal with at this particular time.

By providing the pertinent passages from transcribed interviews voluntarily, I did my best to avoid this sidebar confrontation, and the defense attorney assured me that would be sufficient. Then on September 16 I received *two* subpoenas: one to appear at the courthouse in Amite, several hours' drive from my home, the week of September 28 to testify on behalf of the Woodfox defense; the other to produce

177

in open court all notes, tapes and statements taken from Murray, Hilton Butler (a subsequent warden at Angola) and Lloyd Hoyle regarding events referred to in Chapter 1 of *Dying to Tell.* It took a week of work by both me and Bob, as well as personal visits from both defense and prosecuting attorneys, to get the subpoenas quashed but they were finally withdrawn simultaneously as I provided pertinent passages from my transcribed interviews.

The withdrawal of the subpoenas was hand-carried to my home by the prosecuting attorney, who assured me that she had done everything in her power to keep me from being involved in the case. The withdrawal notice stated that the subpoenas were no longer necessary since I had voluntarily complied with the attorney's request for information. I thought that was the end of that.

Then on Friday evening just after 5 p.m., very carefully timed to arrive after all government and legal offices had closed for the weekend, I received another subpoena to appear in Amite the following Monday morning and be present for the duration of the *entire week.* This subpoena was issued by the state's prosecuting attorney, though when I called her she insisted it was coming from both defense and prosecutor and involved my having served on the grand jury which re-indicted the defendant.

I surely could not spend the week before Murray's trial out of town; this was the time Scott Gardner had scheduled for all his personal interviews with the witnesses and for strategy sessions in St. Francisville where he had only been for two quick visits beforehand. But in the Baton Rouge newspaper on Saturday an article appeared announcing the delay of the Woodfox murder trial for at least one day so hearings could be held on Monday to consider several last-minute motions by the defense—one to throw out the defendant's second indictment because of my being on the grand jury that re-indicted him. Scott Gardner advised that I obey my subpoena and appear in the Amite courthouse.

And then the "law case from hell" took one more strange twist when Hurricane *Georges* appeared in the Gulf of Mexico and began barreling toward New Orleans with sustained wind speeds of 110 miles an hour and gusts clocked at over 170 mph. One and a half million people were ordered to evacuate from below-sea-level areas of New Orleans and the low-lying Louisiana coast, and they streamed up the highways, clogging traffic arteries and filling up motels all the way to Memphis.

The course Hurricane *Georges* was on would take it right across Lake Pontchartrain and practically on top of the Amite courthouse on Monday. My prayers for the removal of this distracting obstacle just might be answered. On Sunday the sheriff called to tell me he'd been notified that the Amite courthouse would be closed Monday and Tuesday.

By Monday we heard that the Woodfox trial had been postponed until December. And who would be sitting in on Murray's trial but both Woodfox attorneys—for the prosecution and for the defense—to see just how their prospective witnesses would perform. The state's attorney in Murray's case even considered calling the Woodfox prosecutor as a witness, for who better to testify to the competency and non-insanity of Murray than an attorney who was planning to build a very important legal case on the strength of his expert testimony.

(It ended up that this attorney was not called to testify in Murray's case, but after that case was over, I would get another subpoena to appear before the Woodfox judge for a hearing on November 4 and to bring with me all of my notes and tapes for that chapter of *Dying To Tell*. The judge would deny the defense motion to quash the indictment based on my service on the grand jury but would insist that I turn over tapes and transcripts of interviews relating to the case. And subsequently, Murray and Lloyd would testify as expert witnesses in the actual trial, which resulted in another guilty verdict just before Christmas 1998.)

CHAPTER 17

Meanwhile, I needed to focus all my energies on my own court ordeal, and I was hardly looking forward to it since everybody involved kept telling me that the only defense Murray would have would be to try to tear me apart on the stand. I knew it would be painful, for me and for my whole family and staff, but I wanted to get it over with and get on with my life. I had lost more than a year to this awful experience, and I was ready for it to be over. I wasn't sure how much faith to put in the court system and hoped I would not be surprised or even terribly disappointed if Murray got off with little or no punishment for what he had done.

By mid-week before the trial was to start, my lawyer cousin Bob, who had nothing to do with the case, had already been subpoenaed by the defense, a legal trick to keep him out of the courtroom so he couldn't be of any assistance to Scott Gardner at the counsel table, and a defense motion was filed reserving the right to ask for a change of venue after jury selection began. Just an indication of the underhanded tricks which would be forthcoming, I was sure.

Scott Gardner kept trying to impress on me how rough it would get in court and that it was essential that I not get mad on the stand since he was sure that would be their main tactic. Take a tranquilizer before court, I was advised, so as not to lose my temper; Big Rose said she would be sitting in the audience with a switch in case that failed!

Just before the trial began, there was an offer to buy the defendant out of jail. The offer was $100,000 in cash, plus one of his monthly retirement pension checks (he gets one from Louisiana, one from Tennessee, one from Social Security, all sizable, and of the three, one goes directly to his first wife as alimony). The offer had been made before. The retirement check would last only so long as Murray lived, which might or might not be very long, and the cash would not even cover my out-of-pocket expenses caused by his criminal act, much less my continuing medical expenses.

But I would be spared the agony of a trial; my witnesses would not be grilled and frightened; my children would not be tortured by the suspense; my friends would not be embarrassed. If I accepted the money, I might be able to pay off a little of what I had borrowed from the bank, but not much, and I would never know to any real degree of certainty where Murray would be or when he would return to finish what he had started. My children began sleeping soundly through the night only after Murray was put in jail, and if he were out again, I knew they'd have no peace. Neither would I. There was no way to put a dollar value on our suffering or to assess a monetary sum that could pay his debt to society or to me. And I had a gut feeling that accepting *any* money—being essentially bought off—would not make me feel very good about myself.

If at any time during the past year Murray had sincerely expressed any regret for what he had done to me, or any concern for my recovery, I might not have felt the need to have a public declaration of his guilt or innocence. His family members, I know, are nice, decent people, and if they had genuinely had concerns about his mental stability, they would have been the first to want him restricted in his movements; instead, they expressed concern only that he might be suicidal and tried to get him help for his depression. Murray's family's concern was only for him, and his *own* concern was only for him. I never received so much as a get-well card.

Somebody needed to establish the fact that what he had done was wrong, and apparently it would take a jury to do that. I talked it over

ꞰUTL

with my children, my sister, Bob, Burnett. We decided not to settle out of court, not unless the monetary settlement was high enough to pay off my debts. I've never been much of a gambler, but this was the second time I decided to go for broke. The gamble paid off the first time when Murray was jailed for not upholding the terms of his bond, but it was hard to say what would happen this time.

#

The trial began on Monday, October 5, 1998, at the West Feliciana Parish Courthouse in downtown St. Francisville, just across from Grace Church. My sister and her husband came from Texas for it, and Bob also sat through the whole thing once a deal was worked out that he would not be sequestered if Murray's son Jerry, also an attorney, was allowed to remain in the courtroom as well. Other friends came and went, and I asked them not to stay for long but just to put in an appearance for support, which I appreciated.

I was so anxious that I slept not at all for the weekend beforehand. My stomach was tied up in knots, I had a constant tension headache, and I was filled with apprehension about what I was putting myself and everyone close to me through. Friends and family began calling and e-mailing from all over the country, and Burnett's church put me back on their prayer list.

Father Dimmick was out of town for a month or so working on a writing project at a seminary in Wisconsin, and I never heard from anyone at Grace Church.

#

Jury selection took one entire day. Of the 150 prospective jurors called, there were only about three left when the grueling selection process was finalized late that evening. The defense had filed a motion to sequester the entire jury venire and permit individual questioning of each prospective juror by the two attorneys in the presence only of the judge, but this was done instead in open court.

Every prospect who had ever even seen me walking down the street, it seemed, was bumped by Mike Small, and everyone who had any connections with my business, with Angola, with my children or with anyone else in my family. One woman, asked if she had ever been in my home, said that she'd been there when I hosted Stewart's fifth-grade end-of-year class party and she had been the classroom aide; she was put off the jury. Another was in timber management and was removed because of business connections; still others had done work at the Bed & Breakfast.

I'd worked in the welfare office when I first returned to Louisiana after graduate school, and one of my old welfare clients from three decades back was a jury prospect. Asked if she could consider my testimony on an equal basis with that of anyone else, she innocently replied, "Oh, *no*! I'd believe anything Miss Anne said." Off she went, as did those who'd had contact with me as Council on Aging director. A couple of prospects didn't even know me personally but said their churches had been praying for my recovery; off they went.

Everyone who attended Grace Church with me was kicked off by the defense, even though all of them knew Murray just as well as they knew me, if not better. One woman admitted to knowing me "only *superficially*," and another said I "used to" attend Grace Church with her, not knowing I'd switched to the early service the past few years.

There were a few prospects who had worked for Murray and who said they could not be fair in considering a case involving him due to their respect for him, and these were also excused, some by the judge and some by the state. The judge also excused an elderly lady with a bad knee who couldn't repeatedly climb the stairs to the second-floor courtroom.

Anyone who had any connections with any of the law enforcement officers who'd be testifying was put off the jury—with the judge himself excusing the former longtime sheriff—plus anyone who had any relatives in law enforcement, and that covered a lot of people. In a little town like this one, nearly everybody knows the sheriff and most of his deputies, not necessarily from being in trouble with the law but through their many community involvements and outreach programs. The defense made a big issue over whether prospective jurors who knew the deputies would be able to hear their testimony and not give it extra weight just because of their law enforcement status.

One factor in the length of jury selection was that the defense, besides having three attorneys (lead defense lawyer Mike Small, a female associate from his office named Sue Ann Kelly, and local attorney Sam D'Aquilla), also had a paid professional jury consultant to assess each possible juror and advise which ones to keep and which ones to remove with the limited number of challenges each attorney has. I'd never heard of anyone besides O.J. Simpson being able to afford a professional jury consultant. Bob and Big Rose and I huddled together in the courtroom and tried to quickly assess the potential jurors as they were called forward—those we knew and those we didn't know—and advise Scott as best we could.

The judge, attempting to get things moving, granted limited breaks, and the only excitement came when one of the jurors who had been picked to serve disappeared during the lunch break. He was eventually found but removed from the jury.

Scott Gardner wanted to know if the jury prospects would be able to consider the defendant guilty if facts warranted it, knowing that even at his age he could face up to 50 years in the penitentiary. Mike Small wanted to know if they would listen to psychological test results, if they had ever had contact with senile elderly relatives or friends, if they would be interested in hearing about what a wonderful career Murray had had in the past.

#

It was well after dark by the time the jury was finally picked, twelve members and one alternate. The presiding judge, the Honorable Wilson Ramshur, carefully gave them their instructions, unfailingly polite and precise in his explanations, and asked them to be in the courthouse promptly at 8:30 a.m. Tuesday for the beginning of the trial. I was exhausted at the end of this first day, both physically and mentally. Murray, pale, with a new short haircut and neatly dressed in dark suit and tie, had sat very alertly throughout the entire day, advising his attorneys and listening carefully to all of the juror interviews.

The young lady lawyer from Mike Small's office sat by Murray and would periodically reach over and solicitously pat him on the shoulder, and he often removed his glasses and wiped his eyes with a handkerchief. The reporter for the Baton Rouge *Advocate* newspaper picked this up and wrote that Murray cried in court, but this is something he does all the time because his eyes water. When I mentioned to the sheriff that I thought I was even more exhausted than Murray was, he said he wouldn't be surprised because most jail inmates consider time in court as recreation and a welcome break from boring jail routine.

When I got home, I had a message on my telephone recorder from a Baton Rouge television reporter asking why Murray had not been handcuffed and why he had been allowed to jump into the front seat of the sheriff's car when they went to lunch. I didn't return the call since I certainly had no complaints about the careful security provided by the sheriff's department, but I did ask about it the next morning and was told that if a juror happened to look out of the courthouse window and see Murray in restraints, there might be grounds for a mistrial.

BUTL

CHAPTER 18

The weather the week of the trial was mild for fall, and the windows in the stair landing outside the courtroom were open. During breaks in the testimony, we could hear the scratch of a bamboo rake as a trustee from the jail raked up the leaves falling from the big old live oaks shading the lush lawns of the courthouse square. Some of the jurors sat in the sun in front of the courthouse door during breaks and smoked cigarettes at the base of the Confederate soldier's statue, which faced toward the South, as they all do.

It was warm enough on the first day of court for me to wear a sleeveless blouse, something I'd been advised to do so the jurors could get just a glimpse of some of my disfigurement. I might not be able to show them my worst scars, all along my stomach, but they could at least see a few of the scars on my arm and notice how little it bends, how little it straightens, how swollen it stays because of the lymphatic damage. The day I testified, though, I had on a suit and did not remove the long-sleeved coat.

Seated in the courtroom audience were two distinct groups. In one were Murray's children and their spouses, as well as his ex-wife Antoinette. In the other, just a few seats away, I sat with Bob, Rose, my sister and her husband. Neither group spoke to the other until the last day when Antoinette and Jerry exchanged cursory hello's with Bob and his wife Liz. No one in Murray's family ever spoke to me at all.

I insisted Chase go on to work, though she would come to court for the last two days of the trial, and I insisted that Stewart go to school. He pitched such a fit that I did finally relent and let him hear Scott Gardner's closing arguments on the final day of the trial, but I didn't let him stay for anything else and I specifically asked that he not be called as a witness, even though he more than almost anyone else could have testified as to Murray's condition on a day-to-day basis, since he was the only one besides me who lived in the same house with him. I refused to permit the exploitation of the emotions of my children, fragile as they were, regardless of the trial outcome, and Scott Gardner let me make that decision. Other friends came and went, and only a few townspeople were tasteless enough to let idle curiosity bring them to the courtroom.

The seats in the courtroom are those awful old wooden-backed movie theater seats, with unmoving rigid backrests and folding padded seats, terribly uncomfortable and close together. We sat and squirmed for four days while the jury sat in relative comfort in padded seats that swiveled and reclined.

During one dull stretch of testimony a juror leaned back a bit too far and then leapt forward when he thought he was about to turn over in his chair, rousing us all from the sleepy stupor that sets in after too many hours listening to the technical jargon of lawyers and psychiatrists and ballistics experts.

"That's all right, Mr. Achord, it will startle you but it won't dump you on the floor," the judge assured the juror with a kindly smile, and Mike Small, who'd been talking at the time, added, "And it woke up anyone who was sleeping."

But the judge's own overstuffed padded chair was the worst offender, squeaking with every shift of his body weight and drowning out some of the softer speakers due to its proximity to the bench microphone. My sister leaned forward and whispered in my ear, "Let's take up a collection to buy the judge some WD-40."

Every hour on the hour, testimony halted briefly as the deep-toned bell in the copper courthouse dome struck the time. Scott Gardner,

soft-spoken as he was, could not have been heard over the tolling of
the bell. But he had such courtroom presence that the jurors often sat
on the edge of their seats as he spoke, leaning forward in rapt attention to catch every word.

Mike Small, on the other hand, could easily have been heard
above the din. He exhorted the jury in loud tones, gesturing and
jumping around as he put on quite a performance. On several occasions the judge had to admonish him to stop shouting at us and to
lower his voice.

Every time Scott Gardner was speaking, Mike Small would remove
his half-glasses with a flourish, whip out his handkerchief and wipe
them vigorously, repeatedly holding them up to the ceiling lights to
make sure every speck of dust had been removed, all to distract the
attention of the jurors. I personally found his attitude toward the jury
condescending, especially when he'd put on his corn-pone *sincere*
act, just a good old country boy like them. Once, when pronouncing
the name of one of the German cities where Murray had lived just
after World War II, he even went so far as to call himself a *redneck.*
Bunch of bull.

#

The state introduced 25 exhibits into evidence. There were evidence photographs of the back porch, of four spent casings found in
a bowl on the back porch table and one found on the floor, of the
belongings emptied from the defendant's pockets, and of his Cadillac,
parked the way he had moved it after he shot me, facing outward,
presumably for a quick getaway.

Besides pictures, there was all of the bloody clothing I had been
wearing, which State Police Detective Steve Dewey had retrieved from
Lane Hospital when he came to check on my condition that night—
the blood-soaked skirt and blouse, even the blood-soaked underwear. I was sequestered and not in the courtroom when these items of
clothing were displayed, which was just as well, but even now my

grandmother's long-ago words of practical advice ring in my ears: for heaven's sake, child, always make sure you have on decent underwear just in case you get run over by a car and have to go to the emergency room, or in case there's a fire and you have to run down a fire escape.

Ironically, this part of the evidence was nearly lost. In the hospital waiting room the day of the shooting, as family and friends anxiously awaited word on my condition, my friend Lily Metz saw Stewart idly pick up a manila envelope and begin looking at the blood-soaked clothing that had been removed from me in the ambulance. Horrified, Lily quickly took the envelope away from Stewart and, without thinking, handed it to a passing hospital aide for disposal. Only later, after it was determined that this envelope contained vital evidence, was a frantic search made and it was eventually recovered intact.

Other evidence presented included the clothes Murray had worn that day, the actual spent bullets removed from my body, the cartridge casings, the pistol Murray had used to shoot me, and a handwritten note found in Murray's shirt pocket (this was not seen by any of the deputies at the scene of the shooting but appeared later among his effects).

There were also state police forms detailing the defendant's individual history and his rights as a defendant, and telephone records showing the times calls had been made from the pay phone at Butler Greenwood and to what numbers (the first call from Murray to Rose about picking up Stewart was made at 11:36 a.m.; the second call from Patrice to Rose calling for help was at 12:30 p.m., both calls of about a minute duration).

#

The judge was very clear in his preliminary instructions to the jury regarding the legalities. Revised Statute 14, Section 14, entitled *Insanity*, he instructed the jury, reads as follows: "If the circumstances indicate that because of a mental disease or mental defect the offender was incapable of distinguishing between right and wrong with reference to the conduct in question, the offender shall be exempt from criminal responsibility." The judge added that insanity as applied here was not to be regarded as a medical diagnosis but as a legal concept.

He continued with Revised Statute 14, Section 27, defining attempt as "Any person who, having a specific intent to commit a crime, does or omits an act for the purpose of, intending directly toward the accomplishing of his object, is guilty of an *attempt* to commit the offense intended and it shall be immaterial whether under the circumstances he would have actually accomplished his purpose."

Second degree murder, the judge informed the jury, is defined in Revised Statute 14, Section 30.1: "*Second Degree Murder* is the killing of a human being when the offender has specific intent to kill or to inflict great bodily harm." This case, the judge continued, "is based on a bill of information which charges *Attempted Second Degree Murder.* The defendant has entered a plea of not guilty and not guilty by reason of insanity."

With respect to the charge of attempted second degree murder, the judge explained carefully, the burden is on the *state* to convince the jury *beyond a reasonable doubt* that the offense was committed. But with respect to the defense of insanity, the burden is on the *defense* to persuade the jury *only by a preponderance of the evidence,* that "it was more likely than not that Mr. Henderson was insane, did not know right from wrong at the time that this offense was committed."

Unanimity would not be required; only ten of twelve votes were needed in order to reach a verdict, the judge explained. "As jurors," he said, "you are judges of facts. It is your duty to consider and weigh the evidence and decide all questions of fact based upon the evidence presented." The judge asked jurors not to read any newspaper articles about the case or to watch any television coverage about it, and then the two lead attorneys began their opening statements.

#

Scott Gardner got right to the point in his opening statement. "On August 24th of 1997, about a year and two months ago," he said, "the defendant Murray Henderson, who had been recently separated from his wife for about a week on what was at that point a fairly permanent separation, loaded a .38 caliber Taurus revolver, went to her house, waited until he was alone with her, and shot her at point blank range, five times, emptying the gun, critically wounding her. And as he did so he said, 'Space, you wanted space, I'll give you space.'"

He backtracked a bit at that point, summarizing the marriage, the relationship, the separations. "During the fairly tumultuous relationship from 1990 'til 1997 there were a series of separations between the defendant and the victim. Many times these separations revolved around who was in charge." But the state's attorney would then describe how the final separation was different, and how it eventually turned into "a money question" when Murray's demand for money apparently transformed a civil back-porch conversation into a nearly fatal shooting.

After describing how normal the defendant had appeared to everyone who'd seen him at Butler Greenwood that morning, Scott Gardner described the shooting and the discovery of it by members of the cleaning staff. Lab tests on the spent bullets and gunshot residue on the victim's clothing, Scott Gardner would tell the spellbound jurors, indicated that some of the shots were fired from as close as 18 inches.

"Anne, to her credit," he said, "probably saved her life because once she was shot, she remained conscious for a great portion of the time in extreme pain, thinking that she was dying, thinking that she would never see her 12-year-old son, her 21-year-old daughter again, but she had the presence of mind to make no movements, to slow her breathing, to keep her eyes closed, and for an unreal amount of time, a time which approaches an hour or perhaps two hours, she lay there bleeding."

He described the arrival of the officers, the two young deputies, not wearing bulletproof vests because of the summer heat, confronting the armed defendant who backed away "with his teeth gritted, reaching into that pocket, the gun got hung up in the pocket," and then the anger of the defendant at being handcuffed, furiously telling the deputies, "Y'all didn't have to handle *me* like that."

The judge, the state attorney continued, in preparation for the trial appointed two doctors to examine the defendant, "court-appointed experts who testify routinely on matters like this . . . They're not paid by the District Attorney's office, they're not paid by the defense attorney, they are paid to do examinations by the Court, they're paid to call it as they see it . . . Both did evaluations of the defendant and both found no signs that the defendant was incompetent to proceed, that he understood everything that was taking place, and likewise no signs that the defendant was unable to distinguish right from wrong at the time of the offense."

The defense team had hired its own psychiatrists who would present totally different conclusions, but the jurors were urged to "scrutinize all of the medical testimony as well as the observations of the persons who saw the defendant before, during and after this offense. You come to your own conclusion of whether the defendant was insane at the time of the offense. I submit to you that he was not, that he may have been suffering from depression because he was separated, because he was angry, because he was disappointed at what his station in life was at that time, but he was *not* insane." And so Scott Gardner ended his opening statement to the jury.

CHAPTER 19

Mike Small began his opening statement to the jury by laying it on thick about how proud he and his colleague were to be here representing Murray Henderson, who he promised to show was suffering from "a mental disease or mental defect, which prevented him from distinguishing right from wrong . . . an obvious mental aberration, mental disease . . ."

He continued by saying, "Now, if I haven't done it by now, let me do it, the operative physical facts are not disputed, oh, there will be some contention about what was said, by whom it was said, when it was said, but the shooting is not disputed, that's by the board. So, to the extent that those elements must be proven and Mr. Gardner must prove them, they're not because we deny them. I told you that yesterday, I reiterate it today. The Judge also read to you, however, the definition in this State of legal insanity. It bears repeating. 'If because of a mental disease or defect a person is not able to distinguish right from wrong as to his conduct at the moment, he is exempt from criminal responsibility.' And therein and therein only lies the issue in this case."

Mike Small went on, "Now, Mr. Gardner, quite appropriately, told you some of the background of the complainant, Anne Butler, something about her life, about her literary efforts, and they're commendable and admirable and impressive. You're about to hear evidence, and I don't mean *lawyer talk*, I mean evidence about a case so bizarre, evidence about a shooting and its aftermath so bizarre as to leave little doubt, I think, in your mind that Murray Henderson on that occasion was acting with an obviously and significantly diseased mind."

He then proceeded to discuss at great length Murray's family history, educational background, career in corrections, then said, "But we can't concentrate just on the good things because I can't sugar coat this in my opening statement, let's talk about what the evidence shows and let's cut to the chase and get to the shooting event because I don't want you to think I'm afraid to cover it, I'm not." The state attorney, Small said, had described already many of the events of the morning of August 24, but "I do want to highlight some things . . . which demonstrate the true character of what happened and the almost unbelievably bizarre and insane occurrences that took place at Butler Greenwood . . . and I want to discuss evidence with you that will show that the actions are consistent only with insanity and not thoughtful planning or preparation."

He then had the audacity to proceed to use my own testimony and statements made in previous depositions to the state police to pay compliments to Murray. Said Small, "This is not to trash any of these witnesses, all of these witnesses are people with whom I have no dispute, but let me talk to you about some of them. The most important witness is obviously Ms. Butler, Anne Butler . . . Ms. Butler will testify that the conversation on the morning of August the 24th was normal in tone, there was no argument, indeed he never raised his voice, and she attested to that as early as September the 5th in a statement to detectives investigating the case. . . . 'Was he ever abusive to you during your seven year marriage?' 'No, he was not.' 'Was he ever physically assaultive to you during your seven year marriage?' 'No, he was not.' 'What about verbal abuse?' 'No, he was never verbally abusive.' She never even heard him curse. We are talking about a quiet, sensitive, gentle man, that from Anne Butler."

Seemed like Mike Small was trying to turn the victim into the best defense witness. "And after in effect admitting killing Anne Butler, did he ever leave? Anne Butler knows that Murray Henderson arrived in a car, had the keys, he could have left at any time. Anne Butler knows that for two hours after the shooting he stayed there without having made an effort to leave, without having attempted to prevent anyone from reporting what happened, and he sat there and was sitting there when the police arrived." (Sitting in the courtroom audience, an aggravated Anne Butler could have added, if asked, that he also made no effort to get any medical help for her or to do anything except make sure she suffered sufficiently and bled to death under his watchful gaze.)

After what Small continued to refer to as "this absolutely outrageously bizarre occurrence on August the 24th," the defendant was hospitalized the day after his arrest, "primarily at that time," Small said, "because of fears that he would *commit suicide*..." (No mention of any familial concern about the possibility of his again attempting to commit murder of someone *else*, but by all means make sure he doesn't kill *himself.*)

The defendant would eventually be examined by two other psychiatric professionals hired by the defense, Dr. Paul Ware and Dr. Ron Gable, who would arrive at the opinion, as attorney Small condescendingly told the jury, "that Mr. Henderson suffered what in psychiatric terms, and I, I *hate those technical medical terms* but they have to be used because they have to attribute a diagnosis, but he suffered from a disassociative episode. And he'll (Dr. Ware) describe to you that it's an episode which is brought on by stress causing one to involuntarily disassociate and during the period of disassociation there is a complete inability to know right from wrong. Dr. Ware will tell you that."

Small continued, "Dr. Ware will also tell you that when he examined Mr. Henderson he saw a need for neuro-psychological testing because of what he thought were signs of dementia and real memory impairment and cognitive impairment... He'll talk to you about the reasons for the disassociation and the type things that can lead to a disassociative episode. He'll talk to you about how in the life of Murray Henderson the abandonment, not ill willed, but having been given up at age six by his own mother, how his own grandmother died when he was but nine years of age. He'll talk to you about the death of his mother and the profound effect that that death and the closing up of her affairs and home had on Murray Henderson . . . And he'll talk to you finally about how at 77 years of age the effect, in his mind and again not attributing ill motives to anyone, of in effect being abandoned again at a time at his point in life when he felt completely unable to fend and cope for himself, a disassociative episode was triggered."

That was just about the conclusion of Small's opening statement, and it would be just about the last time we would hear this abandonment defense. Murray's mother, lovely loving woman that she was, would be turning over in her grave. Murray adored his grandfather and it was his own decision to live with him, and as he described his childhood he made it sound absolutely idyllic. Nor was he overly affected by the death of his 96-year-old totally bedridden and deeply religious mother who'd been ready to go and completely at peace about dying for years, a vital active woman who'd hated being confined to her bed for so long. Certainly he was never abandoned, nor did he ever feel that way. And as for his being helpless and unable to cope or demented, I couldn't believe he would stoop so low as to allow that hogwash to be seriously presented in court.

The tedium of the testimony was relieved periodically by the wry humor of the judge. At one point, when a witness was being asked to estimate the distance of the pay phone at Butler Greenwood from the back porch, Mike Small pointed to a row of vintage photographs along a rear wall and asked, "So, the outside phone by the gift shop is approximately from the back, the wall behind you to the wall at the end of the courtroom where the pictures of former judges are?"

"Those are district attorneys, Mr. Small, don't elevate them," the judge would admonish.

"You are right, your honor, you are above district attorneys."

"We sit higher," answered the judge from his elevated bench.

"And district attorneys are above defense lawyers," Mike Small rejoined, always wanting to get in the last word.

Near the end of the trial, in the final moments of rebuttal testimony, with everyone in the courtroom exhausted, Mike Small began cross-examination of Dr. Davis by saying, "Dr. Davis, it's late and you're gonna get the benefit of the hour, my cross examination won't be as lengthy. I know they're saying 'Yeah, right.'" And as he finished his questioning, he said, "Thank you, Doctor, I was a little shorter than usual." And he tendered the witness to Scott Gardner, who quipped, "I've been short for a long time," to which the judge would reply, "I won't make any follow-up statements."

When Dr. Davis wrapped up his rebuttal testimony with a description of Murray as depressed, distrustful of the motives of others toward him, over-controlled and overly sensitive to criticism, basing his opinion on the results of the MMPI tests, the judge asked the defense attorney if he wanted to cross-examine Dr. Davis. "Mr. Small," the judge asked, "that stuff about the MMPI and sensitive to criticism, that was new stuff, do you want to cross on that?"

"Uh, no, Your Honor, I do not," answered Mike Small. "I thought you were suggesting maybe that I was sensitive to criticism."

"I don't know you well enough to make that conclusion," answered Judge Ramshur. But by the end of the trial, we could have all made a pretty good guess.

#

After jury selection and opening statements, witnesses who were to testify in the course of the trial were sequestered until after their testimony, then allowed back into the courtroom as long as the lawyers had no plans to recall them later. I spent the first morning of the actual trial in the sheriff's office waiting for the deputies to testify; I would be called right after they finished. The sheriff's executive assistant chatted with me and helped to pass the time, trying to keep me from getting too nervous.

I was very apprehensive about testifying in court with Murray sitting a few feet away from the witness chair; in the past year and a half I'd seen him only once briefly at the hearing to revoke his bond in March. I'd been told how rough Mike Small could be on witnesses and had already seen his flamboyant interrogation style to a certain extent in jury selection. Everyone kept advising me to keep my cool, not get mad or emotional, and answer as briefly as possible any questions put to me. I think now that I followed that advice a little too well, coming across as cold and unemotional in my efforts to remain under control.

When my turn to testify came, dear Glenn Daniel, my former husband, who was fortunately one of the deputies assigned to courtroom duty throughout the trial, walked me up the stairs, holding my hand and patting me on the back, reassuring me that I would do fine. Later in the trial when Chase took the witness stand, he recognized her deep fear of Murray and positioned himself as close to her as possible, a friendly reassuring presence there to protect her—and this gave her, and me, a lot of comfort.

CHAPTER 20

Scott Gardner is a neat, well-dressed young man with close-cropped blonde hair and a sincere demeanor. He looks all of about 15 years old, the quintessential freckle-faced boy next door, straight out of *Tom Sawyer*. Mike Small, on the other hand, has a sort of flashy super-sophisticated presence, with expensive suits and long flowing graying hair styled and sprayed into a real *coiffeur*. There were a few scattered showers the first day of the actual trial and to relieve the tension my sister and I tried imagining what Mike Small would look like if he got drenched by one of these sprinkles.

When Small cross-examined me, he opened by solicitously reassuring me in honeyed tones that he knew what physical discomfort I must be in and that I could ask for a recess whenever I needed. I bit my tongue to keep from responding that a near-death experience such as I had had often left one, and certainly had left *me*, with an absolute intolerance of bullshit. I could see Scott Gardner watching me carefully, and in my mind I could hear Big Rose whopping her hand with an imaginary switch. I said nothing.

Throughout the proceedings, I tried simply answering both lawyers' questions as succinctly as possible, having been cautioned against adding too many details. There were so many things I thought of after my testimony was over that I wished I'd said. I told very matter-of-factly about the shooting and described my injuries only briefly. I wished later I had gone into more detail since I didn't feel I had given the jury much appreciation of the misery I had been through or of the lasting consequences (I didn't know it then, of course, but it wouldn't be a month after the trial before I'd be back in Dr. Mazoch's office with internal problems for which more surgery would be performed in December, and when that wasn't sufficient, even more surgery the following summer, the summer of 1999).

#

Scott Gardner began his direct examination of me by asking questions about what led up to the shooting, before I was asked about the actual attack.

I told of Murray's arrival that morning, our low-keyed conversation on the back porch, his demands for money, and my first noticing the gun he pulled from his pocket.

"And how was he holding the gun," Scott Gardner asked me, "do you recall?"

"Just holding it out," I answered.

"What happened?" he asked.

"Then he shot me in the stomach and I sat up like this and I said, '*Stop*, what are you doing, you *know* I have children to take care of,' and he shot me some more and then he shot me in the arm and it flung my arm out and just shattered the elbow and that was extremely painful, the arm went out this way and then he shot me in the shoulder and dislocated all that, and the bullet went into the chest here. But once it hit the arm then my focus was on the arm, which was the most painful."

"Do you recall any statements on his part?"

"Yes, he said, 'Space, you wanted space, how's *this* for space?'"

"How much more do you remember of the minutes or hours involved?"

"I remember saying one more thing which was to say that someone would have to pick up Stewart at the airport, I was most concerned that he not get there alone. And then I just could see that he was standing over me with the gun and so I decided the best thing for me to do was to just look dead, so I tried not to move again and sat there and tried to breath very shallowly and just let my head sort of fall to the side. I was in and out of consciousness, I was not conscious the entire time but I was conscious for a great deal of it."

"When you first encountered him, did you smell any alcohol on his breath?"

"Absolutely not."

"Did you notice any slurred speech?"

"No, he was perfectly normal and in total control."

Attorney Gardner asked how much time passed between the time I was shot and the time the deputies arrived, and I answered that it was about two hours, perhaps a little more.

"During that period of time," the lawyer asked me, "did the defendant have ample opportunity to commit suicide?"

"He was standing there holding a loaded gun," I answered.

#

I was asked if I had observed any decline in Murray's mental abilities, and answered that during the course of our marriage, "he went from age 70 to age 77, and there is a normal progression there that you would expect, but there was certainly nothing out of the ordinary at all." During the seven years I served as director of the local Council on Aging, providing direct services to every single person in the parish aged sixty or above, I had certainly had the opportunity to observe first-hand the effects of aging, and in Murray's case there had been nothing unusual or extraordinary or even unexpected.

I described his active participation, usually quite successful, in trading on the stock market. "He enjoyed following the stock market, he did some investing, he didn't have enough money to invest in a real major way but he did invest and he did extremely well, he was very good at spotting the trends that were coming up and knowing when to buy and when to sell. He was very sharp with that."

"Did you ever," Scott Gardner would ask me, "notice at any point or ever have the feeling that you needed to intervene on his part to handle his personal affairs?"

"I never interfered in his personal affairs and he never needed any help with them either."

"Did you notice anything to indicate a precipitous decline in his judgment or mental abilities?"

"There was no decline in his judgment or mental abilities that I could see."

"The majority of the conflict or conflicts that you had with the defendant, what did they revolve around?"

"Control."

"Control of what and who?"

"Everything."

"Did that include control of the Bed & Breakfast . . . and in particular what types of control issues sparked conflict over the Bed & Breakfast?"

"Anything he didn't agree about."

"And once the focus of your arguments shifted away from that and once separation and divorce were contemplated, what did the arguments then move on to?"

"Money."

Scott Gardner asked one more time about symptoms. "Did you at any time, either prior to the shooting or during the two hours that you survived after the shooting, at any time during that period of time did you see the defendant experiencing what appeared to be an out of body sensation?"

"No, he just sat there."

"At any time prior to that did you see him experiencing demented behavior?" When Mike Small objected to the use of "demented," Gardner asked, "Or any symptoms that you noticed?"

And I answered, "I saw nothing out of the ordinary at all, nothing that would have alarmed me, nothing that would have made me be careful with him, nothing different."

"And if you had noticed anything which would have tipped you off that the defendant was insane, would that have been something that you would have noticed?"

"I certainly would not have invited him to come in for coffee," I answered.

#

After I finished answering Scott Gardner's questions, Mike Small cross-examined me, but only briefly. I think he must not have wanted to give me the opportunity to open up, and perhaps wisely so. He had already made me mad by his insincerity in his initial address to me. "My name is Mike Small, as you know. I have some questions, I don't think they'll be too lengthy to ask you. If at any time during my questioning of you, you feel the need for a break for any reason, if you tell me, you'll get it, okay?" Such heartfelt concern.

And later, when he got to the events of the day of the shooting, he said, "Uh, now, if I could move to the day of the 24th, and uh, Ms. Butler, I don't intend to discuss any more of this than I think is necessary, because I realize that it's not a pleasant topic and it's at this point that I don't intend to cause you any unnecessary distress but should you feel it please bring it to my attention, okay?"

"Thank you," I answered, in what I hoped was a sufficiently frigid tone of voice.

I think maybe I scared him a little with a few quick answers. Once he asked about Murray moving back in with Antoinette during our separations. "Is it your understanding that there was a room in the house which she allowed him to move into on those occasions when he separated from you?" he asked.

"I have no understanding of what went on in the house, it's not my business," I responded flatly.

And according to the exact trial transcript, he replied, "Okay. Uh, now, during the, and you indicated that at least on, on at least one day

I should say, during the week of the separation he had called to discuss the possibility of returning?"

And again later, he asked me whether I had personally heard Murray conversing with either Patrice or Rose about picking up Stewart at the airport.

"No sir, I believe that that was outside and I was in the chair bleeding to death."

"And uh, Ms. Butler, that concludes what I have to ask you concerning the events of the 24th." He definitely took a minute to hit his stride again, and he definitely didn't want to let me get started.

#

There was a whole lot I wanted the jury to know, but I never really had the opportunity to tell them. I didn't ever even show them my scars, the visible ones. I guess it wasn't necessary, since even Mike Small admitted to the jury that the shooting took place and was done by Murray.

"The facts are not in dispute," attorney Small said. "The shooting is not denied. Insanity is the only defense."

And after the state police forensic and ballistics experts testified, conclusively linking the Winchester bullets taken from my body—four intact bullets and two fragments that came from one or two additional bullets—to the gun in Murray's pocket, the Taurus .38 special five-shot revolver, serial number MH63112, there wasn't much else the defense could do.

The experts would also verify that the revolver was the type where spent casings have to be physically removed, rather than ejecting automatically. That meant that the gun, once all the shots were fired, would have to be physically opened, the cartridge cases emptied out, the gun reloaded and closed before firing again, and the bullets would have to be reloaded one by one. A lot of coordinated activity for a shooter in a disassociative state who supposedly could run into walls and not notice.

\#

After I finished testifying, I had to make the decision whether to stay in the courtroom or leave. If I wanted to be recalled to the stand later for rebuttal testimony, I would have to remain sequestered out of the courtroom, not hearing any further testimony from the other witnesses or experts. But if I left, there would be no one present who could advise Scott as to what was true and what was not.

Scott left the decision to me, and I decided to stay so that I could hear and observe the rest of the trial. At times I regretted the decision since there were a number of issues raised later that I would have welcomed an opportunity to address, but perhaps I was most helpful to the case by listening intently to all the other testimony and providing personal comment on it for the prosecutor.

I was, after all, the one who knew Murray best. I knew what was being said that was true. I knew what was being said that was a lie.

There was a lot of the latter. It was almost as if Murray were reaching out through the prison bars to drag down as many people with him as he could. Of course he never took the stand, and the jury was cautioned not to hold that against him since no defendant can be required to testify against himself. They were told not to consider that an admission of guilt. Most defendants who are innocent, I feel sure, are anxious to testify, but in Murray's case he did not take the stand at all. The jury might not be able to consider the implications of that but surely the public could.

What Murray did instead was to make carefully considered comments, regarding what the prosecutor would refer to as "highly selective" memories, to the examining psychiatrists so that they would become part of the court record in the psychiatric reports; and in that round-about way he managed to accuse me—without ever opening his mouth in court—of having spent all his money, of having thrown him out of what he considered his retirement home, of having called him a mother-fucker as we sat talking quietly on the back porch just prior to the shooting, of having asked him to hire a hit man to kill

Stewart's father, of having an affair with "a carpenter who worked at Butler Greenwood."

Vicious, venomous, and very skillfully done, the master manipulator at work. These were all meant to be considered potential triggering elements in his disassociative disorder defense—mentioned to the Sanity Commission members only after Murray's evaluation sessions with the psychiatrists hired by the defense, after defense strategy had been mapped out, no doubt. I never called him bad names in the entire course of our relationship; I had too much respect for him to do so, but the name-calling was what his defense team called the main emotional trigger that set him off into the disassociative state that purportedly robbed him of his awareness of right and wrong.

As for the other awful allegations, I could have put a number of witnesses on the stand to correct these lies, but the prosecutor didn't want to. He would insist, "Anything that helps the jury believe he had a motive to hurt you, we want to allow. We *don't* want to do anything that encourages them to believe his plea of insanity." I was *furious*. I felt that I was being victimized again by the court system, and yet again by the press when these insinuations by Murray were reported as if they were proven fact or had been testified to by him under oath. He never perjured himself; he got other witnesses to do his lying for him.

Lloyd was waiting in the courthouse to testify to the fact that I spent my own money, not Murray's, on building up the Bed & Breakfast business; Burnett was on standby to testify as to our business and family relationship; other witnesses had come forward to volunteer to address the issue of Murray's supposedly sterling past character—but the prosecutor insisted that these were incidentals not important to the verdict and could be addressed only after the trial was over.

I didn't like it, not one bit. I would be the one who'd have to continue to live in the community and try to salvage something of my reputation. Nevertheless, I told Scott Gardner he was the lawyer and he could call the shots.

As it turned out, he was right.

CHAPTER 21

The second full day of testimony was taken up mostly with psychiatric testimony. The court had appointed two unbiased and thoroughly experienced professionals to the Sanity Commission to examine Murray, and they both testified that they found him perfectly competent to stand trial and capable of knowing right from wrong at the time of the crime. Dr. John Thompson, in particular, spent a great deal of time evaluating Murray, returning for a second interview with him after giving him witness statements and evidence documents to read. Asked why he was specifically asking about certain things in the reports and collateral data, he explained that he suspected that Murray was more aware of some of the things that were going on than he'd indicated in the initial interview.

He asked Murray if he had spoken to me about "space" at the time of the shooting; Murray said he didn't remember that. He asked Murray if he told the police that he'd been "screwed and tattooed," as one officer reported being told. Murray said he didn't remember that, either. And Dr. Thompson asked him if he remembered telling Patrice to leave and not get involved, that I was already dead. He "did not recall making those statements."

"Why were you so interested in those three particular areas of the offense reports?" Scott Gardner would ask Dr. Thompson.

"Well, because they point to him having some appreciation of the wrongfulness of his actions around the time . . . and they also point to

BUTL

a non-psychotic motive for what happened. If, in fact, as he was shoot-ing Ms. Butler he said to Ms. Butler, 'You want some space, I'm gonna give you some space,' or 'Here's some space,' or right after he shot her, you know, that's an indication that the relationship or the strain of the relationship played a part in his motive for doing this, not that he was out of touch with reality or there was some other psychotic motive."

The motive indicated here, Dr. Thompson explained, seemed more anger or revenge, as opposed to delusional reasoning that would explain the shooting, perhaps, as an attempt to cement the relation-ship for all eternity. "I can never be with Anne together in a relation-ship here on earth," Dr. Thompson would paraphrase such delu-sional reasoning, "and the only way I'll be in a relationship with her is in heaven, and if I do away with her and do away with myself, then we'll be together." Dr. Thompson did not find any such motivation; in-stead, he saw anger, he saw goal-directed behavior, he saw cover-up, he saw diverting attention from the scene instead of calling for help—none of which indicated mental illness or uncontrolled behavior.

Continuing to direct anger toward the victim by telling the police after his arrest that "'I was screwed by her,' rather than 'I just did something horrible,'" the doctor continued, drew him to conclude that Murray was not just mad but also cognizant of the wrongfulness of his actions. "So all those things all came together and more or less pointed to someone who recognizes that something is going on, and there's a motive for that going on, rather than there's a psychotic process going on or he doesn't really understand what's going on or he's doing it for a delusional reason." Motive, not mental illness, concluded the psychiatrist.

In his testimony in court, Dr. Thompson also added that even when Murray was admitted to the Lady of the Lake psychiatric ward in Baton Rouge soon after the shooting, the treating psychiatrist there noted that the hospitalization was primarily focused on treating his depression, but in the progress notes specified the issue of "unre-solved anger toward his wife." Other than this brief hospitalization,

Dr. Thompson noted, Murray had never before received psychiatric treatment as best he could determine, and he would stress that in most cases of severe mental disorder, there is a history of prior problems or hospitalizations.

But Dr. Thompson was also careful to point out Murray's in-depth studies in psychiatric social work over many years and his prior position directing the state forensic hospital, both making him privy to the psychiatric profiles of a large number of patients and certainly familiar with symptoms associated with most psychiatric disorders used in criminal defense cases.

For ten years, as head of the state forensic facility where the accused were sent to have their mental status and legal competence determined prior to trial, Murray had been intimately involved with nearly every criminal case in Louisiana involving an insanity plea. He was thus certainly aware of the criteria for competence or incompetence to stand trial and be held accountable for criminal behavior, of the symptoms and differing diagnoses required to meet the incompetence ruling, of the medications and treatments, of the genuine mental illnesses and just as many malingering cop-outs.

As a frequent expert witness in court cases, and just as frequently a defendant in dozens and dozens of cases filed by suit-happy inmates against the state which he as warden or CEO represented, Murray also had a thorough knowledge of the court system and an intimate acquaintance with most of the judges and lawyers in just about every one of Louisiana's sixty-four parishes, since both Angola and Feliciana Forensic Facility held inmates from around the state. Add his direct knowledge to the defense expertise of Mike Small, and together they could come up with a pretty professional psychiatric defense for nearly anything, I would think.

Dr. Thompson was certainly aware of this, and he made that very clear to the court. I, on the other hand, had very little knowledge of courts or legalities, and had been scared nearly to death when Dr. Thompson had contacted me for an interview in preparation for the trial. Although I am sure he said he was on the Sanity Commission appointed by the court, all I heard in my mind was "psychiatrist" and I assumed he was working for Murray, especially when he said he did contract work with Feliciana Forensic, Murray's former realm. "Exactly why," I asked him hotly on the telephone in our initial conversation as he requested an interview, "would you think I should help you establish a defense for someone who tried to kill me?"

But between the time of the phone contact and our actual meeting, I had occasion to chat with another forensic psychiatrist staying at my B&B while doing some consulting work at Forensic. He happened to mention that he had gone to school with Dr. Thompson. Without going into too much detail, I conveyed my apprehension about his involvement in the case, and he assured me that Dr. Thompson was highly competent and thoroughly trained, "and part of that training involved being completely fair and objective. You don't have a thing to worry about." And indeed I did find Dr. Thompson to be all that and more in our pre-trial interview—polite, considerate and quite even-handed, but hardly one to be fooled. His powers of perception had obviously been tested by some of the best, and Murray would have to number among those.

Still, Dr. Thompson announced to the court his studied conclusion. "My report says, and this is my opinion to date, that although he was depressed, Mr. Henderson was able to distinguish right from wrong with respect to his conduct, that is the shooting of Ms. Butler on the day of the alleged offense."

#

Asked by the prosecutor to explain the basis for his opinion, Dr. Thompson summarized, "Mr. Henderson's behavior was goal-directed on the day of the alleged offense. The things that he did on that day appeared to be goal-directed by the people who saw him and the people who were around him that day. He acted reasonably up until the time he went into the Butler Greenwood Plantation and up until the time of the shooting, by everybody's report . . . He did practice shooting that morning, what he was thinking while he was practicing, I think only God only knows that, but he was practicing in the morning. He did bring the gun and extra bullets with him into the house and that showed some planning and preparation . . . He was well dressed and well groomed that morning . . .

"There was no irrational or bizarre behavior, he wasn't driving his car irrationally, he wasn't standing on the street corner talking to God or communicating with interplanetary beings or anything like that, no one witnessed any of that kind of stuff happening. His behavior does not appear to be motivated by psychotic thought and I think that's really one of the critical areas, it's important to understand that, because in order for you to say that a mental disease causes someone's behavior, you have to be able to say that there was a psychotic thought process that drove that."

Murray's insistence that he did not remember the actual shooting, Dr. Thompson explained, was no indication of psychosis. "If you look at people that kill other individuals, that don't kill for a living—they're not in Murder Incorporated," he said, "it's a very stressful thing to shoot another person . . . and a good percentage of them will report that they can't remember . . . actually shooting someone. And so the fact that he had amnesia for that is not something that points to he's got a serious mental illness and the amnesia caused his behavior, it's just that he can't recall it." Amnesia about shooting someone, particularly someone who'd been close, would in fact be a perfectly sensible sign of a logical mind at work, Dr. Thompson added.

"I didn't see anything in Mr. Henderson that would make him incapable of distinguishing right from wrong," Dr. Thompson stressed as he concluded his testimony. Nor, he added, did he see any signs of senile dementia, either in his own examinations or in the more detailed neuro-psychological testing done by the other member of the Sanity Commission, Dr. Robert Davis.

Under cross-examination by Mike Small, Dr. Thompson insisted that in his opinion, "a person can disassociate and be performing goal-directed behavior and know the wrongfulness of their action while they are disassociated." When Small asked if there were not another school of thought in the psychiatric profession holding that the disassociative process does indeed preclude the ability to distinguish right from wrong, Dr. Thompson admitted that there were some doctors who believed that, but that they were in the minority.

Depressed, suicidal, disassociated—were any of these states of mind sufficient to justify a conclusion that the defendant was not able to distinguish right from wrong, Scott Gardner asked Dr. Thompson. "No," the doctor answered, "because a person can be depressed and have suicidal ideation but not be out of touch with reality and not be psychotic. And to not be able to appreciate right from wrong with respect to your conduct, it is my opinion—and I think the opinion of many other learned scholars—that the person has to be psychotic, they have to be out of touch with reality in order to not appreciate that. People appreciate at a very young age the wrongfulness of shooting someone and killing them. And certainly Mr. Henderson *with his background* appreciates the wrongfulness of what it means to kill someone."

Of course the psychiatric professionals hired by the defense, on the other hand, testified that they found the defendant showing clear signs of mental dementia and *incapable* of distinguishing right from wrong.

One of these defense witnesses bore an unnerving resemblance to creepy Hannibal Lector in the movie *Silence of the Lambs*, and I was glad I didn't have to sit too near him. Even the jurors seemed to shrink back in their seats when he leaned forward to make a point to them.

Dr. Ron Gable, a clinical neuro-psychologist, explained his field as "using psychological techniques, tests and behavioral assessments to detect and quantify, or measure, the degree of brain impairment, brain damage or brain illness on a person's mental functions." Clinical neuro-psychology focuses mainly on the human brain, Dr. Gable explained, and the relationship between human behavior and the brain's health and functioning.

Dr. Gable testified that his colleague, Dr. Paul Ware, had asked him to use neuro-psychological techniques "to determine if Mr. Henderson's brain was working as well as it should for someone his age and educational background," using the Halsted-Raton Battery, a collection of behavioral tests with dozens of different components to measure close to a hundred different brain functions.

Basing his testing on the premise that Murray "was 77 years old and that he had *20 years* of education *at the college level and beyond*," Dr. Gable also administered the Wexler Adult Intelligence Scale IQ test, and testified that he had been shocked to find that Murray scored only an average 98, not 120 or higher as he had expected for a person of his background.

The tests administered by Dr. Gable gave two IQ scores, a verbal one of 107 and a performance one of only 83—the latter in the low average range—and Dr. Gable called the 24-point difference between the two scores significant, pointing out that not only is the over-all IQ lower than expected, "because if he was always superior compared to other people his age at an earlier point in his life, he should still be an equal amount superior in the later stages of his life, compared to other people his age; that's not the case. . . . The two IQ's are enormously different. That can implicate one half of his brain is not functioning as well as the other half. That can indicate other things as well, it can also indicate depression. Usually depression doesn't cause this big of a difference. But both of these things are very abnormal in spite of the fact that the overall score is in the average range."

Other tests were done to examine brain function, including the General Neuro-psychological Deficit Scale, and Dr. Gable said they also indicated moderate brain impairment, especially in comparing the two sides of the brain. Said Dr. Gable, "Mr. Henderson's verbal IQ was high, his performance IQ was low, if that's because of brain damage that would suggest left hemisphere relatively ok, right hemisphere

3UTL

not ok. We then look at some neuro-psychological tests, 42 of them, turns out that's the same pattern we're seeing there, left side relatively ok, right side not ok, right side of the brain . . ."

The left side of the brain in most right-handed people, Dr. Gable explained, generates speech and language, comprehension and our ability to understand what is being said to us. The right hemisphere, on the other hand, controls motor function, sensory and spatial perception, the ability to put a puzzle together or get from one point to another in a strange environment.

I had minored in Psychology in college, and retained great respect for the field and the trained professionals working in it. But as I sat in the courtroom listening to this testimony, I couldn't help thinking that it wouldn't take a rocket scientist to tell that this essentially verbal man Murray, highly skilled in conversation, well read and scholarly but a real klutz when it came to using his hands, would certainly score higher on verbal tests than those measuring manual dexterity.

Later in the trial, testimony was elicited by Scott from Murray's ex-wife Antoinette that he was not now and never in his life had been skilled with his hands. I could have told them the same thing.

But Dr. Gable would make much of his low scores on tests measuring such motor skills as fitting oddly shaped blocks into appropriate holes while blindfolded, or connecting dots in remembered sequences, and would conclude that the Halsted-Raton data with its five different measures put Murray "in the brain-damaged range, not just a little bit but way into it, much further into it than you would find on the basis of aging alone. So, the first question that I looked at the data to ask was, 'Is this a normal brain or is this a diseased brain?' These five measures consistently vote this is a diseased brain."

Asked Mike Small, "Was the question as to whether or not Mr. Henderson has a diseased brain a close issue in view of the results you analyzed?"

"No, sir."

"Ok. I would assume you've seen close cases that are difficult to call?"

"Yes, I have."

"And was this one of them?"

"This one you'd trip over in the dark."

Later, in rebuttal testimony, Dr. Robert Davis, the clinical psychologist appointed by the court to the Sanity Commission to determine Murray's fitness to stand trial, mentioned doing similar testing and finding no significant impairment whatsoever. Of the five dimensions assessed by the dementia rating scale, measuring such things as concentration, executive functions like planning and organization skills, constructional ability, conceptualization, memory—of all of these, Dr. Davis found all to be within normal ranges except for slightly decreased powers of concentration.

When compared to a normal population of the same age and not on anti-depressant medication, Murray's scores were normal; when compared to a population of demented individuals, his scores were much, much higher, said Dr. Davis, "so it's not like he's approaching a demented condition at this point in time." He added that he found the defendant to be "intellectually operating on an average to high average level in general," with no evidence of organic brain disorder which would cause him not to know right from wrong.

#

Scott Gardner's cross-examination of Dr. Gable elicited admissions that Murray's tests had sometimes been compared with norms of a younger age group in the absence of specific data on his own age level. After leading the doctor to reiterate his diagnosis of moderate to severe brain disease in both hemispheres of the brain, Gardner asked, "And both of those hemispheres would then affect motor skills of a different side, is that correct?"

"Yes," Dr. Gable answered.

"And those you would expect to have an effect on the ability to drive?" attorney Gardner asked.

"Not necessarily, no," Dr. Gable hedged.

"They would have an effect on one's ability to have fine motor coordination?"

"It could, but not necessarily."

"If you had severe brain damage to the extent that it affected motor skills, it wouldn't affect one's ability to fire a weapon accurately?"

"No, no sir."

"It would not affect one's ability to unload a revolver and reload it with five shots?"

"If you're gonna talk about a severe damage to the motor strip, I would say yes, but you can have detectable damage or a deterioration of motor areas but not have it be so severe that you can't do simple motor functions or even complex activities like drive a car, which are highly over-learned."

"So, the concept of severe brain damage as you have applied it in speaking to this jury doesn't encompass performing those types of fine motor skills, is that a fair statement?"

"Well, I think, I think both ways of saying it are correct . . . When we ask you to perform fine motor skills on a Halsted-Raton battery, we are looking for evidence that your brain is or is not functioning correctly . . . This is so sensitive we can find that evidence way before a casual observer would notice it in their friend or relative."

"So," Scott Gardner asked, "you can through this very sensitive test detect brain disease or defect which does not affect such tasks as loading and unloading a gun, driving a vehicle, making phone calls from a cellular phone and things of that sort, is that what you're trying to distinguish?"

"Well, I don't know that I can say it doesn't affect it, I might say it doesn't affect it to the degree that it would be noticeable. But it could. It doesn't have to."

Gardner bore in: "The questions you asked also were more in terms of testing rather than gauging a person's knowledge of right or wrong, is that correct?"

"That's correct. I was not asking any questions about right or wrong."

"That is, you did not ask Mr. Henderson whether he knew it was right or wrong to shoot his wife?"

"I did not ask."

"And so, based upon your testing, you are not here rendering any opinion as to whether or not the defendant was sane at the time of the offense?"

"No, sir."

CHAPTER 22

In a surprise move, the defense psychiatrist, Dr. Paul Ware of Shreveport, introduced into evidence an MRI of Murray's brain showing what he described as extensive cortical atrophy and chronic ischemia, a lack of oxygen indicating vascular dementia caused by gradual hardening of some small arteries. Done in Shreveport at LSU Medical Center on August 6, 1998, a year after the shooting, the MRI was called by Ware "the most sensitive x-ray picture of the brain to reveal the structure of the brain and how the structure of the brain is."

It had never been shown prior to trial to the prosecutor, nor had it even been mentioned, and I'm not entirely sure this is standard courtroom procedure. What little I know of the rules of evidence, admittedly limited, is that the lawyers for each opposing side must be granted the right to prior knowledge and examination of the other side's evidence as they plan their courtroom strategy.

Why was this MRI allowed to be admitted, with feeble excuses for its late introduction? Was the judge favoring the defense? I watched him sitting there on his raised platform in his black robes. A tall, distinguished looking man, Judge Ramshur treated the jurors, the attorneys, the officers of the court and the witnesses with the same dignified and respectful manner. He had a reputation for being highly intelligent, and I had never heard anyone question his integrity or fairness. But one of his best friends was the mayor of St. Francisville, and the mayor was one of Murray's best friends. And he *had* let Murray out of jail within twenty-four hours of his crime. I hoped his judicial integrity was stronger than personal friendships.

The psychiatrist for the defense said he had asked for the MRI when he felt "there was clear evidence that Mr. Henderson did show features of a dementia, impaired brain functioning . . . some impairment of memory and judgment as well as developing a progressive clinical depression . . . significant difficulty with his present memory, which is the first and most sensitive impairment that one experiences with a dementia."

But the main thrust of Dr. Ware's testimony for the defense centered around Murray suffering from what he called a "disassociative disorder" at the time of the shooting. Between that disorder and brain abnormalities indicating dementia as shown in the MRI, Dr. Ware said, he reached the conclusion that "because of the mental disease and defect Mr. Henderson was suffering, he was not aware of the wrongness of his action at the time that he shot Ms.Butler . . . In my opinion he was clearly demonstrating a disassociative disorder at the time, or disassociative state, at the time that he fired the gun and that was the reason that he had no memory of the event and he remembered after the fact and first was aware of what had happened when his awareness of his surroundings returned and he saw some shells had been shot and he also saw his wife bleeding and sitting there, he thought, 'My God, I must have done that.'"

Disassociation, Dr. Ware explained, is an "interference" between a person's thinking and their memory and their feeling state and behavior, all working together. "Normally we feel, think and we do," he said, but in a disassociative disorder, "when a person is under certain types of mental conditions, that combined function of thinking, feeling and behavior no longer works that way, and one or more may be impaired. So, if there is an impairment of memory and the person disassociates, they do not remember and are not aware of their behavior from the time they disassociate until their memory returns." A disassociated person, said Dr. Ware, is like a sleepwalker or someone in a trance; they'll walk right out in front of a car. Said Dr.

Ware, "They are not then aware of and responsible for their behavior at that point in time."

The deterioration of Murray's brain which Dr. Ware indicated he found on the MRI might partially explain his disassociative disorder, the doctor said. "Any type of brain impairment that interferes with your options, your ability to think and deal with options and make decisions and adjust quickly and accordingly, the more that's impaired, the less options you have, and the more likely you are to have more primitive and regressive phenomenon to deal with the stress, and a disassociative disorder is such a mechanism . . . Stress nearly always produces a disassociative disorder, at the basic and regressive level."

The MRI results, Dr. Ware explained under Mike Small's guidance, indicative of brain disease, made the indication of disassociative disorder even more likely. With the neuro-psychological testing showing decreased function and declining ability to adjust to new situations, the patient would have fewer options for handling stressful situations and would be more likely to feel overwhelmed. "This is a man that earlier in his life," the doctor explained, " . . . was in many situations that were very stressful, where his life might have been in danger, but he could sit and talk and be calm and figure out how to handle those situations. But that's when his brain was working normal."

"And is his ability to clear up and to cope diminished significantly by virtue of the brain disease," the doctor was asked.

"Very definitely . . . In fact I was shocked because this man is, in my opinion, he's bright enough and he can cover enough that I suspected that he would have had a mild dementia. From my evaluation I would have said, 'Yes, he has a dementia, it's mild.' And from the actual function of the brain on the neuro-psychological testing, he has almost a severe dementia, it's three points away from a severe dementia, so it's much more severe than I thought it was."

#

While Scott Gardner snorted under his breath about "hokey, made-up psychiatric disorders" and tried unsuccessfully to introduce dozens of other legal cases where the *same* diagnosis was used by the *same* psychiatrist working with the *same* defense attorney to try to free all sorts of murderers and rapists and other criminals, Dr. Ware insisted that a person with disassociative disorder was so removed from his body that he could run into a wall. This removal, this protective mechanism, would have rendered Murray incapable of distinguishing right from wrong at the time of the shooting, according to Dr. Ware.

"In my opinion," Dr. Ware concluded, "he clearly was not aware of the wrongness of his actions and that's within strong medical probability."

In later testimony Dr. Robert Davis, Sanity Commission clinical psychologist, rendered a different and more restrictive interpretation of disassociation, which he said is most often associated with a traumatic event, often manifesting itself in children who block out horrible sexual or physical abuse as a protective mechanism, or in soldiers reacting to wartime trauma and overexposure to violence and death.

"Disassociation is categorized in the new Diagnostic and Statistical Manual," explained Dr. Davis, "as a disorder in which there are several types, disassociative amnesia is one type, or disassociative identity disorder, you may have heard of it, is a multiple personality disorder, it is an extremely rare disorder, rare occurrence. Disassociation as it's been used in the course of this trial, at least what I've heard . . . it's been used more as a defense, and by defense I don't mean in the criminal sense, I mean in the psychological sense. Defenses are those internal processes that we have that operate unconsciously to distort the world around us to protect us from threat."

Dr. Davis continued, "And so an individual, a young child . . . may be horribly sexually abused by someone and have no memory that that event ever occurred. In that case, the disassociation of the memory

BUTL

and the emotions is just moved away out of the way so that he does not have access to that horrible information, and in doing so the mind is protecting that human being from something horrible . . . So disassociation in many ways is a process that is used by the mind when we experience something that is horrible and traumatic and terrifying to us, and by operating, it takes the memory away from us and the emotions away from us so that we're no longer anxious and scared and horrified."

Asked Scott Gardner, "Disassociation in that context is often brought on by a significant trauma, is that correct?"

"Uh, my reading of the literature is the disassociation is *always* brought on by significant trauma. Significant child abuse, sexual abuse, physical abuse, rapes, war, the horrors and atrocities of war, things of that nature."

"Any reported cases where a documented disassociation has been onset by somebody being called a bad name?"

"I'm not aware of any literature to that effect," answered Dr. Davis.

Actually, it came to me about this point in the trial that *I* was the one who should be suffering from disassociation, if *anybody* was. If anybody should have erased the memory of the shooting, it was me. Yet I remembered every moment, every detail, and I remembered it all vividly.

#

Dr. Ware, who proudly admitted in testimony that he had worked with Mike Small many times before in similar defense cases, got so enthusiastic about his testimony that the attorney had to rein him in at one point.

Talking about what happened immediately prior to the shooting, he said that both accounts (mine and Murray's) indicated that Murray "at no time demonstrated any anger toward her, any aggression toward her, before her suddenly realizing, this guy is shooting me, it's like they were carrying on a conversation, not raised voices, whether or not it may be that because of his own mental state she may not have said, she may not have actually said to him, 'You no good mother fucker . . .'"

Mike Small quickly interrupted, "And, Dr. Ware, I want to say this, are you repeating that because that was part of the history, we do have ladies . . ."

"Part of the history, excuse me, I'm sorry, that's part of the history that he gave me, and so I'm just giving the details."

"And in the future we might just say 'MF.'"

"I will, yes, I'm sorry."

And later, as Scott Gardner cross-examined the psychiatrist, he would bring up the MF word again to elicit some very telling admissions by the doctor.

"Now, the disassociative episode begins with the statement, according to the defendant, MF, and that's obviously a pretty charged term, would you agree?" asked Scott Gardner.

"Yes," Dr. Ware would respond.

"Particularly between two people who for seven years had treated each other civilly and genteelly despite having differences about the control of this Bed & Breakfast?"

"Yes."

"And so that word is the onset of the disassociation?"

"If he, if the word was actually said, from his perception it was, yes."

"When he is out target practicing at Bayou Sara earlier, with the gun which he used to shoot her, he's not in a disassociative episode?"

"No."

"He knows right from wrong then?"

"Yes."

"When he reloads that gun after he shot it, because we know it was fully loaded when he walks into the house, he is not in a disassociative episode?"

"No, it's my understanding that the ruling is 'the person is not aware of the wrongness of his action *at the time*,' not two minutes before or five minutes after, but at the time."

BUTL

"Exactly, what I'm establishing is you're not saying that he didn't know it was wrong to shoot his wife when he reloads that gun after discharging it at Bayou Sara?"

"When he became aware of his wife being shot he knew . . ." The judge interrupted at this point: "Doctor, Doctor, answer the question. The question is did he know it was wrong to shoot Ms. Butler at the time that he reloaded the gun down at Bayou Sara?"

"Yes, at the time he became aware of her being shot." Still no answer to the question.

#

Dr. Ware insisted that only after the shooting, after Murray noticed spent cartridges in a bowl on the table and blood all over me, did he come to any awareness that there had been a shooting.

"The end of the disassociation begins with the recovery of the memories later on?" Scott Gardner asked.

"That's correct."

"And so, when he recalls looking down and seeing that she has been shot, seeing the spent casings that he has apparently removed from the revolver, since we know it's a revolver, that's the point at which this disassociation begins to end, is that correct?"

"That's correct."

"And at that point he realizes what he has done?"

"Yes."

"And at that point returns to his prior non-lethal, or non-homicidal, persona, is that correct?"

"Yes."

"And summons assistance?"

"That's correct."

Only of course he did *not* summon assistance.

CHAPTER 23

The psychiatrist appointed by the court, Dr. John Thompson, had earlier in his testimony ruled out any disassociative disorder as an excuse for the shooting. Murray had very carefully described to this psychiatrist a feeling of being out of his body watching himself, no doubt in anticipation of the defense case (he was examined by the psychiatric professionals of the Sanity Commission months after the shooting, when his defense strategy would have been at least in the planning stages, if not already completely finalized), but Dr. Thompson felt that the absence of delusions ruled out the disassociative diagnosis. He said it looked more like revenge to him, powered by a non-psychological motive, probably anger.

And Scott Gardner would point out rather forcefully to the jury that the supposed disassociation—which Dr. Paul Ware insisted would allow the defendant to run into walls without noticing—didn't render him incapable of reloading the revolver, moving his car, making telephone calls, carrying on conversations.

Gardner would carefully direct Dr. Ware's cross-examination testimony, almost toying with the psychiatrist like a cat playing with a mouse.

"It is my understanding," Gardner would say to Dr. Ware, "that you have a fundamental belief that the disassociative disorder relieves one from criminal culpability?"

BUTL

"Well, it may or may not, depending on what behaviors, but yes, if it is a complete disassociative state it does. It makes that involuntary behavior on the person's part without the ability to willfully control that."

"You're in no way intimating to the jury that the dementia, which you have noticed to be moderate to severe, precluded the defendant the day before this act from knowing that killing was wrong?"

"No."

"And you're in no way intimating to this jury that afterwards, the day after, that the defendant, because of dementia, did not know that killing was wrong?"

"No."

"As a matter of fact, you would not tell them today that the defendant because of dementia does not know that killing was wrong?"

"No, I said dementia, I think was probably the main factor that caused the disassociative disorder or disassociative state, but not the dementia by itself would not make him not aware of wrongness of killing someone."

"So, the disassociation was an out of character experience for the defendant?"

"An out of character and out of awareness experience."

"And you believe that the onset of this period of disassociation took place after the defendant believes that he heard his wife at the time say the word 'MF'?"

"Or after he was engaged in some type of disagreement or argument with his wife, yes."

"And one of the foundations of that belief is because there was no expression of anger or rage leading up to his shooting her five times?"

"That's correct."

"And you indicated to the jury that your belief was that him saying that he was going to give her all the space that she needed was an innocuous statement, or an incongruent statement with his actions of shooting?"

"That's correct."

"It's your belief that this man who eight days before separated from his wife, the last statement between them was 'I need some more space,' he loads a gun, goes to her house, says 'Space, I'll give you space,' and shoots her five times, that's not an expression of hostility towards her?"

"No, that was an expression before when he said 'I'll give you all the space you need' and he moved out. And I was very aware of that statement, he told me."

"Then your statement that this was a disassociative disorder does not rely on him saying 'Space, I'll give you space,' and shooting her five times?"

"No."

#

Scott Gardner's cross examination of Dr. Ware would focus also upon Murray's voluntary commitment to the psychiatric ward of Our Lady of the Lake Medical Center in Baton Rouge, where Dr. Frank Silva's discharge notes stated that the patient "tolerated all pharmacal therapy well, his affect improved, he also has some unresolved anger toward his wife."

Gardner asked Dr. Ware, "During the period of time he was free to walk away from that hospitalization at any time, is that correct?"

"That's correct," Dr. Ware admitted.

"He was not committed there because he was a danger to himself or others?"

"That's correct."

"During the period of time that he was there, he was treated for depression, is that correct?"

"That's correct."

"He was not treated for dementia?"

"It was not picked up."

"He was not treated for disassociative disorder?"

BUTL

"No, he was treated for a clinical depression, and his clinical depression did respond to appropriate treatment."

"The defendant had had no previous psychiatric history, is that correct?"

"That's correct."

"And the defendant had had no previous psychiatric treatment, is that right?"

"That is correct."

"And so what you're conveying to the jury is that the defendant was angry with his wife, you acknowledge that?"

"Was angry with his wife?"

"Yes."

"Before the fact?"

"Yes."

"No, I see no evidence to show that he was angry with his wife before the event."

#

Toward the end of the trial, for ultimate impact on the jury when it retired for deliberations, Mike Small put on his most emotional witnesses, Jerry and Antoinette. Murray's ex-wife described what a close family they had been, what a wonderful marriage they had had, and went into great detail about her international background, the number of languages she spoke, and other bits of information whose relevance seemed rather tenuous.

In a quavering voice, she described forty years of marital bliss. No mention of the excessive drinking, no mention of the womanizing, no mention of the sexual harassment suits, no mention of leaving all the high-powered jobs under a cloud of suspicion. It must have been very difficult for her to testify, and I felt sorry for her on the stand.

Poor Scott Gardner said he'd just as soon cross-examine Mother Theresa. He asked her very little, simply eliciting testimony that she had not noticed any bizarre behavior on Murray's part, any untidiness or physical change, any forgetfulness, any senility.

When Jerry was asked to describe his parents' marriage, he answered, "Well, they uh, they were close, they did things together, uh they were very active socially, they had, they loved to entertain, have people at the house, cooked together, uh they had a good relationship. It wasn't, you know, *Leave It To Beaver* or anything, but, I mean, there were problems, but overall they had a good relationship."

Jerry cried on the witness stand as he said he couldn't believe what his father had done. "I couldn't believe he shot Anne. I still can't believe it. *I thought he was going to kill himself.*" He said he'd watched his father exhibit marked eating and sleeping disorders for months prior to the shooting, nodding off in the midst of conversations and showing other signs of deep depression.

I know Jerry was sincere in his testimony. I know how much he loves his father—enough to do anything for him. "We're going to take care of him," he said. "That's what we're going to do." And he wept on the stand as he described how he had put his father in "the psychiatric lockdown" facility at Our Lady of the Lake Regional Medical Center in Baton Rouge because he thought he was going to commit suicide. (Actually it was a voluntary commitment, Murray had his own car there and was free to leave whenever he liked.)

This was the only point in the trial when there was an outburst in the courtroom audience, and it would come from Chase, who'd heard enough. Here a big deal was being made over the distress of Murray's "children," both pushing 50, while the two *real* children in the case, *mine*, were discounted. Two small dependent children were supposed to cope with their mother being shot nearly to death while all the sympathy of the jury was being directed to two self-sufficient married adults whose main concern was that their father—the one who had after all committed the criminal act—might go on to harm *himself*. Chase clapped her hand over her mouth and burst out of the courtroom in silent anguish. I had begged her not to come at all, and it

229

broke my heart to see her suffering. My sister followed her out, and both soon returned to take their seats in silence.

Mike Small would continue to make a big issue of how devastated Murray's children were, how distraught—even after the verdict was announced. He would announce to the media that Murray, who was allowed by the sheriff to visit with his son and daughter in a small private room at the conclusion of the trial, "was doing amazingly well. He is comforting his children, who were devastated."

One evening before the end of the trial, about the second day, after St. Francisville Inn waitress Donna Price had given her testimony about Murray coming in the Sunday morning he shot me and ordering a bottle of red vermouth and a glass of cognac and soda, Donna was absolutely horrified when Jerry appeared before her at the bar and ordered the exact same drink. The owner of the inn said Donna was white as a ghost as she related what had happened, not knowing if it was done to scare her or as a sick joke. I told her I was sure that Jerry had not meant her any harm and was probably just trying desperately to understand what his father had been experiencing that day in an effort to make some sense of an essentially senseless morning.

#

The last testimony in the trial came from the prosecution's two rebuttal witnesses, Chase and Dr. Robert Davis of the Sanity Commission. Chase testified only briefly about Murray's lack of noticeable symptoms during the summer she spent at home just prior to the shooting and of his attempts to always control everything.

Dr. Davis addressed the issue of the MRI of Murray's brain, which the defense found to show such shocking organic damage. Asked by Mike Small if he would agree with Dr. Ware about the MRI results, Dr. Davis replied, "Mr. Small, Mr. Henderson is a 77-year-old man, he's had 30 years of hypertension, he's not gonna have a clean MRI, period. He's gonna show atrophy, he's gonna show some small vessel disease, and it is up to the neurologist and the neurosurgeon to determine in a subjective way whether that is more than we expect for his age . . . My responsibility as a psychologist is to figure out, aside from that, if the individual's function is impaired . . . And their brain can be not correct and their functioning can be intact. My testing finds his function to be intact."

And more than any other witness, Dr. Davis spoke for everyone present when he began to sum up his testimony by saying, with heart-felt emotion, "I certainly understand the terrible position that everyone in this courtroom is in. This is a very tragic circumstance, and there's no one more than I who wanted to provide an explanation, psychological explanation for why this thing happened."

Continued Dr. Davis, "I'm telling you that I was unable to find a cognitive reason, a neuro-psychological reason, if you will, a dementia. I was unable to find an intellectual reason. I was unable to find a psychiatric or a psychological reason that explained everything that occurred and the manner in which it occurred."

BUTL

CHAPTER 24

Before the jury retired for its deliberations at 10:40 a.m. on Thursday, October 8, 1998, each side had an hour for closing arguments before the judge instructed the jury about the possible verdicts in the case, carefully explaining the definitions and ramifications of each: Guilty, which would mean Guilty Of Attempted Second-degree Murder; Guilty Of Attempted Manslaughter or Guilty Of Aggravated Battery, lesser charges carrying lesser punishments; Not Guilty; or Not Guilty By Reason Of Insanity.

Mike Small waxed poetic in his closing arguments: "The rule on burden of proof, like my burden of proof, has been called by a writer long ago as the precious child of our system of justice. I'm asking you not to drop that precious child. You breathe life into it; you give meaning to it. And when you evaluate this evidence and you evaluate it fairly, really think about have I shown by a mere preponderance of the evidence (whether) Mr. Henderson could distinguish right from wrong. Ladies and gentlemen, if you do, if you do, I think you will have to conclude that that kind and gentle 78-year-old man did not plan a murder. His mind left him, but he did not plan a murder. I don't want your sympathy, I don't want favors. I want you to follow the law. I want nothing more than that, nothing less, and nothing else, and if I get that, Mr. Henderson will be found not guilty by reason of insanity."

Scott Gardner, on the other hand, told the jury, in his calm but moving closing, "Insanity is a decision for the jury, and each of you have your own feelings about what constitutes insanity, each of you have your own feelings about what constitutes somebody who was so impaired that they literally don't understand that fundamental concept 'Thou shalt not kill.'"

Dr. Thompson, attorney Gardner reminded jurors, had found nothing to show that the defendant did not understand that killing was wrong, emphasizing the psychiatrist's explanation that "people who don't know that killing is wrong suffer from a psychosis or a psychotic state in which they believe that killing is not wrong. Not that they can't remember, not that they choose not to remember, not that they choose not to talk about it, but that it's not wrong, that it's okay, that there's a reason to do this, that in killing this person or shooting this person I will do something good, or at least I will do no evil, that I'm so mentally ill that that is the reason that I do it."

Concluded Gardner, "Selective recall from the defendant . . . 'I don't remember shooting my wife, I don't remember shooting my wife . . . I don't remember it, therefore I'm not responsible for it.' Walking into a wall. This is a situation where Anne Butler didn't want to be here. I guarantee you she'd give anything not to be here. And each of y'all did not want to be here but you didn't have a choice about it. She didn't have a choice about it. She's here because of what the defendant did. You are here because of what the defendant did. You're here to speak the truth, and the truth is that the defendant is guilty of the offense, and he was not insane at the time of the offense."

#

Over the course of the past year, as I struggled to recover from my physical injuries, a number of well-meaning friends have raised with me the issue of Christian forgiveness as a prerequisite for mental and spiritual healing. You *must* forgive Murray, they insisted. You can never put the issue behind you until in your heart you have completely forgiven him, they said. One B&B guest even told me the story of her mother, brutally murdered in her home by an intruder just recently executed at Angola after years of last-minute stays, a man this guest told me she had totally and completely forgiven for his actions. I could tell she was absolutely sincere, that she truly meant what she said.

I thought about it. I examined my conscience, and I searched my feelings. Did I forgive Murray? Well, not *exactly*. After a number of months, I did finally add him to my nightly prayers, but in a kind of resentful, less than whole-hearted way. "Give to Murray," I would pray, "dear Lord, an awareness of the hurt he has caused, an appreciation of the harm he has done, and make him feel sorrow." *I* wasn't sorry; I wanted *him* to be. And the Lord in his infinite wisdom, I have no doubt, ignored my prayer.

It would not be until the middle of the trial, actually, when I suddenly realized that forgiveness had come, unbidden, into my heart. I did not care about his punishment, I did not want him to suffer. I felt great and overwhelming pity for him, seeing him up there at the table with his lawyers. I knew perfectly well he wasn't crazy or demented or senile; I could watch him sitting there calling the shots in his defense. He avoided looking at me at all, but I sat where I could watch him throughout the entire trial, and I no longer felt any anger, any bitterness. I guess it was at that point that the forgiveness became complete.

Chase and I walked over to Grace Church for a few quiet moments when the jury retired to attempt to reach its decision. We walked beside the family plot which runs parallel to the church along its right side, passing the graves of my parents, my grandparents, and on back through the generations, clustered around the big stone Mathews cross. We sat in the lovely empty church, light streaming through the stained glass windows and the acoustics so magnificent that even the very silence reverberates.

We walked back across the street to the courthouse, and then I left alone and did not return. I didn't hold out much hope for a guilty verdict. But I did not care what the jury's decision would be. It no longer mattered to me. What mattered was that the ordeal of the trial was over.

I handed the newspaper reporter a statement I had written that morning about 5 a.m. as I wandered sleepless through the dark house. It said, "I'm leaving before the jury finishes its deliberations because I will take no satisfaction from the verdict, whatever it is. If the defendant is found guilty I still feel nothing but sorrow for him, but at least the message is sent that everyone, no matter how influential, must be held accountable for their misdeeds. If he is found not guilty, it will be obvious that a defendant with the funds and connections to manipulate the system can sometimes escape responsibility. Unlike the defendant, the state could not afford three attorneys, three psychiatric professionals and a professional jury consultant. There were a number of unfounded lies disseminated by the defense in their efforts to win a not-guilty verdict, and these have hurt innocent, uninvolved people, showing yet again how often the victim is victimized not only by the perpetrator but by the legal process as well.

"In either case, my poor children and I will put our lives back together and move on after this horrible ordeal we have been through. I appreciate the thoughtfulness of the jurors and their attentiveness to testimony throughout this case, and I deeply appreciate the efforts of Scott Gardner, the prosecutor for the state in this case. I am grateful to the law enforcement officers and medical professionals who helped me to live through all this, and I am especially appreciative of the love and support of my family and friends who have done so much to help me as I struggled through months of hospitalization, six major surgeries and a full year of almost daily physical therapy."

"Anne Butler and Burnett Carraway in front of the duck
pond at Butler Greenwood"

235

I drove home and sat in the warm sunshine by the pond, watching Burnett paint the outside walls of the Cook's Cottage. I told him a little about the day in court. He was unhappy with the newspaper coverage and felt I might have been wiser to have settled out of court and not put everybody through the horrors of a trial. I felt bad enough, and that made me feel worse. When the phone rang, I was almost reluctant to pick it up.

Scott Gardner was on the phone. The jury had been out for not much more than two hours, part of that for lunch. By 1:19 P.M. they had returned a verdict with the requisite majority of ten votes in the case of State Of Louisiana Versus Charles Murray Henderson, Number W-97-10-532, Division B, 20th Judicial District Court, Parish of West Feliciana. The verdict? Guilty as charged. Attempted Second-Degree Murder. The two dissenting votes, apparently, had been not for finding him not guilty or insane, but for charging him with a lesser crime like manslaughter so the mandatory minimum sentence wouldn't be so long.

As I had predicted, I took no satisfaction from that. But I felt great relief that it was over, finally at long last over. Chase, Bob, Mary Minor and Mike had been in the courtroom for the verdict and said there was no visible reaction from Murray at all. At home, I cried. I cried for me, and I cried for him.

#

And then I had to set about correcting some of the lies he had been telling. I called Stewart's father as soon as I could get to the phone. No, I told him, I had not tried to have Murray hire a hit man to kill him. He laughed. He said, "I'd never believe anything that old buzzard said." Actually, the newspaper report had said that Murray told the psychiatrist I wanted him to hire a hit man "to kill my fourth husband," and since Murray was my fourth husband, I doubt I'd have asked him to hire someone to kill himself. Hit men and other violent responses were more in his realm of experience than mine, anyway.

It was harder to try to address what Murray had attempted to do to Burnett, so the Sunday after the trial I went to his wonderful little Baptist church in Mississippi. Just before the sermon, Burnett called me up to the lectern and asked me to say a few words; he stood there beside me for support, and I found that what I had thought would be difficult really wasn't all that hard at all.

First I thanked this warm and giving group for their prayers, visits, cards and most especially the healing service they held for me, and then I explained that in the trial I had just gone through, there were no winners, not in a sad situation like that. I explained that I had to try to counteract some of the meanness, and I reminded them how Burnett and Ruby had been not just friends but really *family* to me and my children for nearly twenty years.

I told them how Burnett had said he had cried his eyes out on the way to the hospital the day I was shot, not just because of what had happened to me, but because he feared he had failed me by not having talked to me more about religion, about my relationship with God.

But he didn't have to *talk* to me, I told his congregation. He didn't have to tell me a thing, because for twenty years he had *shown* me, with his character and with his conduct, what a good Christian life is, what true Christian love means.

I told them that as I sat in that chair on my back porch, bleeding to death, I had not a moment of fear, not a moment of regret. Had I been quite as awful as Murray tried to imply, I said, I had no doubt that I would have at least been a little uneasy being that close to meeting my maker—but instead I felt totally at peace.

It was probably then, I explained, that I began being carried by the angels I later told Burnett about, and I felt today that there were at least a few of those angels right there in that church.

There was hardly a dry eye in New Salem Baptist Church that day. Even Burnett was crying. I might not have been able to address Murray's lies in the courtroom, but maybe I could do so where it counted even more. The congregation would be amazed a few weeks later, when Burnett reported to them that I planned to attend the sentencing hearing and ask the judge for leniency for Murray.

CHAPTER 25

After the trial had ended, we awaited the pre-sentencing hearing and then the sentencing, all delayed by the defense. Mike Small told the press that it was unlikely Murray would be incarcerated at Angola where he had once been the warden. "Most likely," Small told the Baton Rouge *Advocate*, "he would be sent to a facility that has a special unit for former law enforcement authorities—although he was so kindly, he could probably be sent to Angola without any trouble."

There would be immediate appeals, first to the trial judge (all denied) and then above his head to higher courts, and word on the street was that Antoinette was running around collecting jurors' phone numbers. We, on the other hand, felt that any contact with the members of the jury was improper and made none, though I really did want to thank them.

Meanwhile, Father Dimmick returned to town and came to visit. One comment he made stood out in my mind. He was talking about some of his early visits with Murray before the bishop suggested that he choose one or the other of us and stop trying to visit both. He said, offhandedly, that Murray had cried and had told him that he still loved me. This was the first time he had told me this. Father Dimmick said he couldn't tell whether Murray was lying or telling the truth.

I suppose it would make it easier to accept if he were really being truthful and not simply trying to make his case look good to Father Dimmick. It is a horrible thing for someone to hate you enough to try

239

to kill you. But then if *that* were the case, it might be easier for me to simply get angry enough to move on.

After the trial, I asked Bob to try to push the divorce through. It had already been filed, then left hanging because Murray would not agree that there was no community property to divide. Now Bob tried again, and Sam D'Aquilla went to Murray about the matter. Sam said Murray began compiling a list of things he thought I owed him, then decided it might be best if he presented it to me in person, asking that I come to the jail to see him. The sheriff agreed to a visit only if it took place in the regular visiting room, with a separating steel wall and just a small viewing window with a speaker grate below it so that we would not actually be in contact; he also promised me that a deputy would be present to further ensure my safety.

I thought about it and decided I could do this. Maybe it would be the final move toward closure in the case. If he were still trying to take away part of my business or home after all he had put me and my family through, it might remove from my mind any lingering doubts about his motive all along. It might, in fact, just make me mad enough to go ahead and file the civil suit everyone in my family had been encouraging me to initiate to recoup some of my losses caused by Murray's actions.

I had actually been asking if I could go to visit him one time anyway. I wanted to see just what he might have to say to me—not to the lawyers, not to the court, not to the jury, not to the police, not to the psychiatrists, not to his ex-wife or children, but to *me*. Maybe he would have nothing to say. If not, I wanted to know that.

And so on Friday the 13th of November 1998, I drove down to the jail and was escorted into the visiting room. Murray was already waiting on the other side of the tiny glass, dressed in a flannel shirt, with radio earphones around his neck. He looked thin and pale, and had a terrible periodic tremor. I asked him why he was shaking, if he were cold, and he said it was the medication he was on to keep him "flat," so that he wouldn't cry all the time as he said he had when he'd first been jailed. He hadn't had the tremor in court during the trial and he didn't have it later when I saw him in court at the sentencing hearing. Maybe he was putting it on for my benefit.

When I said that Sam had mentioned that he wanted to see me, he countered that he understood *I* had wanted to see *him*. I said I'd heard he had a list of things he wanted to present to me, and he said it contained "all the things I bought, you know, community property." I didn't want to get mad, and I was determined not to show emotion in front of him. I replied that I too could present quite a long list of expenses I'd incurred in the past year because of him if I wanted to.

But I wasn't there for that, I told him. "I came," I said, "to see if you had anything to say to *me*. Do you? Do you have anything to say to me?" He lowered his head so that his forehead was almost touching the glass. Then he looked at me and said, in a low voice, "I wanted to tell you how very, very sorry I am. I was sick. I *must* have been sick to do something like that to the person I loved most in the world. I have cried a million tears."

I said I'd never heard any expressions of remorse on his part from anyone who'd talked to him for the past year, nor had I had the first expression of sympathy from anyone in his family. "Jerry tried," he said, "Jerry came to see you in the hospital, and tried again but there was an injunction issued to keep him from contacting you."

I said I'd never heard of any such court order, only the one to keep Murray from contacting me or Stewart. He said he'd tried to find out how I was, that he'd called Rose for information and that a nurse from the home health agency where he worked had a friend at Lane Hospital who gave him periodic up-dates on my condition. He said he couldn't understand why the hospital or family wouldn't give out information about me while I was recovering from surgery, and I replied that it was because they were all afraid he was going to try to kill me again.

He said he'd even sent me a get-well card mailed from Shreveport, I guess while he was up there being examined by the defense psychiatrists. He said he hadn't signed his name or put a return address. I would later look back through all my cards and letters and find only one unsigned card postmarked Shreveport, the one quoted earlier which had given me such comfort during a particularly desolate stretch of recovery.

The handwriting on the envelope was not Murray's, but perhaps someone addressed it for him. If I'd known who it was from, would I have found it as comforting? It is ironic, though, that of all the hundreds of cards and letters I received, this would be the one I had chosen to actually quote in the book, before I ever knew who had sent it. *If* he indeed sent it.

I told him that I would have to have more surgery, and he said I'd better keep the insurance coverage and not go through with the divorce. "I can pay for it myself," I said; "I can pay for the insurance coverage to be extended for 18 months."

He said Stewart and I still had dental coverage under another policy he had. "We haven't used it," I said. "Yes, you have," he answered. "Stewart had $800 billed for dental work." Stewart has only had two cavities in his whole life and just has regular periodic dental cleanings, but I knew the dentist had tried some new enamel coating on some of his permanent teeth, and that might have been expensive—though I doubted it could have possibly been *that* expensive.

I could see, though, that Murray was keeping up with every little detail. When I later asked the dentist to check his billing, he explained that his office had been requested to send a summary of all of our dental charges and that the $800 was practically a lifetime charge for Stewart, covering the entire period he'd been on dental insurance. I guess the defense had compiled an accounting of every penny Murray had spent during our marriage. Well, I had my own account of money I had spent as well.

Murray surprised me by leaning close to the little 8x10-inch window so that he could see me better. "You look pretty," he said gently. "I like your hair like that." I tried to keep sounding angry. I had meant to react with hostility; instead, I felt so sorry for him. I had to keep reminding myself how terribly mean and hateful this man could be.

He made that easier by suddenly reverting to trial strategy. He said he couldn't remember shooting me. He had been getting depressed for a month or two beforehand, he said. "You remember that, don't you?" he asked. I didn't.

The first thing he remembered after the shooting, he said, was my asking him to see that Stewart was picked up from the airport, and he said it was at that point that he noticed spent shell casings and blood all over me and only then realized that he must have shot me. This was right after the shooting before I started playing dead so very little time elapsed between his action and his admitted awareness of what he had done—at least by my calculation.

He said he went out to the pay phone to call Rose about Stewart, knowing what he had done. If he was aware of my condition at that time, as he'd just said he was, he could surely have called for an ambulance. But he didn't. He would wait nearly two hours more, never calling for help, and surely aware of what had happened.

I knew that his attorney had told him not to discuss the trial with me, and I had no interest in rehashing all the details of his defense—but there was one question I just had to ask him. I wanted to know what he had planned on doing with Stewart when he arrived from the airport, since Murray had the money loose in his pocket to pay Rose's daughter for meeting his plane. He told me he hadn't planned on still being alive at the time.

I asked him what he thought would happen to him next, and he said he figured he'd go to the penitentiary for ten years (the minimum sentence) and die there, that he would never live through a sentence. "It's terrible here," he said, "there's nothing to do. I have just a tiny little TV that Jeannie gave me, and I read all the time. I stopped counting when I finished 60 books. They have me in solitary confinement."

Actually, the sheriff bent over backwards to make him comfortable, especially because of his age and law enforcement background.

243

But it surely isn't a pleasant existence in jail, not any jail, and I felt a growing sympathy for him, I couldn't help it, even though I could see what he was trying to do. This was why he had wanted me to come see him, I knew.

He had nothing left, he said, nothing. The defense had been so expensive. I said that I'd heard Mike Small was representing him for free as a professional courtesy to Jerry. "No," he said, "I had to pay him $50,000, and I had to pay the psychiatrists and some of the other professionals. I have nothing left."

I said that I had never wanted anything from him, and he retorted, "You wanted $300,000 to settle out of court, and I didn't have it and my children didn't have it." That wasn't for profit, I replied, just enough to cover my expenses and debts and continuing medical needs, and I knew that with help from his family—his son a successful lawyer, his son-in-law a childless international oil executive—they could easily have come up with it if they hadn't been so cocksure that he'd walk free.

But, I told him, I hadn't come there to argue. I had just wanted to hear what he had to say to me. He said it again. "I would never cause you any harm, never again. I know the signs now, I could see if I were getting sick again and could get help. I would never hurt you or your children." I guess he said this so that if the judge allowed him to get out of jail and he wanted to live near me, I wouldn't object.

"You asked me to kiss you, do you remember that?" he asked. "You asked me to kiss you, and I did. I kissed you." No, I answered, I did not remember that, and I do not believe it ever happened.

"I can't remember *shooting* you," he said, "and I'm *glad* that I can't remember. I don't think I could ever forgive myself if I could remember."

"I *can* remember," I answered him, not unkindly, "I can remember in vivid detail. But I *do* forgive you. I want you to remember that. I do forgive you."

And I put my hand up to the glass, touching it softly, and then I left. I drove home and was telling Burnett about it when Bob arrived to find out how the visit had gone. Both were skeptical, to say the least. "He's just trying to get you to feel sorry for him before the sentencing hearing," both would caution me. But I already *did* feel sorry for him. I'd felt sorry for him before I ever went to see him.

#

I told Bob to go ahead and try to get the divorce finalized, and if Murray's lawyer presented him with any demands for a share of the property here, he should at that point, and *only* at that point, file a civil suit. "Make it for $300,000 so that I can pay off my debts," I told Bob. "No," he said, "a million."

It wouldn't have made a bit of difference. All Murray had—at least all that I knew about—were his retirement checks and Social Security; he'd sold his stocks and car. He wouldn't need those in jail but they might make a little dent in the expenses I'd incurred because of what he did to me.

Before I went to the jail to visit Murray, I anticipated feeling either great sorrow or great anger, and maybe a little fright as well. As it turned out, I felt not the least bit afraid of him—not locked away as he was—but did experience a bit of both anger and sorrow during the visit. But my predominant emotion afterward was a strange and strong sense of elation. I think I felt great relief at having been able to actually confront him face-to-face *without* being overcome by emotion or anger, and I also finally felt an ability to put it behind me.

It was over, for me. It was actually over.

#

Or so I thought. I had gone to see him on Friday, November 13, 1998. Just a week went by before suddenly it wasn't over after all.

On Sunday, November 22, I attended little Mandi Tynes' baptism at Burnett's church; Mandi was the child who prayed for me every night, and I was so pleased that she had called and invited me to

245

share this special moment with her. When I returned home, Murray telephoned. He was calling from the pay phone at the jail. It was not a number I recognized, showing up on the Caller-ID simply as "Pay Phone," so I answered.

"I really want to thank you for coming to see me," he began. "I felt a lot better."

What he wanted me to do for him, he said, was to tell my children that he had loved them and still loved them, that he had never meant them any harm. "You asked me about Stewart," he said. "I would never have hurt Stewart. Of course I would never have meant to hurt you either. It was my sickness."

He continued, "I loved you very much. I always will. I hope we can be friends."

He added, "I'm sorry I was so grouchy and restless the last few months we were together. I wrote you a letter. Did you get it?" No, I answered, I had not received any letter. In my mind, I wondered if the letter contained his list of demands. And then he was called to another phone call and had to say goodbye quickly.

A requested visit. A letter. A phone call. A genuine concern, or a returning obsession? The following day he would call twice, leaving a message on the recorder when I didn't pick up the phone, saying that he had not ever meant to follow through on any demands for community property or a share of anything here; that had all been Mike Small's idea.

He said for me to go ahead with the divorce and he would not raise the issue of community property. I was glad of that because I hadn't really wanted to file a civil suit; I hadn't wanted to go through it all over again in court, and I certainly hadn't wanted to appear to be profiting from anyone's misfortune—his *or* mine.

I knew I should not have let him make me feel sorry for him again. I knew that he was just preparing for the sentencing hearing and wanted my sympathy before then so that I wouldn't make a victim's statement requesting a harsh sentence. I knew that all of the interviews conducted with him over the past year by the court-appointed psychiatric professionals and law enforcement officials showed him to be accepting absolutely no responsibility for his actions, no regret for the consequences of those actions, and no concern for anyone but himself and his family. It was as if he considered himself above the law, concentrating solely on his own problems, his own medical condition, his own mental state—a very large ego so inflated as to block out the view of anyone else but himself.

I knew I should have immediately called the attorney prosecuting him for the state, or Bob at least. But I didn't.

And so naturally the next day he called again. Could there be any question now that he was getting obsessed once more? He said he had written me two letters. He asked if I had tried to call him back. "No," I replied, I had not tried to call him back.

He apologized again for what he had done, then began telling me how expensive his defense had been. Besides the attorneys, he said, he'd had to pay each psychiatric professional $5,000 apiece, and had to pay the professional jury consultant $5,000, plus $2600 for expenses, "and she wasn't worth a thing."

He'd had to sell all of his stock, he said, and his children had had to help him with expenses. "I could have thrown myself on the mercy of the court," he continued, "and done just as well. I *told* Mike Small a rural jury wouldn't understand an insanity defense."

He actually was expecting me to sympathize with his problems in defending himself against charges of shooting me nearly to death! I guess he was forgetting that there had been a board-certified forensic psychiatrist in the jury pool, but he had been excused by the defense for possibly being able to exert too strong an influence on other jurors because of his professional expertise in the field; obviously the defense had not *wanted* a knowledgeable jury. But it was pretty obvious how involved Murray had been in planning his defense, putting to use his years of psychiatric studies and work in the forensic field, no doubt planning on cashing in on all those years of contacts with and favors for friends in the legal professional at all levels.

"How's your car?" Murray asked suddenly. I told him that I'd had to get rid of the car he'd bought for me. "Why?" he asked. "Because people thought it would be a target," I replied. He couldn't understand, he said, why anyone would think he was a continuing danger to me. When he'd called Rose, he insisted, it had been just concern for my welfare, just to see if I was being taken care of properly. "That's why I would ask if anyone was staying with you at night, just to make sure you had plenty of help."

He added that he'd had to sell his Cadillac, too. When I mentioned having seen Antoinette driving around in it, he said he'd sold it to her. I had to wonder if this might not have been a way to make sure there were no assets in his name, in case of continued litigation.

He'd hated having to sell his stock, he said. And then he said, "Say, that Hibernia Bank stock that you have. If you would deed it to me, I would manage it for you and we could split the profits." I told him that I'd had to sell every bit of stock I'd had to cover my own expenses. "You haven't got a clue what this past year has cost *me*, have you?" I asked. "You just really have no *concept* of how expensive it has been. You talk about you having nothing. *I* am the one who has nothing!"

"I don't want our conversation to deteriorate to material *things*," I continued. Even *I* had to notice that the conversation from his side was strictly about him, his problems, his expenses, his needs—very telling. Never did he inquire about my health, my well-being.

"Nor do I," he replied. "I wish we could go back six years. I loved you very much. I still care for you very much. I will always care for you. You go ahead and get the divorce and say there is no community property. What I did for you, I did because I loved you." And then a guest knocked on the back porch door to check out, and I had to get off the phone.

I called Bob and Scott Gardner, both of whom advised an immediate end to the phone conversations, seeing through the sweet talk to his real intentions. They reminded me how, right after he was incarcerated in the West Feliciana jail, he had told someone, with bitter satisfaction, "Well, that's the last time she'll screw *me*!" His present stay in jail, they pointed out, would have only increased this anger and bitterness. And Burnett, furious, would say, "You want him to get fixated again and come back here? You never should have gone to visit him at the jail. Next time, he's not going to shoot you in the stomach. He's going to shoot you in the *head*!"

#

On the 25th of November, the day before Thanksgiving, Bob and I went to court and applied for the final divorce. It took about ten minutes, and was granted on the grounds that we had lived separate and apart for more than six months. Sam D'Aquilla represented Murray and said there was no contest to the divorce or dissolution of the community. After it was over, I asked Sam to tell Murray, not in an ugly way, that it would be better if he did not call me again, but that he could write to me if he wished.

When I got home, a letter from him was waiting for me. "Dearest Anne," it began, "I just got off the phone talking with Jerry. He feels and I feel that we should not keep the issue of community property open. We only did that because Mike Small did not want to give it up at that time. I would like to say never ever did we intend to pursue that route."

(I could tell from the letter that Jerry was assuming more control in advising Murray legally. The anticipation of future hearings was ever-present, but in a kinder, gentler way than with Mike Small in charge, and within a week I received a very carefully worded letter from Jerry himself saying that he really had been concerned all along about my recovery and hoped that as I healed, so would our relationship.)

"How I wish I could relive those first years we had together," Murray's letter continued. "We had fun doing those two books and traveling around. It's my fault the years haven't been as good lately. I loved you and was so proud of you. I wasn't as considerate of you as I should have

249

been. I wish I could have done more for you to show you how I really felt about you"

He added, "Please do not be afraid of me. I am o.k. now. I had never ever in my wildest imagination thought about hurting you or anyone else except me. I feel a failure in my life and career. I loved you so much but I promise if I am ever released I will make it a point to have no contact with you."

Why should I feel so disloyal, so *intrusive*, even quoting from the letter? I knew that when this book was published, Murray would be among the first to get a copy, and I could hear ringing in my head his likely comment, "Horseshit!" But I knew in my mind that I had tried my best to be honest, not to present *my* side, not to present *his* side, but to show what had really happened as I struggled to understand just what that was. As English poet Cecil Day-Lewis says of all of us writers: "We do not write in order to be understood, we write in order to understand."

I think I have revealed nearly as many unflattering sides of my own self as I have of Murray, and Lord knows neither of us was without fault. But of all the critical or complimentary comments I had made about him throughout the text, I hadn't felt nearly as bad as I did when I was quoting from private letters speaking of the love that had been between us. I had to keep reminding myself that he was saying all those things in anticipation of his sentencing hearing, that the words were carefully chosen to have the utmost impact on me.

Maybe Murray was being truthful with me, maybe he wasn't. As skillful as he is at masking his own feelings and manipulating those of others, I wasn't entirely sure I could tell. But it no longer really mattered. I doubted I would ever really know what his motive had been, and as long as he was away from me and my children, I didn't care what his sentence would be, because I felt no need for vengeance.

What I felt predominantly was a sorrow, a loss—mostly a loss of shared memories, I think. The seven years we shared were ones that no one except my children and Burnett really knew much about, years we kept to ourselves. As Murray himself said in one letter, "We had something special once." Was there anything left of those years?

At the onset of this book, I had to concentrate, for my own survival, on strictly negative aspects of our relationship and of his character. My early writing, while not really bitter, had to emphasize the downside. But now, now that it was almost all over, a sensitivity to the other side crept in, unwanted, uninvited. Beneath all the bluster, I've always been a tender-hearted soul, and Murray always knew just how to appeal to that side of me. I guess he still does.

BUTL

CHAPTER 26

I did not see or hear from Murray again until the sentencing hearing on Thursday, January 7, 1999. I bought a new long, loose floral skirt and teal-colored long sweater to wear for the hearing. I didn't want to appear in anything Murray had bought for me or anything he'd ever laid eyes on. I even splurged and bought a pair of earrings to wear with my new clothes. I ordered them—small greenish marble hearts—from the Sundance catalogue and referred to them (to myself) as the ones Robert Redford had sent me. I'm not quite sure why, but I wanted to look good for what in all likelihood would be the last time I'd ever see Murray. I guess I felt it would be my last chance to make him feel sorry for what he had done.

Scott Gardner was there to represent the state and would present me as his only witness. I let him read my statement in advance, and he was not happy with the end of it, feeling it would open the door to problems on appeal; but I had figured out exactly what I wanted to say, and I insisted on saying it. Mike Small and his associate, along with Sam D'Aquilla, were there to represent the defense, and put on a parade of witnesses testifying to Murray's honorable character and outstanding career.

His two doctors testified not so much about his physical condition as his gentle and kind character; several female colleagues talked about how wonderful he had been to work with; an elderly friend appeared as a character witness; and his son Jerry took the stand once again to reiterate much of his trial testimony about what a good father Murray had been.

Once again Murray's family and witnesses sat on one side of the courtroom and I sat on the other with Bob and Chase. Despite the letters and calls leading up to the hearing, none of them spoke to me, and I did not approach any of them. Chase was agitated by the testimonials to Murray as such a kindly old soul, but I thought they were touching, for the most part truthful, and only to be expected. He *had* been a gentle man—I'd said that myself in my own testimony. But did that excuse picking up a gun and shooting someone?

Much was made over his liberalism, his racial fairness, his integrating the prison at Angola (under impending court order), and I began to wonder myself just what any of this had to do with anything. If you're liberal, you can pick up a gun and shoot another person? I don't think so. I'm liberal myself. I remember that when the Council on Aging, for which I served as first director, could not find suitable office space because no one at that time would rent to a racially mixed organization, I provided an office on my own property, free of charge. That doesn't give me the right to try to kill anybody, does it?

#

The judge listened patiently to all the testimonials, as he did to my own statement. What I said was more for myself than for any legal purpose. These were points I had wanted to make in the trial and had not been able to. I needed to say them, and I needed to have them become part of the court record. I was very nervous, and my voice cracked with emotion as I read this statement:

253

SURVIVOR STATEMENT

"Because of some of the defense tactics used throughout this case, it's been difficult to remember if I was the victim or the villain, so I'll call this a survivor statement, and in doing so remind the court that it is only through the grace of God, along with my own strength and struggle, with help from family and friends and medical experts and law enforcement personnel, that there can be a statement at all, that this is not an actual murder case. I do not tell my children, and I hate for the defendant to have the satisfaction of knowing, how many days there are when I hurt so much and when it is so difficult for me to do even the simplest, stupidest little task, that I am almost sorry that I did live.

I'd like to first address a few things raised by the defense in the trial which there was not an opportunity to follow-up on at that time or which the prosecutor considered not relevant during the course of the trial proceedings. At the time of the shooting, I did not call the defendant a bad name, nor had I ever used that name toward him. I had a great deal of respect for this man, and to the best of my recollection I never used any foul language directed toward him.

It was widely disseminated in public and in print that the defendant had spent all of his money restoring my home and establishing the Bed & Breakfast business there as his retirement home. I have loans and mortgages on my separate property totaling nearly $300,000, in my own name without his co-signature. In addition I sold a great deal of stock and timber, all of which I had inherited, and put that money into the place. This is my separate money which was used to restore the home and develop the B&B. The defendant did purchase a few appliances here and there, and well he should have, since I was paying all living expenses for the family and providing the home. The business was never his and there was never any question that it would ever be his; he had his own separate property. While I understand he had considered trying to claim part of my place and business as community property, never was there a mention of his claiming part of my sizable debt as community debt. During the course of the trial I had the business bookkeeper standing by to testify to these facts as well as to the fact that the defendant was never paying his fair share of living expenses there, but the legal decision was made not to interject this tangential information. I will say that at the time of the shooting, I had a legal will leaving to the defendant the right to live out his life in whichever of the Bed & Breakfast cottages he desired in the unlikely event that he outlived me; I don't think he was aware of this, and I did not owe him this, but had done it out of concern for him.

I have no intention of profiting from this miserable ordeal. My bookkeeper added up all the extra expenses out of my pocket over the twelve months immediately following my shooting, expenses I would not have incurred but for the defendant's action, and they reached nearly to $100,000 just by the middle of last year—not things covered by insurance, but strictly out of my own pocket, and not counting any loss of business due to the adverse publicity and fears for guest safety. When an attempt was made to settle out of court for this sum, it was rejected, for this would not have covered even the expenses already incurred and did not begin to address the continuing on-going medical expenses and problems I can expect to have for life. I have just in fact had my seventh surgery in December, and this will be something I will face forever. I would remind the court that I surely could have filed a civil suit to recoup some of these costs, but not only am I sure the defendant's assets are no longer in his name—his Cadillac for example—but also I have no desire to profit from something which has been so tragic for everyone involved.

I would also like to set the record straight by saying that never did I suggest that the defendant hire a hit man, and never during the course of our marriage was I involved with anyone else. I do not say I was the perfect wife for him, but never did I do anything to him that would warrant murder. Mr. Small made so many references to the sterling character of the defendant that it certainly opened the door for the prosecution to address past failings in his life, but again it was decided not to introduce this tangential information despite numerous witnesses ready and anxious to testify to such. He should count his blessings that the prosecution took the high road and did not trash him in the press the way the defense tried to do to me. It would surely have been easy to do.

The defense has made much of the devastation of the defendant's two "children." I would remind the court that there are only two real children involved in this case, and they are my two children—both minors at the time of the offense, both totally dependent on me, both in school full time, and both permanently traumatized by the ordeal they have been through. The defendant's so-called children are both in their fifties, self-supporting adults with families of their own. I know the defendant's family has been sincerely upset by this case, most particularly by the effect upon the defendant's own lifestyle. But until you spend a night in a home with a child who cannot sleep through the night for nightmares, a child who leaps from her bed with every passing backfire in the night, a child who insists on sleeping in the bed with his mother to protect her, you have no concept of real devastation. These are the children who were hurt by the case— my children—but I was not willing to exploit them by flaunting their emotions on the witness stand.

As I struggled to recover from months of hospitalization, from seven surgeries, from an entire year of painful physical therapy, I should have been able to concentrate upon my own physical and mental recovery and that of my children. Instead I was harassed and tormented by private investigators and lawyers intruding upon my privacy, interfering with my staff, and trying to turn the community against me through lies and innuendoes. At no time during this year was there any expression of sympathy or concern from the defendant or his family, other than one visit from his son Jerry when I was heavily medicated in intensive care, a visit of which I have no recollection but which my family considered threatening enough to implement security precautions during my initial six-week hospitalization when I was totally helpless. As the time for the sentencing hearing approached, I did begin receiving contacts from both defendant and his son, perhaps sincere in their concern, perhaps focused more upon the victim statement which they knew would be forthcoming.

I would like to say that these efforts were not necessary. Anyone who has been as close to death as I have comes away from the experience with heightened perceptions and an absolute intolerance of bullshit. These contacts have not increased my sympathy for the defendant for the simple reason that I was already sorry for him. I would of course like to see him take responsibility for what he did instead of shifting all the blame onto me, onto a mental disease, onto senility or dementia or depression or anything handy. But I personally have no need for revenge, and the sentence he is given by the court means nothing to me as long as my children and I are safe from him. I do not hate him, I do not feel any compulsion to have him locked away forever. I would urge the court to be as lenient in its sentencing as is possible while at the same time considering the absolute necessity of ensuring the safety of my children and me.

I appreciate the opportunity to make this statement to the court."

#

I never looked at Murray as I was speaking. I did not look at him as I took the witness stand, and I did not look at him as I went back to my seat in the courtroom audience. I do not know what his reaction was to my statement.

257

His attorney Mike Small handed the judge eleven letters written on Murray's behalf by various friends and family members, many of whom had already given similar testimony in the trial or at the sentencing hearing, and he urged the judge to be lenient, to consider that any sentence given such an elderly defendant was tantamount to a life sentence.

Scott Gardner, in his quiet soft-spoken way, merely pointed out the legal parameters of sentencing for the crime for which Murray had already been convicted, the mandatory sentence range of ten to fifty years for a conviction of attempted second-degree murder.

Judge Ramshur, speaking softly, addressed the court, all eyes upon him. He began by pointing out certain circumstances involved in this particular crime, a crime which he said had been without provocation or justification, had involved a lethal weapon, had been particularly heinous, causing grievous permanent injury to the point of near death, and for which the defendant was still, when taken into custody, indicating merely a feeling a "continued aggrievement." Even after being charged and released on bail, the judge went on, the defendant continued to contact the victim, causing alarm to her and her family.

Murray stood erect and attentive before the judge, one of his attorneys at each side. And then the judge pronounced the sentence: the maximum allowable, *fifty* years without benefit of probation or parole or suspension of sentence.

Mike Small went ballistic, literally shouting at the judge that the sentence was cruel, unusual and excessive, flinging around appeal papers (already prepared so that all he had to do was fill in the number of years of the sentence handed down) and announcing in rather belligerent tones his intention of immediately appealing not only the conviction but the sentence as well. He argued that the judge had ignored testimony from defense witnesses, had not even read the letters seeking leniency, and "gave short shrift to mitigating factors" in the case.

The judge, visibly displeased, ordered the defendant remanded to the custody of the Department of Corrections, and by the very next morning Murray was on his way in the sheriff's car to a processing and protective custody satellite of David Wade Correctional Center near Homer, in north Louisiana. I knew he would be taken care of there, as his friend Kelly Ward, a very capable younger man Murray had hired years earlier at Angola, was the warden at Wade.

I also knew this parish was relieved to no longer be responsible for him, especially since his medications alone were costing several thousand dollars a month, way too much for a little parish like this one to absorb into its meager budget for long; and Murray had been in the local jail for nearly a year, from March to mid-January. The sheriff's office had been grateful that some of his medicine costs were paid by his health insurance, but still he was an expensive prisoner.

I took Chase and Stewart out for dinner the night of the sentencing hearing so we might, not *celebrate*, but be together in our relief that we could now concentrate on other more agreeable matters. There would be interminable appeals, we knew, that would go on for a year or more, but hopefully they would concentrate solely on legal issues, not requiring my presence or testimony again unless another trial should be granted—God forbid.

As we sat down to eat, a nice-looking gray-haired gentleman approached our table. "I just want to tell you," he said to me, "how moved I was by your statement in court today. It was excellent." I thanked him, and he introduced himself as the probation and parole officer for the Feliciana parishes. I was glad at least someone had heard what I had to say.

The following day, Bob received a visit in his office from a long-time professional associate of Murray's. His comment: "He figured he could beat the system the way he always has, and this time it just didn't work out."

#

I felt sorry that the sentence was so harsh, but it had not been at my insistence. Vengeance was not mine, and I did not need or want it to

BUTL

be. Scott Gardner noted that the fifty-year sentence might be reduced on appeal.

Then I found out that Murray had never signed the property settlement part of our divorce, as he had promised to do, and I had to face the fact that all of his contacts with me prior to the sentencing hearing had probably been strictly of a manipulative nature, just as everyone had tried to tell me. Apparently he hadn't meant a word he'd said. Now we'd have to go through the whole process of property settlement again. I had not answered any of his letters from the local jail, but now, trying to keep the lines of communication open, I wrote and asked if he would like me to correspond with him in his new location. It seemed safe enough now, with him so far away.

There was a distinct change in tone in the letters Murray sent from Wade, letters written *after* the sentencing hearing. There was an undercurrent of bitterness and anger as he enumerated what he felt had been his contributions to living expenses: "I bought food in Baton Rouge; there were steaks and seafood in the freezer the most of the time. I bought Chase tires last summer, paid Hoyle for six months and Baker (both bookkeepers) for the time I was there; Mustang, weedeaters, etc . . . Certainly I have never thought of using you or anyone else . . . I feel that in the past I may have been manipulated some . . . but I am not a manipulator whatever I am. You know that."

Almost as an afterthought, he added a postscript: "I want you to know that I live a life of regret and remorse. You certainly did not deserve that." After saying that he'd known after the trial that he'd go to prison and would die there even if he received the minimum sentence, he added, "I don't mind being here. I earned it. Although I still don't remember what happened."

#

I wanted so badly to have it all be over. I really had meant what I said about not caring what Murray's sentence would be, and I sincerely felt sorry for him, but the sentence he would have to serve without me. I was not going to do the time with him. I wrote him back saying that I did not like to hear such bitterness and anger as had been in his last letter. I said that we had both paid dearly and surely did not need to compete to see who had suffered most. We both needed, I said, to put it all down, to let go of it. I meant to do just that, and I hoped he could do it as well. I *did* care about him that much; I guess I had always loved him best from afar.

And just before Valentine's Day he wrote that he did not want to correspond any more. "Certainly I have no 'anger and hatred' toward you," he wrote. "It is directed inward toward me. I am having a real difficult time at this. Still trying to adjust to this place, and I have some rather serious health problems which have been exacerbated in this setting. I ran out of anything to read and started reading a Bible in contemporary language and I have found it interesting.

"I hope you understand what I am going to say. I can't handle getting letters from you. It tears me up and I can't sleep after I get one. You know I love you very much but I can't turn back the clock. God knows I would like to. This is a hell of a way to end up a career that otherwise was fairly honorable.

"I know you understand what I am saying. I can never forget what I did to you. You did not deserve that and I think you know I never would have in my right mind done it. Anyway, I have to adjust to life here and maybe I can find a way here to help others . . . I wish for you the best things in life. You have a lot of years left. For you I wish nothing but happiness and a long life. Take good care of yourself and remember some of the good times we had."

I wrote him once more, asking that he sign the property settlement so that we could both put everything behind us once and for all, at least as much as possible given our individual circumstances. "We both have our crosses to bear, but maybe from here on out we can do so with dignity and grace and put the rancor away," I wrote. "I don't want to add to your unhappiness, or to mine."

#

And *still* we continued to exchange letters after that. For my part, I mostly just sent him newspaper clippings I thought would be of interest to him: Wilbert getting nominated for an Academy Award for a prison documentary he helped produce, and the chubby warden at Angola being investigated by the state auditor for questionable entertainment expenditures including cases of Moon Pies and SlimFast, perhaps in anticipation of the trip to Hollywood he jokingly threatened to take so he could pick up Wilbert's Oscar (there was never any question of *Wilbert* being allowed to go to pick up his own award if he won one, which unfortunately he did not, competing as he was against a Steven Speilberg Holocaust documentary, but the warden and his wife actually went).

Murray's letters to me were a litany of complaints about his health, the heat in his non-air-conditioned prison unit, regrets about his lifestyle change, reviews of his apparently unlimited supply of reading materials, his many letters and visits, his plans to move to Singapore (or later, Texas) with his daughter when he got out of prison, which he felt he might be able to do, given the fact that he was a first offender with what he called an inappropriately long sentence (he would tell this to me as if I had no connection with the case and should certainly be expected to sympathize).

He said he got to go outside and walk on the track, so that he was very tan and fit, and enjoyed raking leaves and working in the flower beds, a job he could do for as long as he felt like it. He found some of the other inmates quite interesting: an artistic pedophile priest, a former college English professor who was writing a novel, a young man he was helping to work toward his GED, some Columbians who were giving Spanish classes that he was taking. "*Hasta la vista*," he ended a note on the birthday card he sent to me, and I had to give him the benefit of the doubt and assume the alibi of ignorance, knowing that he'd never seen any *Terminator* movies.

Nowhere in these letters was there the first sign of senility or dementia, but he still took no responsibility for his actions. In one letter he implied that I had driven him "nuts" by sometimes being warm and sometimes being cold. In another, he blamed his actions on over-medication, saying that the prison doctor at Wade had found "toxicity" in his system and had reduced his dosage of medicine, after which he had performed much better on problem-solving tests—over 70 *percent* better on one test, he boasted. (Just maybe he'd been over-medicated on purpose so that the psychiatric tests administered prior to the trial would indicate the mental disease and deterioration which defense psychiatrists made such a big deal over in court.)

When he dropped his dentures down the drain, he actually wrote and asked me to look in the bathroom to see if he'd left his extra set there, as if I would have enshrined his false teeth after his departure.

I did not mean to be unkind. But I could not help noticing that nowhere in his lengthy missives was there the first expression of concern about *my* health, *my* recovery, *my* constant pain, *my* lifestyle changes brought about by his actions. I don't believe any of *that* ever even entered his head, he was so focused on his own world of woe. When I mentioned this in one letter, he would reply, "I *did* say for you to take care of yourself. I thought you had made a full recovery." This as I scheduled my eighth surgery for Dr. Mazock to insert even more artificial mesh to try to hold together the intestines since, after four major stomach surgeries with full-length incisions, there was almost no fascia left to keep things in place internally.

I drew him a diagram, delineating exactly what he had done, where the scars were, what the limitations were, what damage was permanent and irreversible, what the continuing surgical needs would be. I reminded him that he'd referred to my full recovery and said I wanted him to see just what that looked like.

BUTL

#

Within a few weeks of the sentencing hearing, I began to experience a rebirth of interest in my place, a reawakened enthusiasm for redecorating and making improvements in the cottages, a renewed clarity of my vision for the future. This was such a good sign, as Burnett noted, all the while grumbling as I persuaded him to add a stained glass window here and repaint an interior wall there.

We planted sample plots of the historic crops grown on the plantation—indigo with its delicate hanging pink flowers, cotton, sugar cane. We put in a delightful little vegetable garden, neat rows of squash and corn and tomatoes surrounded by a picket fence with a lichen-covered gate, a clawfoot tub filled with goldfish, on one fencepost a simple wooden nesting box occupied by a pair of bright bluebirds, sunflowers and one hanging purple petunia, and the most wonderful house meticulously crafted by Burnett of sticks with a steep pitched roof and heart-shaped vine windows for the running butterbeans to climb over.

It was as if all my creative energies had been bottled up for the past year and could suddenly begin to flow freely once more, coming out in a great gush of enthusiasm and ideas for new projects. All of this energy, I guess, had gone into simply surviving for a long time, and now it was no longer diverted to mundane matters like recovering from surgery after surgery after surgery.

The writer Sarah Ban Breathnach in *Simple Abundance*, her book of daily essays, has a great little piece comparing life's tragedies and trials to pruning plants in the garden, when the cutting away of what appears to be thriving may not seem sensible at the time but permits more abundant growth later. Pruning, she explains, is really a necessity for complete growth, and so is a bit of pain in our daily lives, for it is the pain which prunes away the unnecessary emotions, non-essential feelings and illusions, and thereby teaches us lessons we either consciously or unconsciously refuse to learn in happier times.

Says Breathnach, "Pain prunes the insignificant details that distract us from what is really important, sapping our days, energies and spirits. When we don't prune in the garden, Nature does it for us through wind, ice, hail, fire and flood. One way or another, the boughs will be shaped and strengthened. If we don't prune away the stress and plow under the useless in our lives, pain will do it for us." And so, pruned by pain and suffering, I was at last ready for abundant growth. As the Psalms say, those who sow with tears shall reap with joy.

"The two children of Anne Butler, Chase and Stewart,
dressed for a friend's wedding"

I began taking Chase and Stewart out for dinner one night each weekend, and we had a good time together. I started attending meetings of civic organizations once more, doing a lot of free writing to publicize various local fund-raisers and non-profit organizations, and people said it was about time I started getting out and about again. "I am so glad to see," one friend called to say, "that you have at last risen from the dead."

I needed to put all the pain and suffering and unhappiness behind me and move on, and I would do so. Any continuing bitterness, any feelings of vengeance that I held onto would give Murray a control over my life that I was not willing to grant him. After all the suffering I had been through, I finally knew I had the power to make that decision, and I could sincerely believe in my heart that the responsibility for what had happened did not rest with me. It had not been my fault, and at long last I fully accepted that fact.

Nor was there any longer a need for me to look for a justification or an excuse for his actions. His behavior was *in*excusable. It was cruel, and cold, and calculated to do the most harm possible—from 18 inches away as I sat still and unresisting in the chair, with his years of marksmanship training, slowly and deliberately firing his pistol directly into my right elbow and right shoulder to totally disable my dominant arm and perhaps even cause its loss, calmly firing directly into the kidney, the intestines, the vital organs, and only missing the spine because of my movement forward as I sat up and said, "*Stop! You know I have children to take care of!*" Oh, yes, he knew just what he was doing, and the responsibility for what he did rests solely with him.

There was one last thing I needed to do in order to be finished with the whole ordeal. I wanted to look at the evidence presented at the trial. I hadn't seen it during the trial because it had been presented by the deputies and detectives and crime lab experts while I was sequestered and out of the courtroom. I don't know quite why, but I felt a real need to confront this as I had everything else, head-on. I didn't want to go alone to the Clerk of Court's office where the evidence was stored in a metal cabinet. I certainly didn't want my children to see it, but I wanted someone there with me. So poor Burnett, protesting all the way that it wasn't a good idea for me to look at the evidence, escorted me down to the courthouse and into the back room of the Clerk's office where stacks of giant leather-bound ledgers held records carefully inked in spidery script back to the early 1800s—the births, the marriages, the deaths, the property transactions, the life of the parish.

A big cardboard box filled with paper bags and manila folders was put on a table for us, and I began sorting through it. Some of the envelopes were sealed, and I didn't open those. But some were open, so I could hold the actual bullets which were removed from my body— huge, heavy, dull metal bullets. I could see the gun, and the unused bullets removed from Murray's pockets.

What I was most interested in was the clothing. In one bag were all of Murray's clothes, even his shoes and belt and tie. I wanted to see if there were any blood spatters on his clothes—and there were a few, on both pants and shirt.

But the worst were my clothes, everything absolutely soaked in blood, still big clots and globs of it, not one inch free of it. My bra and panties were so soaked it was impossible to even tell what color they had been; and my skirt, which showed definite signs of having been literally ripped off just as I had remembered in the ambulance, was covered in blood from waistband to floor-length hem. For some reason my blouse did not seem to be in the box of evidence; perhaps it was in one of the sealed envelopes.

Why was it so important for me to see this evidence, to lift it out with shaking hands, to smell the deteriorating blood? I think it was because I needed to have a clear picture of what I looked like to Murray in those last two hours as he sat there with reloaded gun and did nothing to get help for me.

Some divine guidance had kept me from looking at myself during that period; I never ever saw any of the blood, I never looked at any of my wounds, and it was probably just as well at that time. But for Murray to have been able to sit there and look at me, covered as I was in blood, and do nothing, that to me was the final proof I needed to see how right the EMT Steve Moreau had been when he

BUTL

had cautioned me to stop looking at the shooting as a crime of passion and to instead see it realistically as it was—a crime of hate. Those blood-soaked clothes pretty well underscored Steve's conclusion.

But I would not answer hate with hate, and in my heart I was finally, at long last, able to forgive—not to *excuse* Murray's behavior, not to judge it, but to forgive it. I had faced it all, and now I could let it all go. And when I did, it was as if I reclaimed some of that feeling of serenity I had experienced as I sat dying in the wicker rocking chair. Maybe my months of pain and struggle had indeed been gifts of growth, even gifts of grace, the cost for returning to me my own sacred space.

My revenge, if you can call it that, will not be court-mandated, but will be in rebuilding my life and my business, rediscovering happiness, and taking pleasure in my home and my family once again. Murray nearly took my life, but he'll never be in control of it again. Not that he ever was, really, not even those two hours he sat over me with a gun waiting for me to bleed to death.

Even then, he was not in control.

OTHER VOICES, OTHER VIEWS

BUTL

PATRICE NELSON
& ROSE PATE, CLEANING STAFF

Patrice Nelson

Aug. 24, 1997, Miss Anne Butler and I were in the laundry room discussing when she was going to go pick up Stewart from the airport, and she told me that she was going to give me the key before she left. And while we were in the room discussing this, Mr. Murray Henderson arrived, came into the main house, and he spoke, Miss Anne spoke, and I spoke also. And I asked him how he was doing and he said he was doing fine. After that I left and went to clean up the cabins.

On my way back I was going to check on the laundry and Mr. Murray Henderson stopped me and asked me did I know anyone to go pick up Stewart from the airport. So I told him, "No sir." So he asked me was Miss Rose Pate home? I said, "I think she's at church, did you call her?" And he said, "No, I don't know her number." So he went to the pay phone, I gave him her number, and he called Miss Rose Pate and he got her on the phone, and what he said to her then, I don't know because I left and went back to finish cleaning up the cabins.

Rose Pate

On Aug 24, 1997, approximately 11:30 a.m., Mr. Murray Henderson called me from Butler Greenwood and asked me if I could go pick up Stewart from the airport. I told him that I had to go to church and he held the phone, paused on the phone. And he said, "Rose, you have to help me." I said, "Mr. Henderson, I can't go, but I can send Carol Lynn, I can get Carol Lynn to go pick him up." And he said, "Lord help this day. Thank you, Rose." He said, "I'll pay $25 for her to go pick him up." And I said, "OK, Mr. Henderson," and I hung the phone up.

Patrice Nelson

I was in one of the cabins cleaning up and I realized it was time for Miss Anne to go pick up Stewart from the airport. I went up to the main house and I opened the door, and I saw Miss Anne scooped down in the chair covered with blood, and I asked Mr. Henderson, I said, "What happened? She needs a doctor." He told me that it's best for me not to get involved, that she'd be ok, that she didn't need a doctor, that she was gone. And he told me that he wasn't going to hurt me.

And I turned around and walked out the door. And at that time I didn't call no one because I didn't know whether he was gonna come behind me and catch me on the phone calling someone, and I didn't want him to shoot me. So then later on I called Miss Rose Pate and I told Miss Rose for to come down right away because Mr. Henderson had shot Miss Anne.

Rose Pate

Sometime after 12 Patrice called me and she said, "Miss Rose, you have to get down here right away," and I said, "What's wrong, Patrice," and she said Mr. Henderson had shot Miss Anne, and I said, "Oh my

God!" I jumped in my truck, I started out and then I realized I shouldn't be going by myself, I turned around and went next door to my nephew's house and got my son Carl and said, "Carl, I need you to go with me," and he said, "What's wrong, Mama," and I said, "Mr. Henderson shot Miss Anne."

We got in the truck and we took off and in 15 minutes we were there. We arrived at Butler Greenwood, Patrice and Rosemary were still there, and also was Mr. Henderson. I told Patrice and Rosemary and Carl to stay there and I was going next door and get Mr. Bob Butler because he would know what to do. I got back in my truck and I went next door to Mr. Bob Butler and I told him what had happened, and he called 911. Then I got back in my truck, I arrived back at the house and by the time I arrived back at the house the police had arrived at the house too.

The police arrested Mr. Henderson and then the ambulance came and picked up Miss Anne, they put her on the stretcher and all three of us, Rosemary, Patrice and I, ran over to see if she was ok. And she was talking, and we asked her if she was ok, and I said, "Miss Anne, what you want me to do with Stewart when he gets here," and she said, "Take him to his dad's," and I said, "What you want me to do about the house," and she said, "Just watch it." So the ambulance went ahead and took Miss Anne to the hospital and about 15 or 20 minutes later Carol Lynn arrived with Stewart.

And when Carol Lynn arrived with Stewart I went out and told Carol Lynn to stop before she got to the house. All the police cars were around and everything, and Stewart looked up and said, "What happened?" And I said, "Stewart, I have to tell you something, I have to tell you something that happened real bad." And he said, "What, what happened?" And I told him Mr. Henderson shot Miss Anne. And he said, "You mean Papa shot Mama?" And I said, "Yeah, he did, but she's gonna be ok, she'll be fine, she'll be all right."

Then he said he had to call his dad, he called his dad's house and he wasn't at home, so he called his friend, and by the time he called his friend, his brother-in-law Kevin Ford came up. And Stewart looked at me and he said, "Where is he?" And I said, "Stewart, the police have him, they've got him all locked up and he won't be able to hurt anybody any more."

Rose Pate

I really found out just how jealous Mr. Henderson was when we were in Florida. It was a lot of little small things that happened at Butler Greenwood, but I really didn't pay a whole lot of attention to it because he was so smooth with it until you had to really like *live* with him to really pick up on just how jealous he was, and he always thought evil thoughts of people.

He was just so jealous of everything we did, like when me and Miss Anne were going shopping in Baton Rouge, or we were going to exercise class, or stuff that she did with the kids or stuff that she did with us, he was jealous of everything. And like on Saturday morning when he'd cooked sausage and we wouldn't eat the food, he'd get all mad about that. And when he'd buy her old-fashioned looking clothes and she wouldn't wear them, he'd be mad about that and just any little thing would really piss him off.

But when we were in Florida, that's when I really knew what was going on. Everything that we did, it wasn't satisfaction with him. All the places we went, he wasn't pleased with the places we went, and if we tried to fix food, he wasn't pleased with the food we fixed. He always felt like he should be the one to do all the cooking, decide what places we should go, decide when we should go, when we should come back. He just wanted to be the centerpiece of everything.

Patrice

Stewart and his class were going to have a class party at the pool pavilion and Mr. Henderson wanted to give them little door prizes like key chains from the place where he worked and Miss Anne told him that the kids wouldn't be interested in that and he got very offended about that. And I remember when Miss Anne used to do a whole lot of house tours and Mr. Henderson would get mad about that.

Rose

One morning when I had gone over to the house, he was sitting on the porch with his legs all stretched out looking at this book with all these pretty neckties, and I said, "Oh, Mr. Henderson, you fixing to order you a necktie?" He said, "I was just looking." I said, "That one's so pretty, it just looks like you." And he said, "Yes, it does." And Miss Anne was just coming out of the laundry room, she was real real busy, and he said, "Look," and Miss Anne said, "Oh wait, just give me a little space, just a minute." And then I came back and there he was with his little suitcase on his arm and all these neckties, getting ready to go out, and that's when he moved out that week.

And the next time I saw him, he came by the Council on Aging with all these clothes on Monday, all packed up in these bags, all the presents they had given him for his birthday, and he gave them to me to give to my brother, and he said, "You know I have left from up there." I said, "Oh, you did?" And he said, "Yeah." And I said. "What happened?" And he said, "Well, she said she needed space, and I'm gonna give her all the space she wants." And I said, "Ok, Mr. Henderson." I had seen enough of him, and I knew this coming and going just wasn't gonna do.

All the other times I had encouraged him and told him that I would pray for them to get back together, but this particular day I told him, "Well, that's good, you go on with your life," because definitely I did not want him to come back, because he was just too jealous and he was just making everybody unhappy, and there was just no way you could be happy with him, because he was too evil. He was just as smooth a walker as he was a talker, he really put it over, but now when you think about it and when you look back at things, little bit of things that he done, if we'd just been smart enough to put it together, we could have warned her what was going on.

BUTL

DR. DONALD FONTE,

ORTHOPEDIC SURGEON

When paged by the hospital communication about an open fracture to the arm, I react, as trained. This is an open fracture—a surgical emergency—and I must drop what I'm doing and respond. I know
that I can't have the luxury of having the ER doc splint "the thing"
and send it to the office the next day. Moreover, I was informed that
the patient was on her way to the O.R. for emergency exploratory
surgery for multiple gunshot wounds to the abdomen.

I peered through the O.R. doors and let the surgical crew know I
was available. The surgeon, Lisa Mazoch, was already prepping the
abdomen, so volunteered to assist on the abdominal portion of this
case. "I'll help Lisa," I thought, so as to hurry the case along and do my
part—the orthopedic surgical care of the fractured arm—before midnight.

Remember that I am an orthopedic surgeon and it's been years
since I've assisted in abdominal surgery. Early in my career as a medical student, I "scrubbed" at Charity Hospital in New Orleans as a
'Moonlighter" for extra coins in my medical infancy (I donated blood
too); I'd been on many "belly cases" during that era of my life and was
used to pulling on retractors.

This was my first introduction to Anne Butler, the victim, with
belly split open and blood pouring from her wounded bowels and

vital organs. "Just like old times on a Friday and Saturday night at the 'Charity' Hospital," I thought, "when the 'cut-n-shoot' club met and victim after victim poured in to the emergency room to be followed by the victims of the sweet revenge later that evening. But wait, this is a married Caucasian lady hauled from the serene antebellum town of St. Francisville, a writer, a mother, and a caretaker of a Bed & Breakfast. In fact, she's the heir of the antebellum home she was shot in. She's truly a Southern lady in her own right. I thought to myself again, 'They don't shoot the massah's wife in the South, do they?"

"Lisa, what the hell happened here?" I addressed our lady surgeon. "Her husband tried to kill her—and came pretty close, don't you think?" she replied. Lisa Mazoch was a woman surgeon of few words. Honest and to the point with her every word and move, she could be jovial and serious in the same breath. With her good judgment, I could tell she knew the severity of these wounds, the grim possibilities of complications of the massive blood loss, and potential for sepsis. She conveyed her pessimism even as her talented and well-trained hands began the life-saving surgery.

"We're going to have to do a colostomy," she decided once the bleeding had been controlled. I hadn't seen a colostomy in a patient this young except in a severe case of strangulated bowel or cancer. How the world has changed. Here I am scrubbing on a case with a female general surgeon in a specialty where machismo prevailed in this field for the past two or three decades. Now I witness an extremely competent pair of hands connected to the clinically sound mind of a mother-to-be. I could not have imagined this drama thirty-five years ago when I entered medical school.

In those days in the '60s, we had eleven female freshmen medical students in a class of one hundred and forty-one, and graduated only seven of those. Now the classes at the same school have more females than males. A recent headline in an alumni bulletin of 1996 read, "More Gals than Guys in Frosh Class." I could, at the beginning of my medical career, name the female surgeons I knew on one hand. Now

I thought, "Ms. Butler would be happy to know she's in the good hands of an all-state surgeon."

As Lisa put on the last strips of tape, she removed her gloves and sighed, "She's all yours. I'm going out to pee and talk to the family." For a mother-to-be, she's done well during a two-hour tug-of-war with this lady's life, I thought with astonishment.

Now for this fragmented and powdered right humerus. I must act. With two arm bullet wounds and no way to assess her neurological function, the patient was lucky to have had no vascular injury. At this venture, the best approach would be to clean out the wound, place drains, splint the arm in traction, and hope she doesn't become infected. There would be a need for additional surgery to secure the fractures, but only when the patient recovered from abdominal wounds.

Again my mind rambled. The last case I saw like this was a drug-related shooting in the war zone of the drug lord in Baton Rouge. I couldn't help but ponder on the idea of her husband shooting her.

As the case progressed, bits and pieces of the story emerged. "He was drinking." "He was sitting across from her with a loaded gun continuing to drink into oblivion." There was also a conflict as to the number of times he shot her. Five? Six? Seven? We surgeons can generally count holes—both entrance and exit wounds—and see the missiles on the x-rays, but in this case there are multiple double wounds and fragmentation of the missiles. This is beginning to sound vaguely like the JFK assassination, I reflected.

Being a recovering alcoholic, I was touched by the speculation that Anne Butler's husband was a drinking ex-warden of the Louisiana penal system. In AA circles, we all hear that a drunk usually makes his exit from his drinking past by one of the "D's"—Death, Dementia, or Detention.

Anne Butler certainly had a near-death experience, her shooter had to be demented to have shot her that many times and left her to die, and detention is likely to happen if he's convicted, but wait, he's a former warden. The great paradox is that he could walk, if he is tried for this deed in West Feliciana Parish (Louisiana for county), where his former prison was.

My formerly alcoholic brain sometimes gets judgmental and my recovering peers tell me that's dangerous, so I'll stop. I'm not a good historian and I'm certain it will take months before we know all the details on the case. The facts have a tendency to trickle in long after our official history and physical exams and surgical reports have been recorded on the day of the patient's admission to the hospital.

After my introduction to this case, I know that I have done what I can do now and don't look forward to my return to the operating suite to attempt to reconstruct Anne Butler's writing arm and elbow. I only hope and pray that her writing future hasn't been blown away by those two ill-placed bullets.

Being somewhat of a closet poet and writer myself, I couldn't help but speculate about what types of books Anne Butler writes. "Did you know that Anne and her husband co-authored a book on the Angola prison?" Lisa reported as she returned from her visit with the family. At this point nothing would have surprised me. "What? This case is getting crazier by the minute." "Wake her up," said Lisa, "let's get her to recovery."

Five days later after a watchful vigilance in the Intensive Care Unit, Anne would emerge to the operating room for her second day of surgery. To this point, I was a minor player in the care of this alias (Anne Butler's name had been changed at the request of the family for safety reasons; we were informed that her husband was still "on the loose," having been released on bail).

Now, with the x-rays on the view box and the patient anaesthetized, I tried to map some approach to this shattered elbow. "I have never seen one this bad," I thought with my arms crossed. "Go scrub, Dr. Fonte," I heard, as if being awakened from a bad dream. For the next several hours, I found myself trying to piece together fragments of bone to stabilize Anne's elbow. I had taken all the courses and read all the approaches to difficult fractures about the elbow, but this case was sailing on uncharted waters. A resection of the joint would have been an easier procedure for all concerned. It sounded like Civil War medicine, as I recalled an individual who had a flail elbow that was very functional.

Visiting a patient daily with tachycardia, anemia, fever, colostomy and functionless right upper extremity is no fun for a surgeon. This was the presentation of an anxious, scared Anne Butler for two weeks. Finally a decision was made to transfer her to the rehab unit once the fever had broken. All I could envision was a stiff shoulder and elbow in a patient I barely knew except in the operating suite. In spite of excellent occupational therapy, Anne's arm was slow to respond and ten days later, desiring to go home, she left the hospital, barely ambulatory, barely able to care for herself, with a stiff weak dominant upper limb—but alive. That was a relief in itself.

From this point forward for seven months, there was a complication with every injury that .38-caliber gun produced. Somewhere and sometime a meaningful firearms legislation needs to be passed and all these handguns melted down and a monument erected in honor of this nation's crime victims, I thought as I approached additional procedures to correct complications related to these wounds.

Lisa Mazoch had to cancel the closure of the colostomy and I had to return for multiple operations for complications of bony non-union of the elbow, a frozen shoulder and an ulnar nerve compression. And yes, there were still retained missiles surfacing beneath Anne's skin of her chest and flank that were removed and graciously accepted by the State Police crime lab. The pieces of the puzzling case continue to be put together, as I observe Anne Butler's recovery from this dastardly deed.

I couldn't help but reflect on the remarkable recovery of Anne's arm as I picked up her heavy charts and read her progress. On one of her early operations, her signature is barely legible on the surgical permit. Just five months later, her handwriting is impeccable. It's much the same with her disposition. She has returned to a pleasant, productive, creative individual through her courage and willpower and the grace of God.

I could write for hours on Anne's case from both the physical and mental aspects and recovery, but I'll leave that writing to her. She's the author. I'm still in the dugout.

BUTL

Douglas Dennis

Angolite Staff Writer, LA State Penitentiary

When Wilbert Rideau, the editor of The Angolite, and I heard about it (and we were among the first here to know), we were stunned speechless, which, as you might suppose, takes some doing. Everyone else's reaction—prisoners *and* employees—was the same.

Only a few people know Anne, but everyone knows C. Murray. What he did was unprecedented, certainly in Louisiana. Never before in history had a warden in this state shot his wife. Far as I and Wilbert know, the same is true for the rest of the country. Of course everyone was stunned. It was like seeing a pig fly.

Add to that the fact that both are "high society" in the community, which means their personal lives are private. When something like that happens, the society closes. Nobody says anything about motive or reasons why. In this case, that includes the authorities. While the facts of the shooting are known, no authority has given a reason why (as they usually do). So everyone is curious, but no one knows and no one approves.

As for statistics about law enforcement officer violence against their families, we've come across studies in the past of the extremely high suicide and divorce rates among cops. In divorce, one of the chief factors was brutality. But C. Murray is not a cop. He is a corrections executive, which could only in the broadest sense be considered law enforcement.

Stewart Hamilton, son

Age 12

When I was driving in from the airport, Miss Rose came up to me and said Murray had shot Mom. At first I thought she was joking, but it was no joke. It was the most serious part of my life. It changed everybody's life a little. It brought some people closer, some farther apart.

I was really scared. I thought Mom was going to die or go into a coma. I prayed every night that she would be ok. I was mad at the same time. I wanted to hurt Murray. I still thank God that my mom is still alive.

CHASE POINDEXTER,

DAUGHTER

AGE 21

Well, I can say that I truly never knew the man. This person had been my stepfather for nearly eight years, yet I could never feel comfortable in calling him anything but Mr. Henderson. I don't know whether it was his age or whether I thought he would come and go like so many other stepfathers that I was scared to get close to him. It was rather difficult in the beginning getting used to questions by friends wondering if this old geezer was my grandfather. This was particularly embarrassing for my little brother, who was even younger, so the age disparity was even more noticeable.

Stewart had felt comfortable calling him "Papa", but I would never feel totally accepting of his presence. I knew deep down he would not be my stepdad forever. I had had two before him. Was anything going to be different with him? He did seem to be the most intelligent of all of them, but I liked him the least. He seemed to win my little brother's heart through treats that he would bring him, but I think he did this because he really could not be a father figure for Stewart; it was not like he could go out and play ball at his age.

August 23, Stewart and I drove to Atlanta so he could help me move into the dorm for my last semester at Emory University. He spent the night and the next day, Sunday the 24th, Stewart flew back home by himself. I tried calling that afternoon to make sure that he made it home o.k. I had to call from the dorm lobby as my phone line was not hooked up yet in my room. I called collect several times, and each time I tried, a man answered the phone. I did not recognize his voice and he did not know whether to accept the charges.

Finally, after three times, he accepted the charge. I asked him who he was; I wanted to know why my mother did not answer the phone. The man said, "This is Deputy Ivy Cutrer." At that point, I knew something was wrong. My first thought was Mama and Stewart had been in a car wreck. Deputy Cutrer told me to call my cousin Bob. He could tell me what was going on. I called Bob. His wife Liz answered the phone. She said that Mama had been in an accident; she was in the hospital. Stewart was o.k. though. She said Bob would have to call me.

At this point, I am sitting in the hallway of the dorm, alone and scared to death. Bob called me on the pay phone and told me that Mr. Henderson had shot Mama. She was in critical condition. I was shocked and then terrified. Was I dreaming? This was something that happened only on the news. It never happened to me or someone I knew before.

I knew that I would have to come home immediately. I went and told my Resident Advisor, who was the only friend of mine on campus at the time. Other friends had not come back to campus yet. She stayed with me and even helped get my phone hooked up so that I did not have to sit in the hallway all night. Unfortunately, I could not get a flight until Monday morning. I should have driven the 10 hours home, but I knew that the state of mind I was in would have put me in a bad driving mode or mood.

The whole town of St. Francisville was at the hospital that night except me, it seemed. This really upset me. I wish that I could have been there to hold Stewart's hand. I thank God that he was still flying when the shooting happened. I came to Baton Rouge Monday morning, having gotten no sleep the previous night, watching the phone waiting for any news on Mama. I have never felt so helpless and scared in all of my life.

The next two weeks proved to be a real test of character for me. I had to make sure that I still had a Mama, first of all. My second priority was Stewart. I needed to spend time with him and find out his feelings on the incident. He was very angry and wanted to shoot "Papa" for what he had done to Mama. I got him back into school on Wednesday; this was the best solution. To get him in a routine schedule and back with his friends, these were the most important things for Stewart's well-being. I don't guess I'll ever truly know what he really feels about the incident.

That day was especially hard as I had to return home to see the yellow crime tape still up on the back porch steps. I needed to remove valuables from the house for safe keeping elsewhere. Mr. Henderson scarred the back porch with her blood on purpose, as this was the center of operations for the business. Mama would later say, "This is my house, and I'll be damned if he's keeping me out of it," but it did keep me out of it. Without Mama there, I could not sleep or eat at home, or run the B & B from the back porch as we usually did.

I reopened the business five days after the shooting. I moved all operations out to the pool house. He had scarred our house for me. The whole place was a ghost town without Mama. Thanks to the help of family like my aunt and uncle and friends from the community, I was able to save the business which provided for my family's well-being. The shooting brought our otherwise very distant family close together. This was a positive aspect of this horrible cruel incident.

Mr. Henderson carefully thought this act out. It infuriates me to this day that he knew Stewart and I were gone and that the cleaning staff comes later on Sundays. He did not love Mama. He wanted to watch her die a slow painful death. He was a jealous and controlling man. In the days after the shooting, there were so many things that I had to deal with that I never had time to sit down and think about what he had done to Mama and our family, but now I can say it has shed new light on my feelings toward my mother. I admire her in more ways than one for living and struggling through this painful ordeal. She was not supposed to live, but she did.

I for one do not believe in the American justice system. For a man to have gone and done this and not be immediately imprisoned for this horrific crime is inexcusable. Besides that, I no longer belong to the church I was baptized and confirmed in, because of the minister's initial attempts to minister not only to my family but also to the perpetrator. Mr. Henderson has not suffered one bit, yet the minister insisted he was a victim, too.

I still have frequent nightmares. Not all women can survive domestic violence, which is a huge problem in our society today, but my mother did. Mr. Henderson did not ruin our lives. He scarred my mother's body, but he did not affect her integrity or determination to continue life and business as usual. Plus, the worst time in my life encouraged me to go back to school after two weeks of absenteeism, finish my last semester, and graduate with the highest GPA of my college career. I even made the Dean's List! Maybe I inherited some of my mother's strength and determination after all. Only time will tell.

BUTL

MARY MINOR
BUTLER HEBERT, SISTER

Weekends at Greenwood were the highlight of an idyllic childhood spent with my sister Anne and my cousins. We rode horses, fished in the pond, climbed all over the barn full of hay. My grandmother had an endless supply of biscuits and fried chicken for us, plus bounty from the garden and the hunters, and the patience to tolerate our tramping everywhere in the comfortable old house.

Growing up, my sister often stated her intention to live at Greenwood. She would be an old maid, she said, surrounded by her pets, but the place would be in the hands of a woman—as it had been since it was built. When my grandmother died, my parents enjoyed a few brief years as owners of the place. Anne moved in shortly after my father's death, and she has devoted her life to maintaining Greenwood—with plenty of pets, but certainly not as an old maid.

When my double first cousin Bob called on a Sunday afternoon in August, my first reaction was "long-distance" (as we still say in my family) meant trouble. He told me to put my husband Michael on the phone. Bob is a man of few words, condescending but always polite. As I wondered about the nature of his call, I told him that Michael was napping and would call him back. Then Bob said, "Get him on the phone now! Anne's been shot."

We got the sordid details of my sister's fourth husband Murray's attempt to kill her. She had been shot several times, had undergone two hours of prolonged torture under Murray's gaze. The back porch of my Greenwood childhood was the scene of an unspeakable crime. Anne was alive, though, and she would prove her strength over the next months of repeated surgeries.

Aside from the medical and emotional nightmare, there was the problem of Anne's children. They were my immediate concern because of their fragility. Chase had just returned to Emory after spending the summer with my family. I had seen her struggling with the stress of a new city, several new jobs, and her own burden of diabetes. She had no father figure to rely on, as Anne's first three husbands had been banished from her life. Stewart, age 12, was in Atlanta with Chase, so at least he was spared the sight of his mother being shot nearly to death.

We called Chase, got her a ticket home, and raced to Louisiana to find a hospital full of frantic friends, relatives, and an unusually demonstrative Stewart. After some reassurance from ICU staff and doctors, we took Stewart with us to the safety of Michael's family farm. Greenwood would not be a sanctuary again because Murray was released from jail almost immediately.

Chase arrived, hysterical of course. We spent the next days and weeks in a series of roles as Michael provided legal counseling, I provided refuge and reassurance for Anne's children. We were stunned and bewildered that Murray would commit such a crime and that the system of justice could fail so swiftly.

The fact that Greenwood was now a vast B&B enterprise left an additional nightmarish dimension. Anne had established an efficient and well-run operation, with the serious drawback that only she knew the details. As it was Anne's first conscious wish to re-open the business, Chase and I and the staff struggled to set up an elementary system to accommodate the guests, the reservations, the finances, the employees. Chase grew up in a hurry, and between the frightening problems of her mother's health and her own health, she managed to get Greenwood going again.

Anne Butler

Security at the best of times can be difficult at a B&B, with guests arriving and departing and wandering all over the beautiful property. When we realized that Murray was not in jail, still in the parish, and possibly planning to try again to kill Anne or anyone in the line of fire, security became a terrifying impossibility. We financed and set up a system—with the help of friends, relatives, staff, sitters and security guards—to keep Greenwood open and providing income for an invalid and her shell-shocked children.

As Anne's physical condition stabilized, Chase and her volunteers organized the B&B; Stewart started back to school, staying with his father; Bob and Michael found competent, unbiased legal assistance for Anne, so we were able to consider returning to our own family and business. Week after week, the cousins who played together at Greenwood returned to help, passing the baton as each was needed from their own lives—we came from Texas, Virginia from Washington, then Sam and Ginny from Chesapeake Bay, and always, Bob, Pat and Murrell from just down the road.

This is an ongoing story, but to balance the thought that as I write this there has been no trial yet, very little jail time for Murray, repeated surgeries and a life of pain and therapy for Anne, we must consider the skill and kindness of her doctors, nurses, staff, and friends. Our emotional, financial, and legal aid for Anne, our counsel and shelter for her children—these pale in comparison to the strength of my sister's vow to live at Greenwood. I've said goodbye to that back porch of my idyllic childhood; I just hope Anne remembers the part about the old maid.

BOB BUTLER,

ATTORNEY AND COUSIN

This book describes a heinous act of cruelty whereby a man attempted to take the life of an unarmed and unsuspecting woman in such a manner that would prolong the agony of death and would attempt to forever tarnish an ancestral home and all those who enjoy it, past, present and future. It was cowardly, premeditated, cruel, inexcusable and poor shooting.

Yet this act, heinous as it was, set into motion a course of events which provide a testimonial of faith, strength, resilience, acceptance, humor and compassion. It describes a woman—lady, my mother never liked the term "woman"—who through an ordeal was allowed first to glimpse death but lived to tell about it, who had a will of iron to live yet had to learn to accept help from others, and who through herself allowed others to come to better understanding of themselves.

You know she's my double first cousin and godmother to boot, so I'd better not say too much about her because she might write something about me.

Glenn Daniel,

EX-HUSBAND & DEPUTY SHERIFF

My name is Glenn Daniel and I am a former husband of Anne's. I would like to tell you my thoughts and feelings of the day and the time following the horrible shooting of Anne.

On the day that Anne was shot, I was in Baton Rouge along with my wife Jennifer and my daughter Rachal when I received a page for me to call my mother. I found this to be very unusual as I had never before been paged by her. When I spoke with her on the phone she told me that Anne had been shot several times by her husband Murray Henderson and that she did not look like she would live. I thanked my mother for letting me know and then told Jennifer what I had been told. To say the very least, I was shocked and appalled at what I had been told.

I have been a law enforcement officer for the better part of my life and have seen and witnessed many terrible crimes throughout the years, but what was done to Anne is probably the meanest act of them all. This sorry excuse for a man was not satisfied with trying to kill Anne but wanted to see just how much he could make her suffer. To be made to sit helplessly while you are shot several times and to wonder which shot will be the fatal one and to think of your children and how they will go on without you must be the saddest thought of all. I don't know if I could recover from such horror.

Weep For The Living

Luckily, Anne did survive and is here to tell the story of that day. I always said that Anne is a tough lady and she has proved it to us all. While Anne and I were married, we had our differences—which led to our parting—but we continue to be friends. I am sorry for all that has happened to Anne and her family because of the horrible crime Murray Henderson committed, but I know that Anne will overcome it all because she is a fighter and will not let Murray Henderson take her from her family who need her, the family she loves dearly.

BUTL

BURNETT CARRAWAY

RESTORATION CARPENTER, BUSINESS PARTNER,

BAPTIST MINISTER, LONGTIME FRIEND

Call came in about 4:15 on Sunday afternoon. Mrs. Ann Weller was on the phone and she said, "Burnett, Murray shot Anne and it doesn't look like she's going to live." I don't know how long it takes for an eternity to pass, but it seemed like that long before I could say anything or talk with her or ask how. She didn't know anything except that Anne had been shot and things looked bad. I hung up the phone and turned around and called Bob Butler, her cousin. His wife Liz answered the phone and confirmed what Mrs. Ann had said, and also said that the possibility of Anne living was indeed slim.

At this point I hung up from talking with Liz and called Monette Freeman, one of our deacons at New Salem Church, and asked Monette to make some kind of arrangements for the service that night, that Ruby and I were going to Zachary to the hospital, thinking—well, *knowing*—that Chase was in Atlanta, Stewart was on his way back from Atlanta, supposed to be in; we didn't know what was going on with that, but we would go and do what we could or see what was going on. Of course that was the easy part.

The hard part was driving to Zachary, while going through my mind a million times was the question, "Why did this have to happen," wanting not to believe that it was happening. If in fact all this had happened, why was my soul being torn apart inside? The answer to that involved the thousands of times I'd talked to Anne, and how many times I had gotten so close to saying, "Anne, I would like for you to sit down and tell me about your relationship to Jesus Christ."

I had joked with her numerous times about where she stood with the Lord and what would happen to her soul, but I had never once in all those times shared with her the real message of Jesus Christ and what Jesus could do in her life. I felt so guilty and I was so troubled. I'm thinking, here's somebody who's a very important part of your life, and if she wasn't important enough for you to share that word with, share that message with, how would you share it with other people that you don't care so much about?

And then there was that old nagging thought coming back at me, of how a lot of times we put off the ones who are closest to us until the very last. We just don't have the courage to bring that up, thinking that we might offend them and be separated from them in some way, knowing that if there really is a good feeling there, a lot of friendship and a lot of love and a lot of caring, then they'll understand that all we're doing is caring about where they'll spend eternity. Somewhere along the line I remembered what Anne would always tell me, that "God's taking care of me." But that time, that day, I wasn't so sure.

We went to the hospital, sat with Bob and some of the family, Father Dimmick and Father Rowe, until the surgeon Dr. Mazoch came out and said, "She's gonna make it, there's a lot of damage but she *is* gonna make it." Of course everybody was just overwhelmed with relief. A little later on that evening, Ruby and I got to go in and see her a minute, and of course she had all the life support and things that she had to have at that time, but as I placed my hand on her forehead and began to pray, she began to move her head from side to side. I knew she knew we were there, even though they said she won't know you and can't respond to you, but she did respond.

So that was the beginning of a newness that I saw in Anne Butler. I can't remember how many days it was before she was conscious and able to speak. The very first words that came out of her mouth were, "See, I *told* you God was going to take care of me." And you know, the only thing I could say, with tears in my eyes and a new feeling of how the Holy Spirit works in our lives, was, "I believe you, Anne."

I can't remember the exact day when I went down there to work and Mr. Henderson was at Anne's house; it's been a long time. You often wonder if you could do something, be somewhere, say something to change things that are going to happen in people's lives, but sometimes Satan has the upper hand in spite of everything, and there's no doubt in my mind this was an act of Satan. Why it happened, I have no earthly idea. Did anyone think it would happen? I don't think so. There'd always been a power struggle at Butler Greenwood from day one. I'd been there for 17 years working, and it didn't take a rocket scientist to figure out who the mistress of Greenwood was, nor who was going to *stay* the mistress of Greenwood.

It's been a long, hard struggle for Anne. This is June the first of ninety-eight as I record this. But in the time since the shooting, I've seen something change inside of her that just thrills my very soul. There's a new beginning in her life. I always believed that things like this happen for a reason. I do believe that God has overcome a lot in Anne's life, that she can show to others just what it means to be a child of the kingdom.

Well, I know she's not *perfect*, don't misunderstand me, but I can understand how she feels in her heart right now when she tells people, "I was carried in the arms of angels." Because having that spiritual experience generates new life. Paul said in his writings he'd put off the old man and he'd become a new creature in Christ Jesus. New creatures do new things, have new ideas, have renewed love and care about some different things. New creatures walk a different path. Those that are born from above know heavenly things and share those heavenly things with other people.

Let me tell you how I came to work with Anne, start at the very beginning maybe. Came to Butler Greenwood in 1981 to do some restoration work. The old three-story addition on the house had been torn down—it was not there anymore—and we were attempting to make the house look like it had in the very beginning, with a side porch and a little office added to match the other side. I'd been working at Grace Church, met Anne, wasn't real impressed. We worked there for two or three months and put that all together.

After a period of time, Anne called, and I came back and did some more jobs and some more jobs and some more jobs. I've been there 17 years I guess now, off and on. It's hard sometimes to be around people and not think that you know them, and sometimes you do and sometimes you really don't. Anne Butler was not a person you got close to very easily, but she was a person that would tell you the truth. If you wanted to know what she thought about you, all you had to do was ask her and she didn't mind telling you. Well now, I can live with that. Most folks ought to be at least honest enough to say what's on their mind or in their heart so you don't have to wonder about it.

I don't know that I ever had a problem with Anne Butler. And I appreciated her wanting to preserve Butler Greenwood, not just the house but every facet of it. Every time you looked around there was history: the old kitchen, the cook's cottage, the summer house out front, the gardens. A part of her life was rooted in all of those things and I appreciated her very much for wanting to take care of that so that another generation and another generation could come and enjoy what our ancestors strived so hard to put together.

As I said, through the years, she had called me and said, "I want to have this," "I want to do that," always to the house, never much to the outbuildings. Then in 1990 she decided that this was just a money pit and if she was going to save all this, she'd have to figure out some way to take care of what was there. So we worked together on it—and I say *we* because my association with Anne started before her marriage to Stewart's father, and went through that period of time until their separation and eventual divorce and then marriage to Mr. Henderson, so I've been involved in a lot of situations and seen a lot of things happen at Butler Greenwood in her life and in her children's lives.

I met Mr. Murray—I know it was in between the book writing and somewhere in there between him coming to live at Butler Greenwood and them getting married and all of that, but I can't remember exactly when. But I do remember a spring morning the latter part of March or first of April in 1991. Like I say, Anne had said there had to be some changes made, some adjustments made, for this place to survive, and so she had decided to open the house for tours. And she had decided to use the Cook's Cottage, which we had already renovated, as a B&B, and now we were working on the Old Kitchen, adding a bathroom and sprucing it up for the second Bed & Breakfast.

My brother Jackie and I were there that spring morning, and it was coming a thunderstorm from out of yonder. Rain, thunder and lightening, big time. And out of the back door of the main house popped Mr. Murray with an armload of clothes. It wasn't a lot unusual, because about once a week, sometimes twice, he'd come out with an armload of clothes to take to the laundry. He came out, trying to struggle with an umbrella and that armload of clothes, unlocked the trunk on his car, threw them in there, latched it back, went back in the house. Wasn't hard to see, we weren't 12 foot from where his car was parked, maybe not that far.

Few minutes later he came out again with a second load of clothes. Jackie looked at me and said, "Taking a lot of clothes to the laundry today." I said, "Yep, sure is." Well, the clothes march continued for three or four more trips. Then as he started to leave, he came out where we were working, and he said, "Burnett, I can't handle a teenager giving orders to me. She runs this house." He meant Chase, who was still home then. And he left. Wasn't but a few days, couple of days maybe, three, I can't remember, he came back to get us to help move the rest of his stuff back to his ex-wife's house off of Bains Road.

I can't remember how many times I helped move him, several, in *and* out. The last time that I moved him back in was the second day of January 1997; he'd been gone about a month and decided to move back in again. Now, like I said, Anne Butler's some kind of good friend of mine, but I never crossed her, 'cause I knew that she could be tough. And over the course of those seven years, Mr. Henderson went and came a bunch of times, sometimes a night, sometimes two nights, sometimes a month, sometimes two weeks, sometimes two months.

And everybody that I knew around there wondered what kind of hold he had over Anne, including myself, that she would let him go and come like that. There certainly wasn't anybody else in this world that could come and go on such a regular schedule. It became kind of a laughing, joking matter with the guys that worked with me. Mr. Henderson would come out if we were working there and he'd speak to us a lot of times before he got in his car and left, and then some mornings he'd just come out and he'd just get in his car and he'd throw rocks as he left, and those mornings they'd tell me, "Burnett, you'd better clean your truck out, you're gonna be moving again today."

Well, that last week wasn't very pretty. I said before, I'd never seen any problems, any fussing or loud voices or cussing or anything like that between Anne and Mr. Murray, but somehow, whether Anne wanted to admit it, this time that he left was different. I don't know, I can't put my finger on what was different, but she was a different person that last week he was gone, before she got shot. That last week was a troubling week for her; I could see and hear a difference. When I came down on Monday morning, she came out to meet me before I got started working on the pool, and she said, "Burnett, I can't afford you but a couple of days this week; Murray moved out this weekend and I had to pay him for the computer and he wants me to pay him for some electrical work Andy did upstairs, and so I'm not going to be able to afford you but a couple of days this week."

Now take in mind that Anne Butler and I have been friends for 17 years. And somewhere along the line I had gotten to know her pretty well, I thought, and I knew that something was eating inside of her. But why she did these things with Mr. Henderson was beyond me. I

299

figured he'd be back in a week, or two weeks. He always had before. And I just said, "Thank God I didn't have to move all that heavy stuff again." Like I say, she was different. I don't know if she was afraid, I don't know what it was. But she wasn't the regular Anne Butler that I'd gotten used to.

So we made it through that week, and then on Sunday, we got the telephone call telling us what had happened. I don't understand a lot of things that happen in this life and I shouldn't pass judgment on anyone, but there are some things that are just uncalled for.

When we set out to build the other B&Bs, Anne kept pouring every penny she could get into them, and on Mr. Murray's recommendations, she hired Mr. Lloyd Hoyle to do her bookkeeping. We built the Gazebo B & B and got it operational, then before we finished it we moved in an old house that Anne had bought and began to renovate it as the fourth B & B, the Pond House.

Somewhere in that time frame, Anne and Mr. Lloyd talked to me about becoming a regular part of the business every week, not just building the stuff but maintaining it, trying to keep it all going, and the general consensus was that they would charge enough up front to be able to cover so many hours a week for me to be there to keep everything going, which was fine with me. You don't stay at a place for 15 years or 20 years and put it back together without losing part of your heart to it, and I feel like I'm a part of Butler Greenwood. Even though I have never owned any of it, I've put a lot of blood, sweat and tears into it, and I'm proud of what it is.

Maybe I ought to add that at the very beginning of this Bed and Breakfast thing, most folks giggled just a little bit and said, "Well, Anne doesn't have the disposition to meet the public or run a Bed and Breakfast or be involved in something like that." And when it became the most popular Bed & Breakfast in the area, they all said, "Well, *I* don't know how she does it." Well, I know how she does it; she's very nice to people and she treats them nicely when they stay there. Oh, she has a run-in with a couple of folks every once in a while, who doesn't, but 99 percent of the people come back to

Butler Greenwood because of the atmosphere there, because of their host. She is very good at what she does.

She's gotten even better in the last few months, because she appreciates what God has given her. And even though she thinks there are still some people she needs to let know what's wrong in their lives, her attitude has changed a lot about who folks are and what God wants. She's the most generous person I know. I have never seen anyone come to Butler Greenwood that needed something that she didn't give it to them, be it money, or time, or whatever.

And she's not bitter about it, even now. She has taken this and decided that God has opened other doors, he's closed those and he's opened some more doors, and I believe she's going to go through those doors because God has a purpose for her life, and I believe she'll be open to serve that purpose. Maybe we all need to get shot a little bit to bring us to a closer realization that there's more to life than things of the world, maybe we all need to suffer to see what we're made of inside.

Did I ever wonder if Anne would make it? Don't think so. Oh, I wondered if she might live, but I knew if she lived, she'd come back. I look up there on the dining room wall at that old oil painting of Mrs. Harriett Flower Mathews, who brought Butler Greenwood through the Civil War and a lot of years after, and I say to myself every time I see it, "Well, look at your great-great-great-granddaughter, she's got a lot of stuff that you're made of inside of her." Both of them are tough. T-U-F-F, *tough*.

ACKNOWLEDGEMENTS

There are so many people who have helped me to make it through this ordeal, all doing far more than their jobs called for or than their blood kinship demanded, people who were generous with their time and talents, giving me weeks out of their lives and a tremendous amount of support in many, many ways . . .

Patrice Nelson and Rose Pate, the first line of defense in getting help to save my life, Bob and Liz Butler who called 911, Deputy Sheriffs Randy Metz and Randy Holden along with Jamie Daniel who risked their own lives and wrestled the gun away from him, Steve Moreau and Albert Jean Webb who provided the emergency medical attention necessary to get me to the hospital alive, and whoever was driving that ambulance careening along at 100 mph . . .

the whole marvelous staff at Lane Memorial Hospital in Zachary, my two wonderful surgeons Dr. Lisa Mazoch and Dr. Donald Fonte and their staffs, the nurses and anaesthetists and others in the emergency room and operating rooms and recovery, the very caring nurses in the ICU, all the floor nurses who gave me so much more than just cursory medical attention, the respiratory therapists (goofy Tammy) and x-ray technicians, the outpatient surgery and special procedure nurses, Lisa Young and the other folks in occupational and physical therapy (Elenora, Jeff, Lisa W., Scott, Bruce, Christy, Chantelle) who in the course of 8 months not only gave me back much of the use of my arm but became close friends in the process, the sitters and aides (Hazel and Emma) who helped me so much with things I couldn't do, the cheerful cleaning staff, the dieticians who were so solicitous, Tamara and the others in social services who helped immeasurably by taking care of the interminable insurance hassles (and my new friend Barbara at my medical insurance company who insisted people were more important than paperwork or profits), all the other doctors and nurses and staff members who sort of adopted me as their miracle baby after I spent so much time in the hospital and came so far with their help . . .

Cecile Castello and her staff who went out of their way to provide special home health care nursing, and newspaper writer James Minton who maintained his friendship for both of us by resisting the temptation to sensationalize the coverage of a story which certainly would have lent itself to sensationalism in less capable hands . . .

the family members who came in from across the country and were there to help from the very beginning—Bob Butler who was the first of the family on the scene and who has never left, taking care of legal matters, cooking, pitching in however he could, and his wife Liz who generously shared his time away from their own three small children; my sister Mary Minor and her husband Mike Hebert from Austin who helped with my children and freely shared legal expertise as well as lots of money; Virginia Butler who came from Washington DC to sit with me (and be mean to me when I needed it) in the hospital; Virginia and Sam Marshall who came from Virginia and spent three full weeks helping me when I first came home helpless from the hospital, then came back for more work a few months later; poor Chase, my daughter, who missed the first two weeks of the last semester of her senior year in college to help me, and did she ever help; my son Stewart, who at 12 was forced to face issues he should never have even heard of, and who protected me every night after everyone else went home; my uncle Ormond Butler, who so graciously shared his home and fed the multitudes; Pat and Lucie Butler and Murrell Butler and his friend Jim who helped with food and rides to therapy before I could drive and fishing trips with Stewart to give him a break . . .

303

Burnett and Ruby Carraway, not related by blood but by choice considered among the closest of my family members, who did everything there was to do, helping take care of my place, my business, my family, myself; and the loving members of their church, New Salem Baptist Church in Liberty, Mississippi, who were so generous with visits, cards, prayers and a special healing service which touched my heart and soul (and worked!) . . .

all of the law enforcement officials involved, from the parish deputy sheriffs on up to now-retired Sheriff Bill Daniel himself (and his wife Vivian), including Charlene Rachel and the ladies in the office, always so helpful and so concerned and so professional, and detectives Steve Dewey and William Davis and other members of the state police force, as well as St. Tammany Parish assistant district attorney Scott Gardner and his investigator Mario who got stuck handling the criminal prosecution for the state and who were so very pleasant to deal with . . .

so many friends who helped with the business, like Mary Lea Dyer who donated her time daily for months to run the B&B, along with Ann Weller and Eleanor Beattie; babysat the house at night, like Jon Gentry and David and Irene Meredith; visited and brought food or flowers, like Mary and Dennis Williamson, Maria and Eric Roberts who helped so much with Chase as well, Susan Davis, Patsy Dreher, Marsha Lindsey, Beryl Gene Daniel, Lucie Cassity, W.C. and Adele Percy, the Rev. Lafayette Veal and his brother Nolan Veal, Edna Veal, Juanita Clark, Bobby and Sharon Wilson, Elizabeth Anne Bennett, May deLaureal, Stella Bourgeois, Charles Smith, Rosana McGuff, Rachel Hall, Jo and Lloyd Hoyle, Lula and Dick Pride, Dorcas Brown, Lynne Parker, Pat and Laurie Walsh, Marianne Giorlando, Patsy Foster, Linda LaBranche, Laurie Fisher, Rob and Lisa Fisher, Mary Brown who after each and every surgery sent enough food to feed an army; spent interminable hours sitting with me in the hospital after surgeries, like Ann Weller and Lily Metz (who served not only as sitters for the body but sitters for the soul); drove me to therapy, like Jeane Peters, Lucile and Butler Lawrason, and others already mentioned;

helped to take care of Stewart, like his father and stepmother Cheese and Jane Hamilton, and his godparents Fay and Danny Daniel, always important in his life; even gave blood for me, as Jeannie Morris did; or came to the hospital and to my home to cut my hair and help me to begin to look halfway presentable again, as Jeff Soulier did; or offered to come to the hospital and sing to me, as did angel-voiced Conan Cleveland; exercised remarkable restraint in trusting me to have the house ready for the pilgrimage, like Libby Dart and Nancy Vinci and Betsy Daniel who provided food for that busy weekend as well as trust, and Lula Pride and Maria Godfrey Roberts who served as my pilgrimage coordinators (and yes, miraculously, we were ready for 3,000 visitors the weekend after I had major surgery), and Lynn and Shane Romero who came to help for the whole weekend, and Toni McVea and Susan Lambert who did all the fresh flowers . . .

my irreplaceable nurses/sitters, sisters Belle Jones Washington and Katie Hilliard (with Belle's daughter Gail Carter pinch-hitting occasionally), who not only stayed with me round-the-clock when necessary but who fit into their already busy schedules home visits to change my colostomy every single morning and evening for more than six months, and were always there when I needed them . . .

my very loyal staff, Rosemary Blakes and Patrice Nelson and Rose Pate, who cleaned the B&B cottages and took over much of the work which I normally did, without complaint or question (and slipped me an occasional can of condensed milk to keep up my spirits), and Johnny Harris, who at 72 years of age singlehandedly kept 50 acres of lawns and gardens manicured while I was here and who kept things looking just as good in my absence, and Rose's son Carl who zealously guarded the grounds at night and her daughter Carol Lynn who picked up Stewart from the airport—all of them protective and caring . . .

the business and professional friends who patiently waited and waited and waited as bills got bigger and bigger and there were no funds with which to pay them for months, most especially banker Conville Lemoine, with whose help the business is almost back to

-BUTL

normal (and his wife Polly, who helped me to switch my Mustang convertible for another one which might not be such a red flag); Louisiana's world-famous chef John Folse who waited for me to get well so he could include this place in his new B&B book and public television B&B series (*Hot Beignets and Warm Boudoirs*); friends at Entergy like Dan and Beth Nilsson, Kathy Beauchamp and John McGaha and his staff; CPA Bob Baker and his hard-working right hand Cathy McKey; Bob Butler's wonderful legal secretary Ginger Card who has the patience of Job; and tourism colleagues at Peter Mayer Agency, the Graham Group, St. Francisville Chamber of Commerce and my B&B friends of St. Francisville Overnight . . .

Father Kenneth Dimmick and Father Matthew Rowe of Grace Episcopal Church, who visited me in the hospital and kept me on the prayer list . . .

the many B&B guests who over the years have become friends and who were so kind about sending cards and flowers, like Kay and Conrad Smith; Pat diMichaeles who has supplied Stewart with Chicago Bulls memorabilia since her first visit long ago; Karen and Ken Bailey, Russell Swindell, the John Conways, the Jerome Chauvins, Philip and Peggy Green, dear Deb Wieland who stayed here when others were afraid to, and so many more . . .

the friends from the writing community who provided editorial advice and marketing assistance, authors/professors Jim Magnuson and Joan Mellen, San Diego mystery writer Abby Padgett who did the great foreword, newspaper editor Paul Hodge and his wife Avis, historian Libby Dart whose editorial counsel I've always treasured, Cyril Vetter and Myra Peak who believed in the book and helped so much to polish it for presentation to the public, computer whiz Chris Adelman, and readers Deb Wieland, Kay and Conrad Smith, Bob and Liz Butler, Scott Gardner, Lisa and Doug Young, Betsy Sledge and Anne Hebert, Jeane Peters, Burnett Carraway and my daughter Chase . . .

and the special peculiar category of ex-husbands, all three of whom, Miles Poindexter III (and his late mother Ellen Jane), Glenn

Daniel (and his wife Jennifer) and Charles Stewart "Cheese" Hamilton (and his wife Jane), were extremely kind and supportive and helpful, when they of all people could very well have instead expressed understanding of how I could easily frustrate someone enough to want to shoot me (but *they* never did) . . .

I have surely been blessed.

-BUTL

AFTERWORD

Chase Poindexter, daughter of Anne Butler, never really enjoyed being at Butler Greenwood again, and moved to France in 2000, but the rest of the family and staff stayed to turn the B&B into a thriving business. Burnett Carraway continued his longtime involvement with the place and with the family, and was made a full partner in the business in recognition of his devotion to it. Father Dimmick and Father Rowe both left Grace Church for Texas. Murray Henderson is still serving his time at Wade Correctional Center in north Louisiana in a protective custody unit with crooked cops, pedophile priests and others requiring isolation from the general prison population. He spends most of his time reading, gardening and doing craft work, and in the 1999 elections made from his prison cell a highly publicized campaign contribution to Sheriff Bill Daniel's opponent. His defense attorneys appealed the verdict in his case to the First Circuit Court of Appeals in Baton Rouge; based primarily on the length of the sentence and makeup of the jury, the appeal was heard in November 1999. In December the court rendered its decision, upholding the conviction and letting the sentence stand, finding it not excessive for a perpetrator who shot his victim five times without provocation, and saying in the written opinion, "We find (Henderson) to be one of the worst offenders and this crime to be one of the most serious offenses." When his appeal to the Louisiana Supreme Court was turned down, he decided to try for a medical furlough, essentially releasing him from prison for health reasons. His plan was to return to St. Francisville. "You wouldn't oppose that, would you?" he asked an incredulous Anne.

Anne Butler had her eighth major surgery in late June 1999, six hours of work trying to hold her stomach together, not entirely successfully, so that future surgery remains a distinct probability. And the correspondence between the two of them never did stop.